105 Hikes In and Around
Southwestern British Columbia

105
HIKES

In and Around Southwestern British Columbia

STEPHEN HUI

Foreword by
T'uy't'tanat—Cease Wyss

GREYSTONE BOOKS
Vancouver/Berkeley/London

For my son, Ollie, who agrees every hike should end with ice cream,

and for everyone dedicated to protecting and maintaining our trails

Greystone Books Ltd.
greystonebooks.com

Cataloguing data available from Library and Archives Canada
ISBN 978-1-77164-286-6 (pbk.)
ISBN 978-1-77164-287-3 (epub)

Editing by Lucy Kenward
Copy editing by Alison Jacques
Cover and text design by Nayeli Jimenez
Cover photograph by iStock
Photographs by Stephen Hui
Cartography by Steve Chapman, Canadian Map Makers

Printed and bound in Singapore on FSC® certified paper at COS Printers Pte Ltd.
The FSC® label means that materials used for the product
have been responsibly sourced.

Greystone Books gratefully acknowledges the Musqueam, Squamish, and
Tsleil-Waututh peoples on whose land our Vancouver head office is located.

Greystone Books thanks the Canada Council for the Arts, the British Columbia
Arts Council, the Province of British Columbia through the Book Publishing Tax
Credit, and the Government of Canada for supporting our publishing activities.

MIX
Paper from
responsible sources
FSC® C016973

Canada

BRITISH
COLUMBIA

BRITISH COLUMBIA
ARTS COUNCIL
An agency of the Province of British Columbia

Canada Council   Conseil des arts
for the Arts   du Canada

PREVIOUS SPREAD: *Moraine above Upper Joffre Lake.*

SAFETY NOTICE

Hiking, scrambling, and all forms of outdoor recreation involve inherent risks and an element of unpredictability. Many of the hikes in this guidebook are not for novices and may not be safe for your party. There are dangers on every road, trail, and route, and conditions can change at any time. While every effort has been made to ensure accuracy, this book may contain errors. You assume full responsibility for your safety and health in the backcountry. The author, publisher, and distributors accept no liability for any loss, damage, injury, or death arising from the use of this book. Check current conditions, carry the ten essentials, exercise caution, and stay within your limits.

CONTENTS

Hikes North of Vancouver

NORTH VANCOUVER

WEST VANCOUVER

Hikes East of Vancouver

MOUNT BAKER

FOREWORD

---

by T'uy't'tanat—Cease Wyss

Chexw men wa ha7lh?
Hello, you are well?

Chet kw'enmantúmi-wit, wa lhtíma sḵw'lhay'alkalh!
We invite you to our cultural places, where the water runs over anything (falls, rapids, stones in the mountain streams)!

Chet kwen ha7lh sḵwálwen!
Our hearts are lifted!

THE SḴWX̱WÚ7MESH PEOPLE, the St'át'imc, and the many tribes of the Stó:lō—Sts'ailes, Skwah, Cheam, Skowlitz, Nicomen, Seabird Island, Kweykwitlem, Katzie, Kwantlen, Slíl'utulth, and Xwmétskwiyam, to name a few—are among the Coast Salish nations whose lands and waters you are blessed to be travelling through. North along the Sunshine Coast and over to the south end of Vancouver Island are the Shishá7lh, Slhay'ámin, Snanáymexw, Sooke, Sx̱imálhalh, Tsalhúlhtxw, and Quwuts'n peoples. South of the border are the Nooksack, Sumas, and Lhaq'temish peoples, among others.

We love our sacred *stséḵtseḵ*, our forests, and we hope you love them too. These forests and *smánit*, these mountains, are the places where we have gathered *s7ílhen* (foods), *ḵ'éytl'tanay'* (medicines), materials for our cultural regalia, and tools for creating the important treasures that we spent centuries learning about. We are people of the forests, lakes, and rivers, and, of course, we are people of the Salish Sea.

Our hope, as Indigenous peoples, is that through your time in our ancestors' homes in the natural world, you will become as deeply connected to these wonderful and beautiful places that have cared for our peoples—as we have, hopefully, cared for them. We trust that you will find your personal healing journey along the rivers, trails, watersheds, and estuaries that you visit and that you will find caring ways to help these sacred places continue to exist for all of our future ancestors!

Huy chexw a' for taking the time to consider where you are and what your intentions and your relationships to these wild places are! Please remember to bring only what you need and want, and understand that the wild places need nurturing as much as we do. Please consider helping the forest to stay clean and loved as you make your way through the many trails you find in this book.

Our forests are filled with rich and wondrous stories of everything—from lesson stories, which we tell our children to keep them self-aware, to humorous and serious stories that are a reflection of our ancestors' stories from long ago. The mythical creatures who helped us to shape these mountains and valleys are very much still present.

Huy chexw a' for your good feelings and positive actions in realizing that you are part of the journey through these places. You are as important to us as the forest is to you.

Huy ma7lh!
T'uy't'tanat kwi en snas!

My traditional name is Woman Who Travels by Canoe.
Cease Wyss is my nickname.

T'UY'T'TANAT—CEASE WYSS (Ṡḵwx̱wú7mesh/Stó:lō/Métis/Hawaiian/Swiss) is an interdisciplinary artist and a Coast Salish ethnobotanist who recently has returned to a textile arts practice through learning Coast Salish weaving techniques in wool and cedar. She is a member of the Aboriginal Writers Collective West Coast and lives in East Vancouver.

A TRIBUTE TO
MARY AND DAVID MACAREE

AS WE LAUNCH *105 Hikes In and Around Southwestern British Columbia,* it is appropriate to salute Mary and David Macaree, who started a long tradition in 1973 with the first publication of *103 Hikes in Southwestern British Columbia.* They worked tirelessly to ensure the 1973 book made it to the printer on time, and for 45 years that book has been continuously in print in a series of new editions.

In 1955 when the Macarees immigrated to Canada from Scotland, however, they could hardly have imagined this legacy they would leave. Both of them were keen on the outdoors—Mary having grown up on a farm and David having served with the Royal Marines during World War II—and they soon joined two local clubs, the North Shore Hikers and the British Columbia Mountaineering Club.

The Macarees were devoted to making sure that others could enjoy the remarkable landscape of southern British Columbia. Long before the current interest in hiking existed, they helped launch that first book—and a second one, *109 Walks in British Columbia's Lower Mainland*—and kept them going through nearly ten editions. They were the trailblazers, and Greystone Books is proud to preserve their legacy.

We are equally proud to introduce Stephen Hui as the author of this new book and the person who will keep the Macarees' legacy alive. Reflecting the spirit of the Macarees and Stephen Hui's wishes, a portion of the proceeds from the sale of this book will go to the British Columbia Mountaineering Club for conservation purposes.

ROB SANDERS, Publisher
Greystone Books

INTRODUCTION

105 HIKES IN and Around Southwestern British Columbia covers recommendable trails and routes in the Coast Mountains and Cascade Range and around the Salish Sea, extending across the Canada–United States border into northwestern Washington. These are the Indigenous territories of the Coast Salish, St'át'imc, Nlaka'pamux, and Syilx peoples, who have lived here since time immemorial. The cultures, economies, histories, and languages of the First Nations are intertwined with these lands and waters, which remain subject to Indigenous governance today.

This guidebook features hikes new and old, long and short, popular and sleepy. Whether the classic hikes of Garibaldi and Manning Provincial Parks, the Skywalk trails in Whistler, hill walks of the Gulf Islands and San Juan Islands, or sections of the Sunshine Coast Trail and Hudson's Bay Company (1849) Heritage Trail, there's no shortage of options for your next adventure. The hikes included in this book vary widely in quality and difficulty, but they generally fit within the following parameters (with a few exceptions):

- Are accessible as a day or weekend trip from Vancouver.
- Are doable in a day on foot, though some are better suited to overnighters.
- Take a minimum of 3 hours (with at least 150 m/490 ft of elevation gain) and a maximum of 12 hours.
- Deserve at least a "worthwhile" rating; there are no "poor" hikes in the book.
- Require no more than Class 3 scrambling. (Class 1 denotes foot travel; Class 2 involves some use of hands; Class 3 entails easy climbing that's typically tackled unroped.)

Lofty summits, turquoise lakes, resplendent meadows, and ancient forests—many a fair-weather hiker tries to pack in as many of these natural spectacles as possible between the long weekends of May and October, the so-called hiking season in these parts. Indeed, Vancouver averages 165 days with rainfall a year, and many high-elevation trails are snow free only from July to September. Therefore, being a dedicated hiker means donning gaiters, waterproof gear, traction aids, and snowshoes and persevering through all kinds of weather.

This guide is intended for use with the ten essentials, avalanche and bear safety awareness, and more than a modicum of caution (see Being Prepared). No one plans to get lost or injured in the backcountry. Before heading out, consult trail reports, check avalanche and weather forecasts, and take note of sunset time. Make sure to leave a trip plan with a reliable person—to help search and rescue teams find you in the event of an emergency.

Once on the trail, please endeavour not to spoil the experience for others. Unfortunately, more hikers often equals more problems: litter, poop, noise, human-wildlife conflict, environmental damage, etc. Indeed, a little knowledge of backcountry etiquette and ethics goes a long way (see Ethical Hiking). For starters, respect the posted regulations, refrain from building inuksuit, silence your cellphone (save the battery for emergencies), keep your music to yourself, and put that drone away. Yield to horseback riders and, when going downhill, to uphill hikers. The minimum-impact practices espoused by the Leave No Trace Center for Outdoor Ethics include hiking in small groups, sticking to established campsites and trails (don't shortcut switchbacks), packing out all food and waste, leaving natural and historical objects in place, and keeping dogs under control at all times (and picking up their poop) or leaving them at home.

Reaction to any hiking guide is often mixed, ranging from astonishment that the author "forgot" a popular trail to outrage over the inclusion of a local favourite. In any case, a healthy appreciation of our natural areas is essential for building the public support needed to ensure their preservation. For decades, the Wilderness Committee has blazed trails as part of campaigns to safeguard wild lands around British Columbia. These trail-building efforts were instrumental in securing the creation of Carmanah Walbran Provincial Park in 1991, Pinecone Burke Provincial Park and Stein Valley Nlaka'pamux Heritage Park in 1995, and the Upper Elaho Valley Conservancy in 2008, among other protected areas. Nonetheless, once established, provincial parks still contend with inadequate funding and staffing and the threat of boundary changes for private development. It's up to us to speak out for our wild places.

Future editions of *105 Hikes* are planned. Please share your feedback, trail and access updates, and suggestions via *105hikes.com*. See you on the trails.

GET INFORMED

AdventureSmart
www.adventuresmart.ca

Avalanche Canada
www.avalanche.ca

B.C. Search and Rescue Association
www.bcsara.com

Federation of Mountain Clubs of B.C.
mountainclubs.org

Get Bear Smart Society
www.bearsmart.com

Leave No Trace Center for Outdoor Ethics
lnt.org

Washington Trails Association
www.wta.org

BEING PREPARED

by Michael Coyle

AS A SEARCH and rescue (SAR) volunteer for eighteen years, I have thought a lot about why some people become lost or need rescuing, whereas others do not. As a hiker, mountaineer, and backcountry skier, I have experience planning trips and returning successfully. As a SAR member, I see the opposite—the unsuccessful trips. Herein I offer my insight so you do not end up in the latter group.

There are two classes of things you take on a hike: those you carry on your back and those you carry in your head. Both are equally important. In your pack, you carry your equipment: the basic things you need for the hike and a few extras—more on them in a moment. In your head, and much lighter in weight, are your training, experience, and knowledge.

Every time you leave your home, you embark on a miniature expedition. You take with you the things you will need until you arrive home again. For everyday needs, you make sure you have money, ID, and probably your phone. For a short hike, you need to take more: some water, a little food, comfortable clothes, and good shoes. You also need to take a little knowledge with you. What are the conditions on the trail? Is it sunny (you'll need a hat) or is it raining (you'll need a jacket)? How long will the hike take?

The longer the hike, the more you need to carry. The physical items you will reasonably need for the hike are the simplest to enumerate—food, water, clothing, and sunscreen are the easy ones to remember. Others, such as navigation equipment (map, compass, GPS), a knife or repair kit, and fire starter, are often overlooked but are highly recommended. Then we come to the resources you'll need only if something goes wrong: a first-aid kit, flashlight,

View of Watersprite Tower from the shore of Watersprite Lake.

and emergency shelter. These last "extras" are the safety net. Together, these items give you the minimum amount of equipment you should have with you for every hike—the things that can make a big difference when something small goes wrong.

Of course, in addition to all the physical items, you're always carrying the things in your head. These come in two main forms: experience, which consists of the skills and information you've learned from previous trips, and knowledge, which is based on training or research. Experience and knowledge work hand in hand. Courses and training in various backcountry skills and techniques come in handy, but you need to exercise those skills for them to be useful. Other kinds of knowledge are specific to the day, the conditions, and the location. How am I feeling? What condition is the trail in? What is the weather going to be like? What is my starting time? When does the sun set? Knowing these things allows you to evaluate how you should prepare—or whether you should set out at all.

When you're on your backcountry trip, it's important to re-evaluate from time to time whether your current skills and resources are enough to handle the conditions you're finding. Has the weather changed? Is the trail as well marked as expected? Have you encountered snow? Is there evidence of a bear in the area, and are you prepared if you meet it? I know I mentioned "success" at the top, but success on a backcountry trip doesn't mean reaching your objective; it means *arriving home under your own power*. Even for simple trips, this re-evaluation is a crucial step—and making the decision to turn back can be the most important one you will ever make.

When your local resources are exhausted, that's when you need to call for help. You can reach this point for many reasons: bad planning, changing conditions, injury, or just plain bad luck. Bad planning comprises a lot of things, including classics such as not considering that a trail might have snow at higher elevations. Snow leads to slower travel, which often results in hikers being out after dark. If a party doesn't have a light but keeps going after dark, they typically get lost or injured quite quickly. Changing conditions include unexpected weather—rain or a thunderstorm, for example—or reduced visibility. Without resources such as warm or waterproof clothing, hikers can become cold and wet and succumb to hypothermia.

By carrying the right equipment on your back, and the right information and experience in your head, you can avoid many of the situations where people need to call for help. If you continually re-evaluate the situation, and understand when your resources are no longer sufficient for the conditions, it is easy to tell when you need outside assistance. Delaying a call for help often makes a rescue more complicated, so as soon as you know you are in over your head, call for help.

May your adventures be exciting for the right reasons!

MICHAEL COYLE is a search and rescue manager with Coquitlam Search and Rescue.

10 ESSENTIALS FOR BACKCOUNTRY TRAVEL

1. Navigation (topographic map, compass, GPS)
2. Sun protection (sunglasses, sunscreen)
3. Insulation (extra clothing, rain gear)
4. Illumination (headlamp or flashlight, spare batteries)
5. First-aid supplies (bandages, blister pads, etc.)
6. Fire starter (waterproof matches, lighter)
7. Repair kit and tools (knife, multi-tool, duct tape, etc.)
8. Nutrition (extra food)
9. Hydration (extra water)
10. Emergency shelter (tent, emergency blanket)

Adapted from *Mountaineering: The Freedom of the Hills* (8th edition, Mountaineers Books, 2010)

ETHICAL HIKING

by Jaime Adams

WE LOVE TO be in pristine, untrammelled wilderness. All of us have different reasons: perhaps to escape our responsibilities and the minutiae of our day-to-day lives, to care for ourselves physically and emotionally, to challenge ourselves, to share the experience with a friend, or to feel connected to something great. It is in these incredible places that we feel proud, accomplished, content, and inspired. They awaken something inside of us that is primal and important.

We can't take any of this wilderness for granted. The future of our parks and wild places is shaped by our own actions. We need to show respect for the land, access natural areas in a sustainable manner, and ensure the environment can withstand the impact of our usage. British Columbia's provincial parks are desperately underfunded, and their rangers cannot keep up with regular trail maintenance—never mind repair all the damage resulting from poor backcountry behaviour. Public land outside of our parks receives even less care, with only scattered conservation efforts led by volunteers.

In order for us to keep enjoying these wild places, we must take collective and individual responsibility for our activities in the backcountry and the effects of our access. By observing minimum-impact practices, such as the seven principles of Leave No Trace, we can protect these special places—for ourselves and for future generations.

There is a learning curve to Leave No Trace ethics. It takes thought, planning, care, and respect. I grew up bathing in the lakes and rivers of the Kootenays. We washed dishes and shampooed our free-ranging dogs in the same places we fished and obtained drinking water. Back then, I had no idea that these activities were environmentally damaging; as an adult exploring the alpine, I learned these things firsthand. We can all benefit from educating ourselves about Leave No Trace practices, and we can all play a role in sharing this knowledge with our fellow hikers.

These days, a growing number of people are accessing the backcountry. Many seek out the gorgeous places they see on their social media feeds, yet they have little idea of the preparation and planning that should go into those trips. At the same time, others chase Instagram followers by posting a stream of epic but irresponsible photos: tents set on fragile meadows or too close to water, campfires built in the subalpine, dogs roaming off-leash in sensitive environments, people feeding wildlife or hiking ill-equipped in challenging terrain, etc. Let's all think twice and use some common sense. There is a whole world of copycats out there itching to replicate your too-good-to-be-true shot. Our thirst for content and "likes" is not a good enough reason to trample vegetation, put wildlife at risk, or encourage reckless behaviour.

We can get a lot wrong on any given day in the backcountry. But the more we try to get it right, the longer our favourite places will stay wild. Here are some tips from the Leave No Trace Center for Outdoor Ethics: hike single file in the middle of the trail, even when muddy; camp at least 70 m (200 ft) from lakes and streams; don't dig trenches or build structures; view wildlife from a distance and avoid animals during mating and nesting seasons; and respect other backcountry users and the quality of their experience. To learn more, visit *lnt.org*.

JAIME ADAMS is the founder and program coordinator of the Forest and the Femme Society, a non-profit outdoor recreation program for marginalized women of Vancouver's Downtown Eastside.

7 PRINCIPLES OF LEAVE NO TRACE

1. Plan ahead and prepare.
2. Travel and camp on durable surfaces.
3. Dispose of waste properly.
4. Leave what you find.
5. Minimize campfire impacts.
6. Respect wildlife.
7. Be considerate of other visitors.

HOW TO USE THIS GUIDE

THE 105 HIKES in this book are categorized by regions north, east, west, and south of Vancouver and arranged by distance from the city. Each numbered trip comes with statistics and ratings, hiking and driving directions, a topographic map, and a photograph. (Note: Trails are not described in winter conditions.) Where possible, I've included public transit information and longer or shorter hiking options. For kid-friendly, backpacking, and rainy-day recommendations, consult Hikes at a Glance. What follows are explanations of the statistics and ratings used in this guide.

STATISTICS

Distance: The length of the hike as described is provided in metric and imperial units.

Time: Everyone hikes at their own pace. Once you've completed several of the hikes in the book, you'll get an idea of how your times compare to the estimates listed. I've indicated whether a given time refers to a round or one-way trip, or more specifically a loop, lollipop, circuit, etc. The estimates include enough time for an average hiker to take short breaks for snacks, lunch, and viewpoints.

Elevation gain (or loss): The net elevation gain (or loss) is simply the difference between the highest and lowest points encountered on the hike. Although both metric and imperial elevations are noted in the text, the maps show contour lines in metric only.

High point: This number represents the highest elevation attained on the hike—often, but not always, a summit.

Maps: The small maps in this guide are no substitute for large, printed maps. For each hike, the required map sheet(s) from Canada's National Topographic System or the U.S. Geological Survey is noted, as are other recommended topo maps.

Trailhead: The geographic position of the start of the hike is given in degrees, minutes, and seconds using the World Geodetic System (WGS) 84 datum. The trailhead is often, but not necessarily, near the parking area.

RATINGS

Each hike is assigned a quality rating and a difficulty rating, with which you may vehemently disagree. Both are inherently subjective, but might help you select the right trip for a given day.

Quality

★ Worthwhile: A decent leg-stretcher if you're in the area.

★★ Good: A tad low on the reward-effort ratio, but definitely has its moments.

★★★ Very good: Great views for the effort required.

★★★★ Excellent: An incredibly scenic and satisfying trip.

★★★★★ Amazing: Among the very best experiences in the book.

Difficulty

● Easy: Minimal distance and elevation gain on well-marked trails.

■ Moderate: A workout with decent distance and/or elevation gain on reasonably obvious paths.

◆ Difficult: Strenuous due to large distance and/or elevation gain, some route-finding challenges, and/or easy scrambling with little exposure.

◆◆ Advanced: Extremely demanding with tricky route-finding, substantial off-trail travel, and/or exposed scrambling—for experienced parties only.

KEY TO MAP SYMBOLS

P Parking

Toilets

Camping

Waterfall

Viewpoint

Ferry Dock

Bus Stop

Backcountry Hut

Chalet/Lodge

4WD 4 Wheel Drive Road

Warning

No Entry/Restricted Access

99 Primary Highway

▲ Mountain Peak

→ Direction of Travel/
Off Map Destination

Roads

Tracks

Trails

Route

Route (off trail)

Alternative Route

Alternative Route (off trail)

Ski Lift

Commercial Rail Tracks

800 Major Contour Lines (100 m)

Minor Contour Lines (20 m)

Streams/Creeks

Forest

Oceans, Lakes, Major Rivers/Creeks

Alpine (1000 m and higher)

Marshland

Glaciers

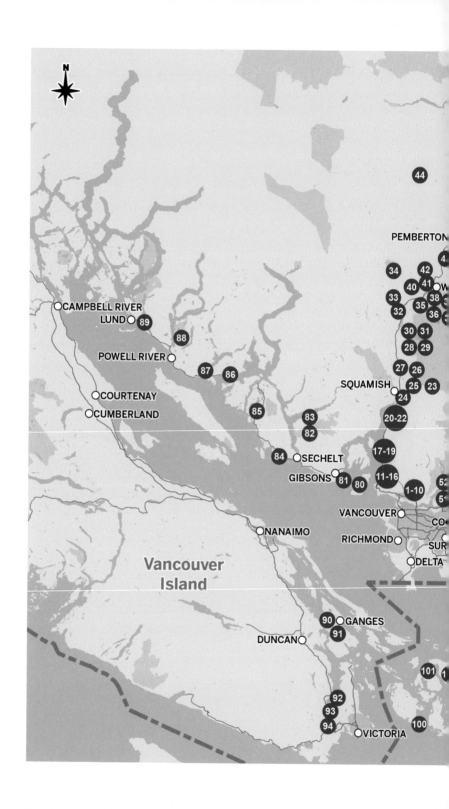

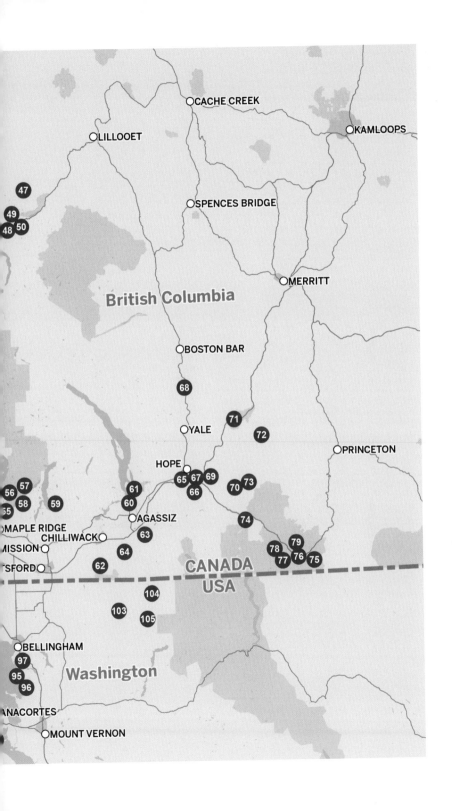

Hike	Quality	Difficulty	Distance	Time
HIKES NORTH OF VANCOUVER				
North Vancouver				
1 Mount Seymour	★★★	■	8 km (5 mi)	4 hours
2 Mount Elsay	★★★★	◆	13 km (8.1 mi)	10 hours
3 Lynn Creek	★	●	14 km (8.7 mi)	4 hours
4 Lynn Peak Lookout	★	■	8.8 km (5.5 mi)	4 hours
5 Norvan Falls	★★	●	14 km (8.7 mi)	5 hours
6 Mount Burwell	★★	◆	25 km (15.5 mi)	10.5 hours
7 Lower Mount Fromme	★	■	10 km (6.2 mi)	3.5 hours
8 Mount Fromme	★	■	11 km (6.8 mi)	5 hours
9 Goat Mountain	★★	■	14 km (8.7 mi)	6.5 hours
10 Crown Mountain	★★★★	◆◆	17 km (10.6 mi)	8 hours
West Vancouver				
11 Capilano Pacific Trail	★	●	14 km (8.7 mi)	4 hours
12 Hollyburn Mountain	★★	■	10 km (6.2 mi)	4 hours
13 Mount Strachan	★★★	■	10 km (6.2 mi)	4.5 hours
14 Unnecessary Mountain	★★★	◆	17 km (10.6 mi)	8 hours
15 Black Mountain	★★★	●	9.5 km (5.9 mi)	5 hours
16 West Knob	★★	■	12 km (7.5 mi)	5 hours
Lions Bay to Britannia Beach				
17 Mount Harvey	★★	◆	13 km (8.1 mi)	7.5 hours
18 Brunswick Mountain	★★★	◆◆	14 km (8.7 mi)	8.5 hours
19 Tunnel Bluff	★★★	■	9 km (5.6 mi)	5 hours
Squamish				
20 Sea to Summit Trail	★★	■	8 km (5 mi)	4 hours
21 Al's Habrich Ridge Trail	★★★	■	7.5 km (4.7 mi)	4.5 hours
22 Stawamus Chief Mountain	★★★★	■	14 km (8.7 mi)	5 hours
23 Watersprite Lake	★★★★	■	17 km (10.6 mi)	7 hours
24 Mount Crumpit	★★★	■	8 km (5 mi)	4 hours
25 Elfin Lakes	★★★★	■	22 km (14 mi)	7 hours
26 The Gargoyles	★★★★	◆	27 km (17 mi)	9 hours
27 Tantalus View Lookout	★★★	●	10.5 km (6.5 mi)	3.5 hours
Cheakamus River				
28 Garibaldi Lake	★★★★	■	20 km (12.4 mi)	7 hours

Elevation Gain (or Loss)	High Point	Kid-Friendly	Best for Backpacking	Save for a Rainy Day	✓
388 m (1,270 ft)	1,455 m (4,770 ft)				
500 m (1,640 ft)	1,422 m (4,665 ft)				
154 m (505 ft)	154 m (505 ft)	x		x	
780 m (2,550 ft)	992 m (3,255 ft)			x	
210 m (690 ft)	420 m (1,380 ft)	x		x	
1,330 m (4,360 ft)	1,544 m (5,065 ft)				
435 m (1,430 ft)	770 m (2,525 ft)			x	
810 m (2,660 ft)	1,171 m (3,840 ft)			x	
1,127 m (3,700 ft)	1,401 m (4,595 ft)				
1,227 m (4,025 ft)	1,501 m (4,925 ft)				
160 m (520 ft)	160 m (520 ft)	x		x	
415 m (1,360 ft)	1,326 m (4,350 ft)			x	
544 m (1,785 ft)	1,459 m (4,790 ft)				
633 m (2,080 ft)	1,548 m (5,080 ft)				
310 m (1,020 ft)	1,224 m (4,015 ft)	x		x	
610 m (2,000 ft)	720 m (2,360 ft)			x	
1,420 m (4,660 ft)	1,652 m (5,420 ft)				
1,560 m (5,120 ft)	1,788 m (5,870 ft)				
640 m (2,100 ft)	700 m (2,270 ft)			x	
850 m (2,790 ft)	885 m (2,900 ft)				
350 m (1,150 ft)	1,235 m (4,050 ft)				
625 m (2,050 ft)	702 m (2,300 ft)				
668 m (2,190 ft)	1,479 m (4,852 ft)		x		
270 m (885 ft)	325 m (1,065 ft)			x	
685 m (2,250 ft)	1,600 m (5,250 ft)	x	x		
905 m (2,970 ft)	1,820 m (5,970 ft)		x		
155 m (510 ft)	385 m (1,260 ft)	x		x	
1,080 m (3,500 ft)	1,650 m (5,400 ft)		x	x	

Hike	Quality	Difficulty	Distance	Time
29 Mount Price	★★★★★	◆◆	27 km (17 mi)	11 hours
30 Panorama Ridge	★★★★★	◆	29.5 km (18.3 mi)	10.5 hours
31 The Black Tusk	★★★★★	◆◆	29 km (18 mi)	10.5 hours
32 Brew Lake	★★★	◆	8 km (5 mi)	6 hours
33 Brandywine Mountain	★★★★★	◆◆	10 km (6.2 mi)	5.5 hours
34 Conflict Lake	★★★★	■	12 km (3.7 mi)	4 hours
Whistler				
35 Crater Rim Trail	★★★	■	10.5 km (6.5 mi)	5.5 hours
36 Half Note Trail	★★★★	◆	6 km (3.7 mi)	2.5 hours
37 Flute Summit	★★★★	■	9 km (5.6 mi)	4 hours
38 Blackcomb Burn	★★★	◆	5.2 km (3.2 mi)	2.5 hours
39 Decker Tarn	★★★★	■	9 km (5.6 mi)	3.5 hours
40 Rainbow Pass	★★★★	■	18.5 km (11.5 mi)	7 hours
41 Skywalk South	★★★★	◆	18 km (11.2 mi)	6 hours
42 Skywalk North	★★★★	■	20 km (12.4 mi)	8.5 hours
Pemberton to Lillooet				
43 Mount Currie Trail	★★	◆	13 km (8.1 mi)	7.5 hours
44 Tenquille Lake	★★★★	■	12.5 km (7.8 mi)	4 hours
45 Camel Pass	★★★★	■	17.5 km (11 mi)	7.5 hours
46 Cool Creek Canyon	★★★★	■	2 km (1.2 mi)	2 hours
47 Twin Lakes	★★★★★	◆	16 km (10 mi)	7.5 hours
48 Joffre Lakes	★★★★★	●	9.5 km (5.9 mi)	4 hours
49 Mount Rohr	★★★★★	◆◆	12 km (7.5 mi)	8 hours
50 Anniversary Glacier	★★★★	■	9 km (5.6 mi)	5.5 hours
HIKES EAST OF VANCOUVER				
Belcarra to Coquitlam				
51 Lakeview Trail	★	●	11 km (6.8 mi)	3 hours
52 Mount Beautiful	★	◆	20 km (12.4 mi)	8 hours
53 Coquitlam Lake View Trail	★★	■	13 km (8.1 mi)	5.5 hours
54 High Knoll	★★★	●	7.5 km (4.7 mi)	3 hours
Pitt Meadows and Maple Ridge				
55 Alouette Mountain	★★★	■	22 km (14 mi)	9 hours
56 Evans Peak	★★★★	◆	9 km (5.6 mi)	5 hours
57 Golden Ears	★★★★	◆◆	25 km (15.5 mi)	11 hours

Elevation Gain (or Loss)	High Point	Kid-Friendly	Best for Backpacking	Save for a Rainy Day	✓
1,480 m (4,855 ft)	2,052 m (6,730 ft)		x		
1,555 m (5,100 ft)	2,126 m (6,975 ft)		x		
1,740 m (5,710 ft)	2,310 m (7,580 ft)		x		
700 m (2,300 ft)	1,430 m (4,700 ft)		x	x	
860 m (2,820 ft)	2,213 m (7,260 ft)				
182 m (595 ft)	1,372 m (4,500 ft)			x	
360 m (1,180 ft)	912 m (2,992 ft)			x	
333 m (1,091 ft)	2,182 m (7,160 ft)				
455 m (1,490 ft)	2,182 m (7,160 ft)				
1,175 m (3,855 ft)	1,860 m (6,102 ft)			x	
236 m (775 ft)	2,051 m (6,730 ft)	x			
890 m (2,900 ft)	1,520 m (5,000 ft)	x	x	x	
1,060 m (3,480 ft)	1,790 m (5,870 ft)				
1,050 m (3,445 ft)	1,784 m (5,850 ft)		x		
1,240 m (4,070 ft)	1,600 m (5,250 ft)			x	
450 m (1,480 ft)	1,710 m (5,610 ft)		x		
1,090 m (3,580 ft)	2,130 m (6,990 ft)		x	x	
320 m (1,050 ft)	710 m (2,330 ft)				
965 m (3,170 ft)	2,215 m (7,270 ft)		x		
360 m (1,180 ft)	1,570 m (5,150 ft)	x	x	x	
1,030 m (3,380 ft)	2,423 m (7,950 ft)		x		
450 m (1,480 ft)	1,660 m (5,450 ft)		x		
150 m (490 ft)	275 m (900 ft)	x		x	
1,130 m (3,710 ft)	1,259 m (4,130 ft)				
600 m (1,970 ft)	920 m (3,020 ft)			x	
165 m (540 ft)	169 m (554 ft)	x		x	
1,110 m (3,640 ft)	1,361 m (4,465 ft)			x	
950 m (3,120 ft)	1,132 m (3,714 ft)				
1,530 m (5,020 ft)	1,716 m (5,630 ft)		x		

Hike	Quality	Difficulty	Distance	Time
58 Gold Creek	★★	■	14 km (8.7 mi)	4.5 hours
Mission to Harrison Hot Springs				
59 Mount St. Benedict	★	■	11 km (6.8 mi)	6.5 hours
60 Campbell Lake	★	■	10 km (6.2 mi)	6 hours
61 Bear Mountain	★	■	18 km (11 mi)	7 hours
Abbotsford and Chilliwack				
62 Teapot Hill	★★	●	13 km (8.1 mi)	5 hours
63 Cheam Peak	★★★★★	■	9 km (5.6 mi)	4 hours
64 Mount Thurston	★★★	◆	16 km (10 mi)	7 hours
Hope and Fraser Canyon				
65 Hope Lookout Trail	★	■	5 km (3.1 mi)	2.5 hours
66 Hope Mountain	★★★★	■	8.5 km (5.3 mi)	6 hours
67 Hope–Nicola Valley Trail	★	●	5.4 km (3.4 mi)	2 hours
68 Tikwalus Heritage Trail	★★★	■	12 km (7.5 mi)	7 hours
Coquihalla Pass to Tulameen River				
69 Manson's Ridge	★	◆	16.5 km (10.3 mi)	7 hours
70 Palmer's Pond	★★★★	■	11.5 km (7.1 mi)	7 hours
71 The Flatiron	★★★★	■	10 km (6.2 mi)	5 hours
72 Illal Mountain	★★★★★	◆◆	13 km (8.1 mi)	7.5 hours
73 Podunk Creek	★★	■	23 km (14.3 mi)	8 hours
Manning Provincial Park				
74 Skagit River Trail	★★★	■	18 km (11.2 mi)	6.5 hours
75 Windy Joe Mountain	★★	■	15 km (9.3 mi)	5.5 hours
76 Frosty Mountain	★★★★★	■	22 km (14 mi)	7.5 hours
77 Lightning Lakes	★★★	■	20 km (12.4 mi)	7 hours
78 Snow Camp Mountain	★★★★	■	17 km (10.6 mi)	6 hours
79 Three Brothers Mountain	★★★★★	■	21.5 km (13.4 mi)	6.5 hours
HIKES WEST OF VANCOUVER				
Howe Sound				
80 Mount Gardner	★★★	■	17 km (10.6 mi)	7 hours
81 Lookout Peak	★★★	●	9 km (5.6 mi)	4 hours
Sunshine Coast				
82 Chapman Lake	★★★	◆	20 km (12.4 mi)	8 hours
83 Mount Steele	★★★★	◆	18 km (11 mi)	8 hours

Elevation Gain (or Loss)	High Point	Kid-Friendly	Best for Backpacking	Save for a Rainy Day	✓
340 m (1,100 ft)	480 m (1,600 ft)	X	X	X	
1,020 m (3,350 ft)	1,278 m (4,190 ft)				
679 m (2,230 ft)	695 m (2,280 ft)			X	
1,000 m (3,280 ft)	1,036 m (3,400 ft)			X	
255 m (840 ft)	310 m (1,020 ft)	X		X	
690 m (2,260 ft)	2,104 m (6,902 ft)				
990 m (3,250 ft)	1,620 m (5,315 ft)				
462 m (1,515 ft)	524 m (1,720 ft)	X		X	
690 m (2,260 ft)	1,844 m (6,050 ft)				
205 m (670 ft)	347 m (1,140 ft)	X		X	
790 m (2,590 ft)	910 m (2,985 ft)		X		
1,210 m (3,970 ft)	1,530 m (5,020 ft)		X		
950 m (3,120 ft)	1,855 m (6,085 ft)		X		
690 m (2,260 ft)	1,898 m (6,230 ft)		X		
745 m (2,445 ft)	2,020 m (6,630 ft)		X		
215 m (705 ft)	1,470 m (4,820 ft)	X	X	X	
60 m (200 ft)	625 m (2,050 ft)	X	X	X	
677 m (2,221 ft)	1,825 m (5,989 ft)	X		X	
1,160 m (3,805 ft)	2,409 m (7,900 ft)		X		
50 m (160 ft)	1,250 m (4,100 ft)	X	X		
600 m (1,970 ft)	1,980 m (6,497 ft)		X		
480 m (1,575 ft)	2,272 m (7,453 ft)		X		
720 m (2,360 ft)	727 m (2,385 ft)			X	
189 m (620 ft)	189 m (620 ft)	X		X	
310 m (1,020 ft)	1,130 m (3,710 ft)		X		
840 m (2,755 ft)	1,659 m (5,440 ft)		X		

Hike	Quality	Difficulty	Distance	Time
84 Triangle Lake	★★	●	8 km (5 mi)	3 hours
85 Mount Daniel	★★★★	■	4.5 km (2.8 mi)	2 hours
86 Fairview Bay	★★★	●	13.5 km (8.4 mi)	4 hours
87 Walt Hill	★★★	■	22.5 km (14 mi)	8 hours
88 Confederation Lake	★★★	■	20 km (12.4 mi)	7 hours
89 Manzanita Bluff	★★	■	10.5 km (6.5 mi)	4.5 hours
Gulf Islands				
90 Mount Erskine	★★★★★	■	5.5 km (3.4 mi)	2.5 hours
91 Mount Maxwell	★★★	■	6.5 km (4 mi)	2.5 hours
Victoria				
92 Mount Work	★★	●	6 km (3.7 mi)	2.5 hours
93 Jocelyn Hill	★★★★	●	9 km (5.6 mi)	4 hours
94 Mount Finlayson	★★★	◆	7 km (4.3 mi)	2.5 hours
HIKES SOUTH OF VANCOUVER				
Bellingham to Mount Vernon				
95 Fragrance Lake	★	■	13 km (8 mi)	5 hours
96 Oyster Dome	★★★	■	14 km (8.7 mi)	6 hours
97 Pine and Cedar Lakes Trail	★★	■	12 km (7.5 mi)	5 hours
Anacortes and San Juan Islands				
98 Mount Erie	★★	●	8 km (5 mi)	4 hours
99 Hoypus Hill	★	●	10.5 km (6.5 mi)	3 hours
100 Cattle Point	★★★	●	8 km (5 mi)	2.5 hours
101 Turtlehead	★★★★★	●	8.5 km (5.3 mi)	2.5 hours
102 Mount Constitution	★★★	■	13.5 km (8.4 mi)	6 hours
Mount Baker				
103 Skyline Divide	★★★★★	■	13 km (8.1 mi)	6 hours
104 Yellow Aster Butte	★★★★★	◆	13 km (8.1 mi)	7 hours
105 Chain Lakes Trail	★★★★★	■	11.5 km (7.1 mi)	5.5 hours

Elevation Gain (or Loss)	High Point	Kid-Friendly	Best for Backpacking	Save for a Rainy Day	✓
185 m (610 ft)	210 m (690 ft)	x		x	
365 m (1,200 ft)	440 m (1,440 ft)	x		x	
95 m (310 ft)	100 m (330 ft)	x	x	x	
890 m (2,920 ft)	1,050 m (3,440 ft)		x		
530 m (1,740 ft)	630 m (2,070 ft)		x	x	
165 m (540 ft)	340 m (1,115 ft)	x	x	x	
380 m (1,245 ft)	448 m (1,470 ft)				
280 m (920 ft)	593 m (1,945 ft)	x		x	
300 m (985 ft)	449 m (1,475 ft)	x		x	
210 m (690 ft)	434 m (1,425 ft)			x	
415 m (1,360 ft)	419 m (1,375 ft)				
541 m (1,775 ft)	559 m (1,835 ft)	x		x	
583 m (1,910 ft)	627 m (2,060 ft)		x	x	
467 m (1,530 ft)	559 m (1,830 ft)	x	x	x	
275 m (900 ft)	386 m (1,266 ft)	x		x	
134 m (440 ft)	134 m (440 ft)	x		x	
88 m (290 ft)	88 m (290 ft)	x			
270 m (885 ft)	325 m (1,065 ft)	x		x	
460 m (1,510 ft)	734 m (2,409 ft)	x		x	
670 m (2,210 ft)	2,000 m (6,560 ft)	x	x		
770 m (2,530 ft)	1,902 m (6,241 ft)		x		
375 m (1,230 ft)	1,640 m (5,380 ft)	x	x		

1
MOUNT SEYMOUR

Distance: 8 km (5 mi)
Time: 4 hours (round trip)
Elevation gain: 388 m (1,270 ft)
High point: 1,455 m (4,770 ft)

Quality: ★★★
Difficulty: ■
Maps: NTS 92-G/7 Port Coquitlam, Trail Ventures BC North Shore
Trailhead: 49°22'03" N, 122°56'57" W

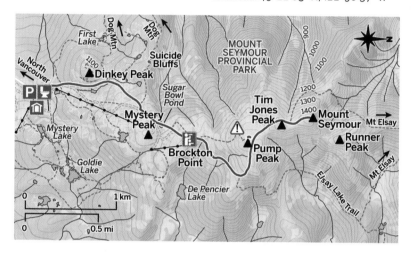

MOUNT SEYMOUR is visible from most parts of Vancouver and therefore one of the peaks most identified with the city and the North Shore mountains. This local landmark lies in the territories of the Musqueam, Squamish, and Tsleil-Waututh First Nations.

From the B.C. Parks kiosk at the top of Parking Lot 4 (1,067 m/3,500 ft), set off north on the Mount Seymour Trail, left of the Manning ski run and Mystery Peak Express chairlift. (Did you bring the ten essentials and leave a trip plan? North Shore Rescue has extracted many injured and lost hikers from these slopes.) Ignore leftward turnoffs for Dog Mountain, Dinkey Peak, and First Lake.

Your trail converges momentarily with the ski run, below the chairlift's top terminal on Mystery Peak. It then leaves to the left (49°22'40" N, 122°56' 39" W) and descends to small Sugar Bowl Pond. Soon Pump Peak, Mount Seymour's first summit, enters the view as the trail rises and continues along the ridge past Brockton Point. Dropping east to circumvent the south face, you come to the start of the Elsay Lake Trail, 2.2 km (1.4 mi) in. Keep left to regain the crest behind Pump Peak (1,407 m/4,615 ft); the top's a quick scramble from here.

Mount Seymour and Runner Peak from Mount Elsay.

Descend north to a col. Go up and over the Second Pump, now officially named Tim Jones Peak (1,435 m/4,710 ft) in honour of the North Shore Rescue team leader who died in 2014. Its summit is off to the right of the main trail. From here, the marked route to the third and highest "pump" can be difficult to follow in fog. Carefully hike by a steep drop-off and down to the next col. You might not notice the start of the Mount Elsay Trail on the left.

Finally, ascend inclined rock to Mount Seymour's main summit (49°23′ 36″ N, 122°56′40″ W). Behold the impressive panorama: Crown Mountain (Hike 10), the Twin Sisters (Ch'ich'iyúy to the Squamish), and Cathedral Mountain on the North Shore; Mount Garibaldi (Nch'kay') in Garibaldi Provincial Park; Meslilloet Mountain at the head of Indian Arm (Say Nuth Khaw Yum to the Tsleil-Waututh); and Golden Ears (Hike 57) to the east. To the north, the Fannin Range continues, with Runner Peak, Mount Elsay (Hike 2), and Mount Bishop. Retrace your steps on your return.

In recent years, Mount Seymour has endured mob scenes, such as hundreds of flag-waving folks greeting the sunrise from the summit while being filmed by a drone. This sort of thing runs contrary to Leave No Trace principles, which advise hiking in small groups, avoiding times of high use, walking in single file on trails, and limiting noise. Dogs must be leashed at all times in provincial parks, and B.C. Parks' permission is required for drones to take off or land.

SHORTER OPTION
Pump Peak is a popular snowshoeing destination. The (free) winter route stays west of the Mount Seymour ski-area boundary. Check Avalanche Canada's forecast for the South Coast and carry avalanche safety gear.

GETTING THERE
Vehicle: On Trans-Canada Highway 1, north of Ironworkers Memorial Second Narrows Crossing, take Exit 22(B). Head east on Mount Seymour Parkway. Following signs for Mount Seymour Provincial Park, turn left on Mount Seymour Road and drive up to the ski area. Winter tires or chains required between October and April. Park as close as you can to the top.

2
MOUNT ELSAY

Distance: 13 km (8.1 mi)
Time: 10 hours (lollipop)
Elevation gain: 500 m (1,640 ft)
High point: 1,422 m (4,665 ft)

Quality: ★★★★
Difficulty: ◆
Maps: NTS 92-G/7 Port Coquitlam, Trail Ventures BC North Shore
Trailhead: 49°22'03" N, 122°56'57" W

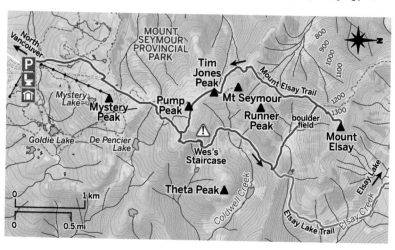

BECKONING WITH its panoramic views, Mount Elsay is the next major peak north of Mount Seymour (Hike 1) in the Fannin Range. Rising in the territories of the Musqueam, Squamish, and Tsleil-Waututh First Nations, the mountain chain constitutes the divide between the Seymour River and the Indian River and Indian Arm (Say Nuth Khaw Yum [Serpent's Land] to the Tsleil-Waututh).

From the B.C. Parks kiosk at the top of Parking Lot 4 (1,067 m/3,500 ft), follow the Mount Seymour Trail north for 2.2 km (1.4 mi) to the junction east of Pump Peak. Embarking on a strenuous counterclockwise loop, head right on the Elsay Lake Trail; leave the music-blasting crowd behind and enter the wild backcountry of Mount Seymour Provincial Park. In winter, this trail (adopted by the Vancouver Korean Hiking Club) is closed due to extreme avalanche hazard.

With Runner Peak and your objective entering the view, plunge down Wes's Staircase, next to a rockslide. Cairns with orange flagging lead north across talus and the headwaters of Coldwell Creek. Salmonberries and blueberries are plentiful in season. Enjoy the descent; it'll be over soon.

Crossing a boulder field below Mount Elsay.

Watch out for a junction in the woods (49°23′53″ N, 122°55′46″ W), on the divide between Coldwell and Elsay Creeks, 4.75 km (3 mi) from the parking lot. A large orange blaze on the left marks the start of the fun ascent. With some flagging, the Mount Elsay route climbs steeply under the trees to emerge in a bowl with a peaceful tarn. Cross a clear creek that feeds it, and clamber up a boulder field all the way to the Elsay-Runner col.

Turn right and head up the rooty forest path, easy slabs, and lingering snow to the summit cairn (49°24′25″ N, 122°56′16″ W). Your 360-degree prize: Mount Bishop due north and Elsay Lake far below, Buntzen Lake (Hike 51) across Indian Arm, Metro Vancouver and the Fraser Valley, Mount Seymour behind Runner Peak, the Gulf Islands, The Needles, etc.

Back at the col, go right to return via the rugged, slippery, and wickedly steep Mount Elsay Trail. Follow the west side of the ridge, cross boulder gullies, and drop to bypass Runner Peak. Finally, after 9 km (5.6 km) of hiking, you rise to the Mount Seymour–Tim Jones Peak col (49°23′29″ N, 122°56′38″ W). Turn right on the Mount Seymour Trail and head south over easier terrain to the trailhead. B.C. Parks discourages bringing dogs to the backcountry.

LONGER OPTION

The rough Elsay Lake Trail continues north to its remote overnight destination. An emergency shelter stands northeast of Elsay Lake, which involves a 20 km (12.4 mi) round trip with 600 m (2,170 ft) of elevation gain to contend with on the return.

GETTING THERE

Vehicle: On Trans-Canada Highway 1, north of Ironworkers Memorial Second Narrows Crossing, take Exit 22(B). Head east on Mount Seymour Parkway. Following signs for Mount Seymour Provincial Park, turn left on Mount Seymour Road and drive up to the ski area. Winter tires or chains required between October and April. Park as close as you can to the top.

3
LYNN CREEK

Distance: 14 km (8.7 mi)
Time: 4 hours (circuit)
Elevation gain: 154 m (505 ft)
High point: 154 m (505 ft)

Quality: ★
Difficulty: ●
Maps: NTS 92-G/6 North Vancouver
Trailhead: 49°18'18" N, 123°02'15" W

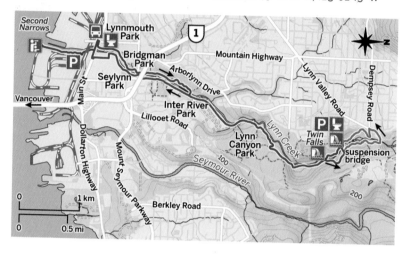

AS ENVISIONED, the multi-use Sea to Sky Trail will eventually span 180 km (110 mi), connecting Squamish, Whistler, Pemberton, Mount Currie, and D'Arcy in the territories of the Squamish, Lil'wat, and N'Quatqua First Nations. Then there's the other Sea to Sky Trail. This lesser-known coast-to-canyon path along North Vancouver's Lynn Creek is delightful on rainy days and in shoulder season and requires only a short hike to complete. It lies in the territories of the Musqueam, Squamish, and Tsleil-Waututh First Nations.

From the Harbourview Park trailhead, start by walking south on the Sea to Sky Trail to the viewing tower at the mouth of Lynn Creek. Burrard Inlet (Tsleil-Wat to the Tsleil-Waututh) and the break-bulk cargo facilities of the Port of Vancouver's Lynnterm terminal make up the industrial foreground.

Turn upstream and follow the trail under a rail bridge to Lynnmouth Park and Cotton Road. Turn left on the sidewalk and cross the bridge. Use the crosswalks at Brooksbank Avenue and pick up the Sea to Sky Trail behind the MEC outdoor equipment store. Join joggers, cyclists, and dog walkers on the suburban path as you head north along the west bank—from Lynnmouth to Bridgman Park (with its black cottonwood and red alder trees) and under the Keith Road and Upper Levels Highway bridges.

Less than an hour in, cross a rusty bridge to the east bank and Inter River Park. Go up the eroded road and keep left to stay with the Sea to Sky Trail as it enters Lynn Canyon Park. With tree roots, slippery boardwalks, and footbridges in your path through the temperate rainforest, you might finally earn some sweat.

Sea to Sky Trail in Lynn Canyon Park.

Thirty minutes past the rusty bridge, head left on the Baden-Powell Trail (49°20′05″ N, 123°00′59″ W) and descend stairs to Twin Falls. Don't cross the bridge yet; go up the stairs on the right. Two hours in, turn left to join the hordes on the Lynn Canyon Suspension Bridge (49°20′38″ N, 123°01′05″ W), which hangs 50 m (165 ft) above Lynn Creek. Heed signs warning against cliff jumping; drownings happen here almost every year.

Once you've had your fill of the bouncy bridge (and perhaps visited the Lynn Canyon Ecology Centre), follow the fence downstream on the west side of the canyon to the Centennial Trail. Stairs on the left lead down to Twin Falls Bridge. From the east side, retrace your steps to the rusty bridge.

This time, stay with the road and path along the east bank to St. Denis Avenue. Pass under the two bridges, and continue down the path from Seylynn Park to the end of Crown Street, by the District of North Vancouver operations centre. Walk east (left), turn right on Lynn Avenue, and cross Main Street. Take the sidewalk west (right) to rejoin the Sea to Sky Trail in Lynnmouth Park.

LONGER OPTION

From the Lynn Canyon Suspension Bridge, follow the trail up the east side of the canyon to Pipeline Bridge. Return via the west side on Rice Lake Road, Lynn Valley Road, and the Baden-Powell Trail, which is accessed opposite Dempsey Road. This loop adds 2 km (1.2 mi) and 50 minutes to your hike.

GETTING THERE

Transit: TransLink Bus 232 (Grouse Mountain) to Brooksbank Avenue at East 3rd Street, or 239 (Capilano University) to Cotton Road at Brooksbank Avenue. Find the Sea to Sky Trail behind the MEC store.

Vehicle: From Trans-Canada Highway 1 (Exit 23A), north of Ironworkers Memorial Second Narrows Crossing, head west on Main Street and quickly turn left on Mountain Highway. On the other side of the Canadian National Railway underpass, go right on Dominion Street, then right on Harbour Avenue. The road curves west to the small parking lot at Harbourview Park.

4
LYNN PEAK LOOKOUT

Distance: 8.8 km (5.5 mi)
Time: 4 hours (round trip)
Elevation gain: 780 m (2,550 ft)
High point: 992 m (3,255 ft)

Quality: ★
Difficulty: ■
Maps: NTS 92-G/6 North Vancouver, Trail Ventures BC North Shore
Trailhead: 49°21'37" N, 123°01'41" W

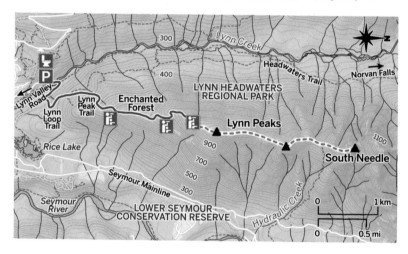

WHAT METRO Vancouver calls "Lynn Peak" is actually a lookout near the south summit of a pair of bumps officially named Lynn Peaks, according to the B.C. Geographical Names Office. Lynn Peaks sit on the south end of the Lynn Creek–Seymour River divide, in the territories of the Musqueam, Squamish, and Tsleil-Waututh First Nations. When the desire to work up a sweat and spend some time in the woods hits in spring or fall, an outing to the Lynn Peak Lookout is short and accessible by transit.

From the Lynn Headwaters Regional Park entrance, cross the bridge over Lynn Creek and fill out a form at the hiker registration kiosk. Head right on the wide Lynn Loop Trail for 400 m (0.2 mi), then follow it left at a junction with the Lynn Headwaters Connector (dogs must be on-leash).

In 0.8 km (0.5 mi), the signed start of the Lynn Peak Trail is on the right. The steep route covers 3.2 km (2 mi), enters the Lower Seymour Conservation Reserve, and may prove difficult to follow in snow. (Just before the trailhead, the unsigned path to Sully's Hangout, a sport-climbing crag, heads off into the woods.)

A rocky path and switchbacks transport you up to the first viewpoint overlooking the Seymour River valley. Up the ridge, the trail penetrates the

Foggy view at the Lynn Peak Lookout.

Enchanted Forest, whose old-growth Douglas fir and western red cedar trees certainly do look magical with a light dusting of snow. Then comes the Blimp Lookout, which offers a vista of the three peaks of Mount Seymour (Hike 1), Suicide Bluffs, and Dog Mountain. This was the site of a balloon logging operation that attempted to salvage timber blown down by the windy remains of Typhoon Freda in 1962.

Eventually, a "Lynn Peak" sign directs you right onto a rocky bluff (49°22′53″ N, 123°01′09″ W) with views—well, when they're not obscured by clouds—of Metro Vancouver and the Salish Sea. Burnaby Mountain, Second Narrows in Burrard Inlet (Tsleil-Wat to the Tsleil-Waututh), and Point Roberts are visible in the smog. Retrace your steps to return to the trailhead.

LONGER OPTION

For a long day of hiking, continue north over Lynn Peaks to the South Needle (1,163 m/3,815 ft) on a rough route littered with deadfall. This is an unpopular, strenuous hike with considerable route-finding challenges.

GETTING THERE

Transit: TransLink Bus 209, 210 (Upper Lynn Valley), or 228 (Lynn Valley) to Underwood Avenue at Evelyn Street. Walk east via Evelyn Park and Evelyn Street to Lynn Valley Road. Staying outside of the Lynn Headwaters Regional Park gate, continue east on Rice Lake Road, turn left on Marion Road, and head north on the Varley Trail for 1.5 km (0.9 mi) to the park entrance.

Vehicle: On Trans-Canada Highway 1, take Exit 19 and head north on Lynn Valley Road. Alternatively, from Exit 21, go north on Mountain Highway and turn right on Lynn Valley Road. If the park gate is open, follow the access road to the park entrance, using an overflow parking lot if necessary.

5
NORVAN FALLS

Distance: 14 km (8.7 mi)
Time: 5 hours (round trip)
Elevation gain: 210 m (690 ft)
High point: 420 m (1,380 ft)

Quality: ★★
Difficulty: ●
Maps: NTS 92-G/6 North Vancouver, Trail Ventures BC North Shore
Trailhead: 49°21'37" N, 123°01'41" W

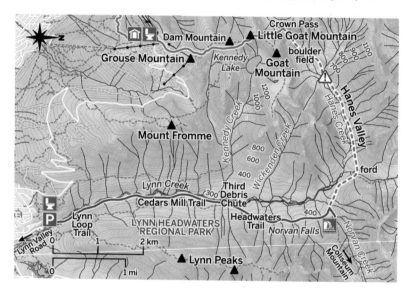

VISIT LYNN Headwaters Regional Park in spring or fall and you're likely to encounter admirable bolete, deer mushroom, apricot jelly, woody bracket, and other noteworthy fungi. Please note: foraging for fungi and plants, including berries and ferns, is prohibited in Metro Vancouver parks—and provincial parks too. One of the seven principles espoused by the Leave No Trace Center for Outdoor Ethics is "Leave what you find." This guideline also applies to the rusty logging relics you'll see on this four-season, transit-friendly outing in the territories of the Musqueam, Squamish, and Tsleil-Waututh First Nations.

From the park entrance (site of the historic B.C. Mills House), cross Lynn Creek using a bridge built near the remains of a water intake dam. Fill out a form at the hiker registration kiosk on the east side. Go north (left) on the wide Lynn Loop Trail for 1.8 km (1.1 mi) and, ignoring a trail to your right, continue onto the pretty Cedars Mill Trail, leaving most of the dog walkers and joggers behind. Here is the site of a logging mill closed in 1927. Reach the Third Debris Chute in 2.1 km (1.3 mi).

Join the northern portion of the Headwaters Trail, an old logging road that leads you deeper into the pleasing forest, away from Lynn Creek, and across several debris-flow channels. Three km (1.9 mi) later, the challenging route to Coliseum Mountain (Hike 6) strikes off to the right; ignore this turnoff. Before going right at the next junction, detour left to check out the nifty suspension bridge over Norvan Creek.

Head back upstream to Norvan Falls, where signs warn hikers to keep back from the steep cliff. Optionally, continue up the slope to (carefully) take in the view of the north peaks of Crown Mountain (Hike 10) from atop the horsetail waterfall. After lunch, retrace your steps to the park entrance.

Winter snow at Norvan Falls.

LONGER OPTION

On the far side of Norvan Creek, the trail continues to a junction. Rough routes carry on to the Hanes Valley and Lynn Lake. The difficult Hanes route is closed in winter and makes headlines for all the wrong reasons: lost, unprepared, injured, and dead hikers. To cross over to Grouse Mountain, ford Lynn Creek, head west up the Hanes Valley, and ascend the boulder field to Crown Pass. Turn south (left) for the steep trail to Little Goat Mountain, and follow the Alpine Trail (Hike 9) to the ski area. Descend the BCMC Trail to the transit-serviced base of the Skyride aerial tramway. One-way distance: 19 km (11.8 mi).

GETTING THERE

Transit: TransLink Bus 209, 210 (Upper Lynn Valley), or 228 (Lynn Valley) to Underwood Avenue at Evelyn Street. Walk east via Evelyn Park and Evelyn Street to Lynn Valley Road. Staying outside of the Lynn Headwaters Regional Park gate, continue east on Rice Lake Road, turn left on Marion Road, and head north on the Varley Trail for 1.5 km (0.9 mi) to the park entrance.

Vehicle: On Trans-Canada Highway 1, take Exit 19 and head north on Lynn Valley Road. Alternatively, from Exit 21, go north on Mountain Highway and turn right on Lynn Valley Road. If the park gate is open, follow the access road to the park entrance, using an overflow parking lot if necessary.

6
MOUNT BURWELL

Distance: 25 km (15.5 mi)
Time: 10.5 hours (round trip)
Elevation gain: 1,330 m (4,360 ft)
High point: 1,544 m (5,065 ft)

Quality: ★★
Difficulty: ◆
Maps: NTS 92-G/6 North Vancouver, Trail Ventures BC North Shore
Trailhead: 49°21'37" N, 123°01'41" W

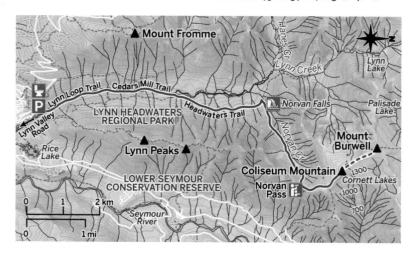

IN 1908, a B.C. Mountaineering Club party made the first recorded ascent of a pleasant peak at the north end of the Seymour River–Lynn Creek divide and called it White Mountain. Mount Burwell, as it is now known, lies in the territories of the Musqueam, Squamish, and Tsleil-Waututh First Nations.

From the park entrance, cross the Lynn Creek bridge and fill out a form at the hiker registration kiosk. Go north (left) onto the easy Lynn Loop Trail (1.8 km/1.1 mi), Cedars Mill Trail (2.1 km/1.3 mi), and Headwaters Trail (3 km/1.9 mi). Just before the Norvan Falls (Hike 5) junction, the gruelling Coliseum Mountain route (4.6 km/2.9 mi) leaves to the right. Follow this trail.

For the next 2.5 hours, make your way up the relentlessly steep slopes of the forested Norvan Creek drainage. Heading northeast, you will encounter a little waterfall and pool, as well as Norvan Meadows at the base of a rockslide. Upon gaining Norvan Pass, a viewpoint overlooking the Seymour Valley lies off to the right.

Continue north along the divide, merging with the rough approach from the Lower Seymour Conservation Reserve. Eventually, arrive on a subalpine ridge with a few small ponds. While the mountaintop seems to keep moving

Cathedral Mountain, Mount Burwell, and Coliseum Mountain from Crown Mountain.

backwards, the blocky summit of Coliseum Mountain (1,446 m/4,740 ft; 49°26'02" N, 123°00'24" W) finally comes 2 hours after the pass.

Wait, there's more: Mount Burwell (49°26'33" N, 123°00'55" W) is higher and tantalizingly close (1 km/0.6 mi). Descend to nearby ponds. Follow marking tapes along the ridge extending north, with the Cornett Lakes below to your right. The easy (Class 2) scramble parallels a drop-off. From the summit, marvel at the gully-incised south aspect of Cathedral Mountain and peer down at Palisade Lake. To return to your starting point, retrace your steps.

SHORTER OPTION

The punishing ascent to Coliseum Mountain—and the impressive views—should be more than enough for most hikers. Turn around at this lesser summit for a 23 km (14 mi) round trip lasting 9.5 hours. Dogs must be leashed on the Coliseum Mountain route.

GETTING THERE

Transit: TransLink Bus 209, 210 (Upper Lynn Valley), or 228 (Lynn Valley) to Underwood Avenue at Evelyn Street. Walk east via Evelyn Park and Evelyn Street to Lynn Valley Road. Staying outside of the Lynn Headwaters Regional Park gate, continue east on Rice Lake Road, turn left on Marion Road, and head north on the Varley Trail for 1.5 km (0.9 mi) to the park entrance.

Vehicle: On Trans-Canada Highway 1, take Exit 19 and head north on Lynn Valley Road. Alternatively, from Exit 21, go north on Mountain Highway and turn right on Lynn Valley Road. If the park gate is open, follow the access road to the park entrance, using an overflow parking lot if necessary.

7
LOWER MOUNT FROMME

Distance: 10 km (6.2 mi)
Time: 3.5 hours (lollipop)
Elevation gain: 435 m (1,430 ft)
High point: 770 m (2,525 ft)

Quality: ★
Difficulty: ■
Maps: NTS 92-G/6 North Vancouver, Trail Ventures BC North Shore
Trailhead: 49°21'33" N, 123°02'08" W

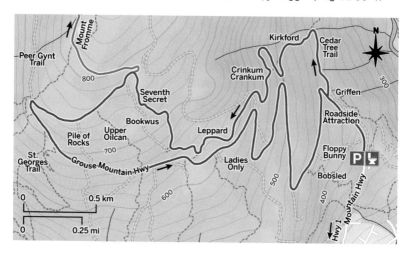

DOZENS OF mountain-bike trails cover the lower slopes of Hollyburn Mountain and Mount Seymour, but lesser-known Mount Fromme is ground zero for free riding on the North Shore. For hikers, Fromme's maze of second-growth forest paths is best saved for rainy days and shoulder season.

From the Mount Fromme parking lot, go past the water towers and up the old Grouse Mountain Highway. Just below the gravel road's first switchback, exit right onto the Cedar Tree Trail to begin a counterclockwise loop. This multi-use, cross-country path heads north to ford a rushing stream. Before it does, turn uphill on the Kirkford bike trail.

Stay right at marked forks, where left leads to Grouse Mountain Highway, to ascend the Crinkum Crankum, Leppard, and Seventh Secret trails. Several older paths diverge, so stick to the maintained trail. Admire (and bypass) the various bridges, ramps, and other artificial obstacles erected by crafty trail builders among the forest's ferns and conifers. The four aforementioned trails are designated as "mountain bike primary." While foot traffic is allowed, hikers should step aside for bikers. On multi-use trails, etiquette dictates bikers yield to hikers. In both cases, avoid shortcutting these paths.

Crinkum Crankum mountain-bike trail.

At the top of Seventh Secret (49°21′50″ N, 123°03′27″ W), turn left on the Grouse Mountain Highway. Follow the road down via six switchbacks to the parking lot.

Mount Fromme lies in the territories of the Musqueam, Squamish, and Tsleil-Waututh First Nations. Find out more about Fromme's bike trails in Wade Simmons and Sharon Bader's *Locals' Guide to North Shore Rides* (MTB Trails, 2011). Want to give back? The North Shore Mountain Bike Association sells trail passes to raise funds for trail building and maintenance.

LONGER OPTION

From the top of Seventh Secret, continue up the Grouse Mountain Highway to summit Mount Fromme (1,171 m/3,840 ft; Hike 8) via the upper section of the Peer Gynt Trail. Elevation gain: 835 m (2,740 ft) from parking lot to peak.

GETTING THERE

Transit: TransLink Bus 210 (Upper Lynn Valley) to McNair Drive at Tourney Road. Walk southwest on McNair, then north on Mountain Highway (1 km/0.6 mi).

Vehicle: On Trans-Canada Highway 1, take Exit 21 and go north on Mountain Highway. Alternatively, from Exit 19, head north on Lynn Valley Road and turn left on Mountain Highway. Drive to the top and pull into the Mount Fromme parking lot, opened in 2015. Pay attention to the posted closing time.

8
MOUNT FROMME

Distance: 11 km (6.8 mi)
Time: 5 hours (round trip)
Elevation gain: 810 m (2,660 ft)
High point: 1,171 m (3,840 ft)

Quality: ★
Difficulty: ■
Maps: NTS 92-G/6 North Vancouver, Trail Ventures BC North Shore
Trailhead: 49°20'57" N, 123°03'58" W

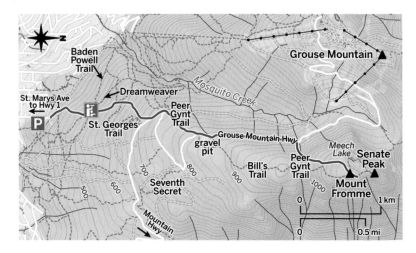

MOST VANCOUVERITES can't pick Mount Fromme out of a lineup, but it's the forested hill immediately east of Grouse Mountain in the territories of the Musqueam, Squamish, and Tsleil-Waututh First Nations. Formerly known as Timber Mountain, Fromme is heavily scarred by logging and crisscrossed by mountain-bike trails (see Hike 7). Still, it's an enjoyable hike that's accessible without snowshoes earlier in the season than other North Shore summits, due to its relatively low elevation.

One of several trailheads for this destination lies at the top of St. Marys Avenue. Head west (left) on the power line access road. Go past a gate and branch off to the right onto a wide trail that goes uphill, passing St. Marys Trail on the right and a radio antenna on the left. Cross a bridge and go up some stairs to the signed start of the St. Georges Trail, which heads uphill to the right. It soon intersects the Dreamweaver bike trail, parallels it briefly, and then forks right and uphill where Dreamweaver goes left. Follow orange markers and flagging tape as the rocky path crosses the Baden-Powell Trail (a bench on the left offers a view of Vancouver) and, higher up, a few bike paths to reach the old Grouse Mountain Highway.

View from the snowy summit.

Go left on the gravel road, passing Executioner on your left, to the next curve. Quickly find the Peer Gynt Trail beginning to the right of the big rock on the spur road. Head up the trail, again following orange markers, to re-emerge on the old highway. Go left on the road, passing a gravel pit. In twenty minutes, look for flagging on the right indicating the rugged upper section of the Peer Gynt Trail.

The rocky, rooty path climbs past a waterfall. Near the top, go straight through a four-way junction. From Mount Fromme's south summit (49°23′00″ N, 123°03′23″ W), spy Crown Mountain (Hike 10), Mount Burwell (Hike 6), and Mount Seymour (Hike 1)—and even Mount Garibaldi (Nch'kay' to the Squamish Nation) in the distance.

Senate Peak, the lower north summit, beckons across a steep gap. Several options are possible for the descent, but you're less likely to get lost if you retrace your steps. (A map and compass are essential.) Mount Fromme is named after Julius Fromme (1857–1941), a former reeve of the District of North Vancouver and owner of the Lynn Valley Lumber Company.

GETTING THERE
Transit: TransLink Bus 230 (Upper Lonsdale) to 200 block of East Braemar Road. Walk up the stairs at the crosswalk to St. Marys Avenue and continue north (600 m/0.4 mi).
Vehicle: On Trans-Canada Highway 1, take Exit 18. Go north on Lonsdale Avenue. Turn right on East Braemar Road, left on St. Georges Avenue, and right on Balmoral Road, which curves left and becomes St. Marys Avenue. Park near the intersection of St. Marys Avenue and Wooddale Road.

9
GOAT MOUNTAIN

Distance: 14 km (8.7 mi)
Time: 6.5 hours (circuit)
Elevation gain: 1,127 m (3,700 ft)
High point: 1,401 m (4,595 ft)

Quality: ★★
Difficulty: ■
Maps: NTS 92-G/6 North Vancouver, Trail
Ventures BC North Shore
Trailhead: 49°22'16" N, 123°05'54" W

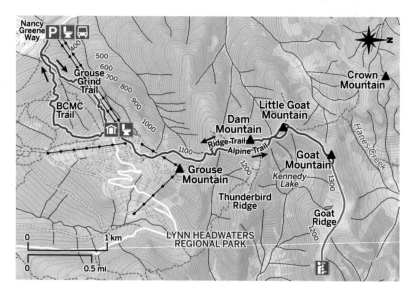

IN 2017, Metro Vancouver established Grouse Mountain Regional Park on the lower slopes of its namesake. Covering 75 ha (185 acres) in the territories of the Musqueam, Squamish, and Tsleil-Waututh First Nations, the park is home to two popular workouts: the Grouse Grind Trail and the B.C. Mountaineering Club (BCMC) Trail. Although most hikers and trail runners just do one or the other, both steep paths are best used to access the higher terrain behind Grouse Mountain (Mumtem to the Squamish Nation) in Lynn Headwaters Regional Park.

To hike Goat Mountain and Dam Mountain, go through the trailhead gate (closed at night and all winter) at the base of the Grouse Mountain ski area. Follow the crowd left onto the viewless Grouse Grind (no dogs or downhill hiking allowed), ascending 853 m (2,800 ft) over 2.9 km (1.8 m), with the help of 2,830 stairs. (Note for later: The BCMC Trail pops out of the woods just east of the Grind.) From the chalet at the top, head north for 1.2 km (0.7 mi), walk up the service road to the left of the Lower Peak ski run, and come to the hiker registration kiosk.

After gaining some height on Dam Mountain, follow the rugged Alpine Trail right, saving this summit for the return. Pass a zipline tower and ignore the Thunderbird Trail leaving to the right. Keep right at subsequent junctions, including one with the trail to Crown Pass. After ascending a steep section with a fixed cord, choose the left fork for the scrambly route through the rocks to the top of Goat Mountain (49°24'13" N, 123°04'44" W). Soak up the terrific view of Crown Mountain (Hike 10) and its subpeak, The Camel, across the Hanes Valley.

On the descent, take the trail dropping east from the summit, then turn right at the Goat Ridge

Crown Mountain from Dam Mountain.

junction. Just after the Crown Pass junction, go right and follow the Ridge Trail over indistinct Little Goat Mountain (1,323 m/4,340 ft) and Dam Mountain (1,349 m/4,425 ft). Continue south to the chalet. Descend the BCMC Trail and hang a right on the Baden-Powell Trail to complete the circuit.

Camping, smoking, balloons, and foraging for plants and fungi are banned in Lynn Headwaters Regional Park. Paying customers can use the Skyride aerial tram to skip the Grouse Grind and/or BCMC Trail.

LONGER OPTION
The Goat Ridge route extends 1.6 km (1 mi) east from Goat Mountain to tarns and a viewpoint.

GETTING THERE
Transit: TransLink Bus 232 or 236 (Grouse Mountain) to Grouse Mountain Skyride.
Vehicle: On Trans-Canada Highway 1, take Exit 14 and head north on Capilano Road, which turns into Nancy Greene Way, to arrive at the base of the Grouse Mountain ski area.

10
CROWN MOUNTAIN

Distance: 17 km (10.6 mi)
Time: 8 hours (round trip)
Elevation gain: 1,227 m (4,025 ft)
High point: 1,501 m (4,925 ft)

Quality: ★★★★
Difficulty: ◆◆
Maps: NTS 92-G/6 North Vancouver, Trail Ventures BC North Shore
Trailhead: 49°22'16" N, 123°05'54" W

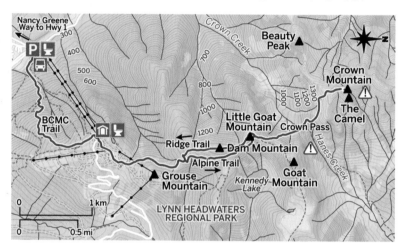

CROWN MOUNTAIN is one of the more distinctive peaks on the North Shore. Rising north of Grouse Mountain, the main peak is fittingly referred to as The Pyramid and the curiously shaped rock formation known as The Camel sits on its shoulder. This classic hike is not for everyone. Novices, kids, and dogs have no business here. Summiting requires negotiating vertiginous trails and exposed scrambling—and is better left to days without rain, snow, or significant wind. One slip on this mountain—located in the territories of the Musqueam, Squamish, and Tsleil-Waututh First Nations—could do you in.

Begin by heading east on the Baden-Powell Trail from the trailhead gate (closed at night and all winter) at the base of the Grouse Mountain (Mumtem in S_kwx_wú7mesh sníchim) ski area. Ignore the mob going left for the Grouse Grind Trail. Take the third left to ascend Grouse Mountain Regional Park's less-crowded B.C. Mountaineering Club (BCMC) Trail to the chalet up top.

Make your way north toward the peak of Grouse—past grizzly bears in captivity and other resort spectacles—and up the service road left of the Lower Peak ski run. Fill out a form at the Lynn Headwaters Regional Park hiker registration kiosk. After gaining some elevation on Dam Mountain,

Crown Mountain and The Camel, viewed from the south.

follow the rugged Alpine Trail right and across its eastern slopes. Pass the turnoff for Thunderbird Ridge on your right. An hour from the chalet, reach the col between Little Goat Mountain and Goat Mountain (Hike 9).

Choose the trail to Crown Pass (1,030 m/3,380 ft), which leads off to the left, and tackle the super-steep and slippery descent, starting with fantastic views of your objective. Fixed chains provide assistance. A half-hour later, the epic Hanes Valley route strikes off to the right, but go straight to start the ascent of Crown Mountain. The well-marked trail passes an imposing cliff as it rises in the woods. Scramble across and up slabs following paint smears on rock. Pick your way through a boulder field and up to a shoulder above the aptly (but not factually) named Crater Rim arête. Crown's southeast face lies before you.

Now the real fun (and danger) begins. The loose path leads up the ridge until it's time for the final Class 3 scramble to the top of The Pyramid (49°24′36″ N, 123°05′31″ W). An alternate route lies left of the ridgetop and goes up the back. While the knife-edge summit is thrilling, it's not exactly a comfortable lunch spot. The North Shore mountains surround you, with The Camel and Crown's north peaks and west summit (Beauty Peak) closer at hand.

After clambering out of Crown Pass on the way back, go right to take the Ridge Trail over Little Goat Mountain (1,323 m/4,340 ft) and Dam Mountain (1,349 m/4,425 ft) en route to the chalet and BCMC Trail.

GETTING THERE
Transit: TransLink Bus 232 or 236 (Grouse Mountain) to Grouse Mountain Skyride.
Vehicle: On Trans-Canada Highway 1, take Exit 14 and head north on Capilano Road, which turns into Nancy Greene Way, to arrive at the base of the Grouse Mountain ski area.

11
CAPILANO PACIFIC TRAIL

Distance: 14 km (8.7 mi)
Time: 4 hours (lollipop)
Elevation gain: 160 m (520 ft)
High point: 160 m (520 ft)

Quality: ★
Difficulty: ●
Maps: NTS 92-G/6 North Vancouver
Trailhead: 49°19'21" N, 123°08'49" W

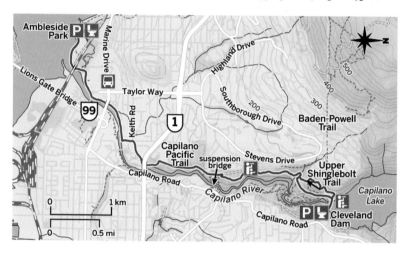

YOU'VE PROBABLY heard of the multi-use Trans Canada Trail, but what about the National Hiking Trail? Backed by Hike Canada and Hike B.C., the decades-in-the-making NHT aims to link existing footpaths between Port Alberni, B.C., and St. John's, N.L. The long-distance trail will span 10,000 km (6,000 mi) from coast to coast, with a spur connecting it to the top of the Pacific Crest Trail at E.C. Manning Provincial Park.

Metro Vancouver has designated several park trails as part of the NHT. One of these is the Capilano Pacific Trail in Capilano River Regional Park, which straddles the West Vancouver–North Vancouver district boundary and lies in the territories of the Musqueam, Squamish, and Tsleil-Waututh First Nations.

The Capilano Pacific Trail (X̱wemélch'stn Shewálh in Skwxwú7mesh sníchim) begins at the east end of Ambleside Park (Ch'tl'am) and runs from the mouth of the Capilano River (X̱wemélch'stn Stakw) to Cleveland Dam. Much of the coast-to-canyon route follows a 1917 rail bed built by the Capilano Timber Company. Popular with joggers and dog walkers (pets on-leash, please), it's best saved for a rainy day.

From the river mouth, head upstream along the west bank, ducking under three bridges—one for the Canadian National Railway, the second behind

Keep dogs on designated trails and out of streams and wetlands.

the Park Royal shopping mall in the Capilano reserve (X̱wemélch'stn), and the third for Marine Drive. In a half-hour, take the stairs on the left, leaving the riverbank, and turn right on Keith Road. Follow the road under Highway 1 until its end, and continue upstream on the gravel path.

After 1 hour (4 km/2.5 mi) of hiking, you reach the back of the privately owned Capilano Suspension Bridge Park. Keep right at the Moyne Drive turn-off, and go right at the next two junctions, trading the trappings of suburbia for lush forest. A wooden viewing platform on the right overlooks Capilano Canyon.

The trail continues over a long wooden footbridge, keeps right at the stairs, and goes straight through the Upper Shinglebolt Trail junction. Join a gravel service road and follow the fence to the roadway atop the 92 m (300 ft) tall Cleveland Dam (49°21′38″ N, 123°06′42″ W), which dates back to 1954 and impounds Capilano Lake. Feel the spray and hear the roar. Backtrack to the concrete dam's right abutment and head west on the Baden-Powell Trail. Turn left to descend the Upper Shinglebolt Trail. Go right to rejoin the Capilano Pacific Trail and retrace your steps to Ambleside Park.

GETTING THERE
Transit: TransLink Bus 239, 250, 251, 252, 253, 254, 255, 256, 257, or 258 to Park Royal.
Vehicle: From Highway 99's Marine Drive–Taylor Way intersection in West Vancouver, north of the Lions Gate Bridge and south of Trans-Canada Highway 1 (Exit 13), drive west on Marine Drive. Go south on 13th Street and east on Argyle Avenue. Park past the Squamish Nation Welcome Figure in Ambleside Park.

12
HOLLYBURN MOUNTAIN

Distance: 10 km (6.2 mi)
Time: 4 hours (lollipop)
Elevation gain: 415 m (1,360 ft)
High point: 1,326 m (4,350 ft)

Quality: ★★
Difficulty: ■
Maps: NTS 92-G/6 North Vancouver,
Friends of Cypress Provincial Park
Trailhead: 49°22'45" N, 123°11'30" W

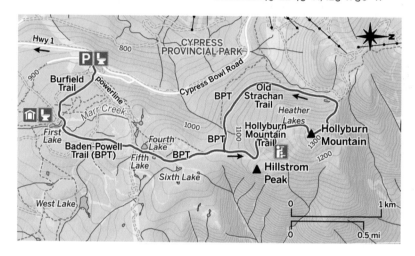

ON TOP of Hollyburn Mountain, you're likely to be visited by whisky jacks and ravens looking for a free lunch. Other birds you might see on this hike include the chestnut-backed chickadee, sooty grouse, red-breasted sapsucker, and winter wren.

From the B.C. Parks kiosk at the base of the Nordic ski area, pass under the power line, briefly go left on the gravel road, and then go right to take the Burfield Trail to First Lake. Here stands the historic Hollyburn Lodge, opened in 1927 and rebuilt in 2017. Follow the path to the left, around the lake's north shore. Turn left on the Baden-Powell Trail to head up Hollyburn Ridge.

Over the next 1.9 km (1.2 mi), pass a warming hut, Fourth Lake, and Fifth Lake. Where the B-P Trail turns west, continue straight ahead (north) on the steeper Hollyburn Mountain Trail for 1.8 km (1.1 mi), coming close to minor Hillstrom Peak (1,159 m/3,800 ft), earning a viewpoint, and visiting Heather Lakes.

Enjoy the sight of the Twin Sisters (Ch'ich'iyúy to the Squamish Nation) and Crown Mountain (Hike 10)—or fog—from the summit knob. Examine the outcrops for chlorite schist, quartz veins, and hornblende diorite dikes

Raven guarding the hikers' access trail in winter.

surrounded by metasedimentary rock. It can be tempting to feed wildlife, but please resist the urge to do so; it's more harmful than helpful.

Once satisfied, plunge northwest down a rough, steep path to the dank col between Mount Strachan (Hike 13) and Hollyburn Mountain. Take the left-hand fork and descend south on the Old Strachan Trail amid old-growth yellow cedar and western hemlock trees, including the Hollyburn Giant (diameter: 3.2 m/10.5 ft). Turn left on the B-P Trail and retrace your steps to First Lake and the Burfield Trail.

Cypress Provincial Park lies in the territories of the Musqueam, Squamish, and Tsleil-Waututh First Nations. During ski season, snowshoers can follow the (free) hikers' access trail from the base of the Nordic ski area to the summit (round trip: 6 km/3.7 mi). It is marked with wands, stays outside the ski-area boundary, and is glorious after a snowfall. Heed the posted avalanche bulletins. Dogs must be leashed.

GETTING THERE

Transit: Better Environmentally Sound Transportation's Parkbus offers coach service on select summer weekends to Cypress Provincial Park's downhill ski area from downtown Vancouver. Walk east on the Baden-Powell Trail to access the Hollyburn Mountain Trail.

Vehicle: On Trans-Canada Highway 1 in West Vancouver, take Exit 8. Head north on Cypress Bowl Road for 13 km (8 mi). Turn right to arrive at the cross-country ski area in Cypress Provincial Park.

13

MOUNT STRACHAN

Distance: 10 km (6.2 mi)
Time: 4.5 hours (loop)
Elevation gain: 544 m (1,785 ft)
High point: 1,459 m (4,790 ft)

Quality: ★★★
Difficulty: ■
Maps: NTS 92-G/6 North Vancouver, Friends of Cypress Provincial Park
Trailhead: 49°23'47" N, 123°12'16" W

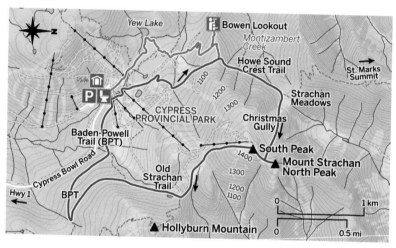

ON A clear day, the satisfying panorama from Mount Strachan (pronounced "strahn") extends far beyond the Twin Sisters (Ch'ich'iyúy to the Squamish Nation) and Howe Sound (Atl'Kitsem). From this subalpine summit in Cypress Provincial Park, your gaze extends to Mount Garibaldi (Nch'kay') and Sky Pilot Mountain to the north and Golden Ears to the east.

Getting there is super fun too, if you climb up the back side and make the hike a clockwise loop. From the B.C. Parks kiosk past the Olympic rings (915 m/3,000 ft), go north on the Howe Sound Crest Trail (Hike 14), which quickly splits into west and east branches. Head right for the old (east) path. The trails reunite by a vista of the Sisters, also known as The Lions.

Continue north on the Howe Sound Crest Trail across forested slopes to lovely Strachan Meadows at the 2.6 km (1.6 mi) mark. Between two bridges over the headwaters of Montizambert Creek (49°24'49" N, 123°12'14" W), a path on the right strikes off toward Christmas Gully, where snow lingers in the shadows. The steepening route heads up the obvious couloir—ducking into the trees for part of the exhilarating ascent—to emerge in the saddle between Mount Strachan's two summits.

North peak of Mount Strachan and the Twin Sisters (Ch'ich'iyúy).

Go left to drink in the sea of Coast Mountains from the higher north peak (49°24′47″ N, 123°11′36″ W). Then head back and up the south peak (1,442 m/ 4,730 ft), at the top of the downhill ski area. For your descent, the Old Strachan Trail stays east of the ski runs, visits the site of a 1963 plane crash, and runs through a meadow to the dank col between Strachan and Hollyburn Mountain (Hike 12). Pay attention to trail signs and markers; it's easy to get off-path.

Stick with the Old Strachan Trail as it descends south amid old-growth yellow cedar and western hemlock trees. At the Baden-Powell Trail, turn right to return to the parking area, 2 km (1.2 mi) distant.

Cypress Provincial Park was established in 1975. Open fires and bikes on trails are prohibited, and dogs must be leashed. Founded in 1990, the Friends of Cypress Provincial Park Society advocates for the preservation of the park's natural and historical features.

SHORTER OPTION

For an easy loop, go up the east (right) branch of the Howe Sound Crest Trail and turn left onto the west branch. Visit Bowen Lookout to see Bowen Island (Nex̱wlélex̱wem; Hike 80) and Gambier Island (Chá7elkwnech) from above. Further down, keep right on the wheelchair-accessible Yew Lake Trail to enjoy the wetlands along Cypress Creek. Go left on the Baden-Powell Trail to finish the 3.9 km (2.4 mi) loop.

GETTING THERE

Transit: Parkbus offers coach service on select summer weekends to Cypress Provincial Park's downhill ski area from downtown Vancouver.

Vehicle: On Trans-Canada Highway 1 in West Vancouver, take Exit 8. Head north on Cypress Bowl Road. Drive up to the downhill ski area and park as close to the top as possible.

14
UNNECESSARY MOUNTAIN

Distance: 17 km (10.6 mi)
Time: 8 hours (reverse lollipop)
Elevation gain: 633 m (2,080 ft)
High point: 1,548 m (5,080 ft)

Quality: ★★★
Difficulty: ◆
Maps: NTS 92-G/6 North Vancouver, Trail Ventures BC North Shore
Trailhead: 49°23'47" N, 123°12'16" W

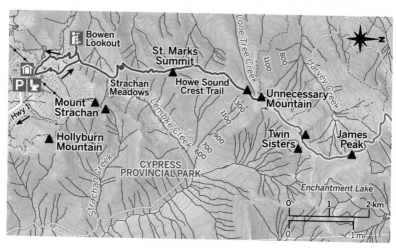

SCALING THE iconic Twin Sisters, also known as The Lions, is taxing enough. Imagine having to surmount another peak on the way there and back. That's how Unnecessary Mountain got its name; the old trail to the Sisters from Lions Bay goes up and over it.

These days, nobody's forcing anyone to visit Unnecessary Mountain. Nevertheless, it's a worthy destination in its own right, particularly as a strenuous day hike on the Howe Sound Crest Trail in Cypress Provincial Park. From the B.C. Parks kiosk past the Olympic rings (915 m/3,000 ft), go north on the HSCT, which quickly splits into two branches. Head right for the original (east) path; save the newer (west) trail and Bowen Lookout for the return.

Where the paths reunite, there's a vista of the Sisters, known as Ch'ich'iyúy to the Squamish Nation. Poet E. Pauline Johnson (Tekahionwake) famously retells the story of "The Two Sisters" in her 1911 book, *Legends of Vancouver*, based on her conversations with Chief Joe Capilano (Sa7plek), a member of the 1889 party credited with the West Lion's first recorded ascent.

Continue north along the forested slopes of Mount Strachan (Hike 13), perhaps spotting an American three-toed woodpecker, to pleasant Strachan

Howe Sound (Atl'Kitsem) from St. Marks Summit.

Meadows at the 2.6 km (1.6 mi) mark. Next, the HSCT negotiates a couple of wooded bumps en route to St. Marks Summit (1,371 m/4,500 ft; 49°25′41″ N, 123°12′23″ W) at 5.5 km (3.4 mi). Turn back here for a moderate, 4.5-hour round trip. The best and worst are yet to come.

Drop 175 m (575 ft) to a col, only to regain it and more on the wickedly steep and rugged ascent of Unnecessary Mountain. A magnificent ridge walk to the south peak (49°26′41″ N, 123°12′01″ W) or farther to the slightly lower north peak (1,543 m/5,060 ft; 49°26′54″ N, 123°11′53″ W) rewards your efforts. Gaze upon the vertically jointed hornblende diorite of the Sisters and peer down at Bowen Island (Nex̱wlélex̱wem; Hike 80) and Gambier Island (Chá7elkwnech) in Howe Sound (Atl'Kitsem).

Watersheds on either side of the ridge supply drinking water for Lions Bay and Metro Vancouver. Open fires are prohibited, and dogs must be leashed in the park. However, B.C. Parks advises that dogs are "not suitable" in the backcountry due to wildlife concerns.

LONGER OPTION

Done in full, the Howe Sound Crest Trail is a 29 km (18 mi) overnight hike. Part of the proposed route for the National Hiking Trail, the HSCT goes between the Twin Sisters, summits James Peak, and ends south of Porteau Cove, off Highway 99. Camp at Magnesia Meadows, Brunswick Lake, or Deeks Lake.

Dehydration and heat exhaustion are real risks on this trail in summer; carry extra water and wear a hat. In winter, this is avalanche terrain; consult Avalanche Canada's forecast for the South Coast before heading out.

GETTING THERE

Transit: Parkbus offers coach service on select summer weekends to Cypress Provincial Park's downhill ski area from downtown Vancouver.
Vehicle: On Trans-Canada Highway 1 in West Vancouver, take Exit 8. Head north on Cypress Bowl Road. Drive up to the downhill ski area and park as close to the top as possible. (Use Parking Lot 3B for overnight trips.)

15
BLACK MOUNTAIN

Distance: 9.5 km (5.9 mi)
Time: 5 hours (circuit)
Elevation gain: 310 m (1,020 ft)
High point: 1,224 m (4,015 ft)

Quality: ★★★
Difficulty: ●
Maps: NTS 92-G/6 North Vancouver,
Friends of Cypress Provincial Park
Trailhead: 49°23'47" N, 123°12'16" W

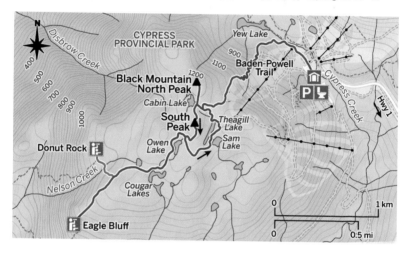

FOR SOME, the cloudy days of fall signal that it's time to put away the hiking boots. Not so fast. Lace 'em up and head to Cypress Provincial Park in the territories of the Musqueam, Squamish, and Tsleil-Waututh First Nations. Autumn is the ideal season for paying a visit to Black Mountain's pretty lakes and woods.

From the B.C. Parks kiosk past the Olympic rings (915 m/3,000 ft), head westbound on the Baden-Powell Trail. Keep left at turnoffs for the Howe Sound Crest Trail (Hike 14) and Yew Lake Trail. The gravel path switchbacks up Black Mountain, paralleling the Maëlle Ricker's Gold ski run. (Between November and May, snowshoers must pick up a free backcountry-access corridor tag at the Black Mountain Lodge to pass through the ski area.)

Reach a major junction in 2.1 km (1.3 mi). Turn right for Cabin Lake, a summer swimming hole, and right again to visit the Yew Lake Lookout on Black Mountain's north and highest summit (49°23'39" N, 123°13'08" W). Back at Cabin Lake, continue on the Black Mountain Loop (counterclockwise) to the rocky south summit (1,218 m/3,995 ft). Rejoin the B-P Trail farther south.

Fall hike on Black Mountain.

Go west (right) for 1.6 km (1 mi), passing Owen Lake and Cougar Lakes and losing elevation, to break out of the trees at wide-open Eagle Bluff (1,050 m/3,445 ft). Lay your eyes on Vancouver and Burrard Inlet (Tsleil-Wat to the Tsleil-Waututh), Bowen Island (Nex̱wlélex̱wem to the Squamish; Hike 80) in Howe Sound (Atl'Kitsem), and beyond to Mount Baker. While you're enthralled with the view, a raven might drop in to snag some lunch.

On your return, stick with the B-P Trail eastbound all the way back to the trailhead. That way you'll see Sam Lake and Theagill Lake and complete the scenic loop of the Black Mountain Plateau. Fires are prohibited in the backcountry, and bikes are not permitted on park trails. Dogs must be on-leash.

The B-P Trail, which this excursion samples, traverses the North Shore mountains for 48 km (30 mi), from Horseshoe Bay to Deep Cove. Built in 1971 by Boy Scouts and Girl Guides, it's typically day-hiked in four sections by completists—or dashed in a matter of hours as part of the Knee Knackering North Shore Trail Run.

LONGER OPTION
A short side trip to Donut Rock is a worthy diversion. Between Cougar Lakes and Eagle Bluff, the rough but flagged Donut Rock Trail strikes off to the north. Trees largely obscure views from the lonely bluff, just 15 minutes from the Baden-Powell Trail.

GETTING THERE
Transit: Parkbus offers coach service on select summer weekends to Cypress Provincial Park's downhill ski area from downtown Vancouver.
Vehicle: On Trans-Canada Highway 1 in West Vancouver, take Exit 8. Head north on Cypress Bowl Road. Drive up to the downhill ski area and park as close to the top as possible.

16
WEST KNOB

Distance: 12 km (7.5 mi)
Time: 5 hours (round trip)
Elevation gain: 610 m (2,000 ft)
High point: 720 m (2,360 ft)

Quality: ★★
Difficulty: ■
Maps: NTS 92-G/6 North Vancouver, Trail Ventures BC North Shore
Trailhead: 49°21'39" N, 123°15'31" W

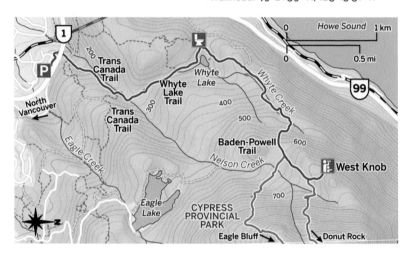

ESTABLISHED IN 2014, Whyte Lake Park is the largest park in West Vancouver. It preserves old-growth trees and provides a vital link between Nelson Canyon Park and Cypress Provincial Park. This shoulder-season hike to Whyte Lake and the West Knob on Black Mountain visits all three parks, which lie in the territories of the Musqueam, Squamish, and Tsleil-Waututh First Nations.

From the Westport Road trailhead, take the service road west and under the Nelson Canyon Bridge to a water tank. Don't cross the old Highway 1 bridge; go right on the Trans Canada Trail.

Soon the easy Whyte Lake Trail leaves to the left of the Trans Canada Trail, bridging Nelson Creek and Whyte Creek on its way north to Whyte Lake, 3 km (1.9 mi) in. Visit the wooden dock and turn right at the lovely outhouse to join the Baden-Powell Trail in the woods above the lake. The rugged trail heads up the dark lower slopes of Black Mountain, with switchbacks.

An old metal plate on a tree indicating "Eagle Ridge" (Hike 15) lies 60 minutes farther on the B-P Trail (590 m/1,935 ft; 49°23'02" N, 123°14'45" W). Here, however, you go left on the rough and sometimes ill-defined Donut Rock Trail.

Macrofungi on the West Knob.

At the next junction, head left and follow yellow signs to the West Knob viewpoint (49°23′16″ N, 123°14′35″ W). Look down at Bowen Island (Nex̱wlélex̱wem to the Squamish; Hike 80) in Howe Sound (Atl'Kitsem) through the treetops. Return the way you came.

Dogs must be on-leash in Whyte Lake Park. No camping, fires, or smoking.

LONGER OPTION

From the West Knob junction, the Donut Rock Trail continues up Black Mountain. Beyond the lonely bluff at Donut Rock, the route rejoins the Baden-Powell Trail above Eagle Bluff (1,050 m/3,445 ft). Turn right to return to Whyte Lake.

GETTING THERE

Transit: TransLink Bus 250 (Horseshoe Bay) to 6300 block of Marine Drive. Walk north to the roundabout and cross the highway overpass. Turn right on Horseshoe Bay Drive and find the Black Mountain trailhead on the left (49°22′01″ N, 123°16′29″ W). Hike up the Baden-Powell Trail, merging with the Whyte Lake approach in 2 km (1.2 mi).

Vehicle: On Trans-Canada Highway 1 in West Vancouver, take Exit 4. From the north end of the highway overpass, drive west on Westport Road, go under the highway, and turn right into the Whyte Lake trailhead and parking lot.

17
MOUNT HARVEY

Distance: 13 km (8.1 mi)
Time: 7.5 hours (round trip)
Elevation gain: 1,420 m (4,660 ft)
High point: 1,652 m (5,420 ft)

Quality: ★★
Difficulty: ◆
Maps: NTS 92-G/6 North Vancouver, Trail Ventures BC North Shore
Trailhead: 49°28'15" N, 123°14'05" W

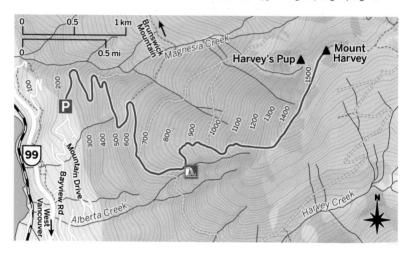

MOUNT HARVEY is the destination of one of the cartoonishly steep trails that snake skyward from the village of Lions Bay. The reward for your considerable efforts is the backside view of the Twin Sisters (Ch'ich'iyúy to the Squamish Nation), also known as The Lions, that most people never get to see.

From the Sunset Drive gate, the logging road climbs relentlessly into Lions Bay's drinking watershed. Keep right—ignoring routes to Brunswick Mountain (Hike 18) and Magnesia Creek—until an orange marker on the left (before the road hits Alberta Creek) signifies the start of the Mount Harvey trail. Early on, a waterfall vantage lies off to the right. Two Howe Sound (Atl'Kitsem) viewpoints, the first looking out at Bowen Island (Nexwlélexwem; Hike 80) and the second at Gambier Island (Chá7elkwnech), break up the sweaty ascent.

The hike culminates with a ridge walk to one of the highest peaks on the North Shore. Breaking out of the forest, an eye-popping view of the West Lion provides ample motivation to continue after a much-deserved rest. Along the southwest ridge, you'll notice a rock tower, called Harvey's Pup by climbers, to

Descending the southwest ridge of Mount Harvey.

your left. A simple scramble earns you Mount Harvey's summit (49°28′31″ N, 123°12′01″ W).

From the panoramic perch, the middle ground includes the Sisters below you; Brunswick Mountain, the North Shore's highest summit; and Hat Mountain, wearing a radio repeater. Under a clear sky, you can make out Mamquam Mountain, Golden Ears (Hike 57), and Mount Baker in the distance. To the northeast, a red emergency hut lies in Magnesia Meadows, a stop on the 29 km (18 mi) Howe Sound Crest Trail in Cypress Provincial Park.

Try not to let thoughts of ice cream at Lions Bay or Horseshoe Bay (Ch'axáy) distract you on the descent. It's easy to go off-trail on the braided forest path. Heat exhaustion is also a significant risk on Mount Harvey.

Founded in 1983, Lions Bay Search and Rescue serves the area between Horseshoe Bay and Porteau Cove (Xwáẃchayay). The team recommends all hikers leave a trip plan with a reliable person, prepare for unexpected weather, and carry the ten essentials. Be sure to stay away from cornices (overhanging shelves of snow), as they can collapse suddenly.

GETTING THERE

Transit: TransLink Bus 259 (Lions Bay) to the Highway 99 underpass or Community Shuttle C12 (Brunswick) to Crosscreek Road. Walk 2 km (1.2 mi) to the Sunset Drive trailhead.

Vehicle: On Highway 99 (Sea to Sky Highway), take the Lions Bay Avenue exit 11 km (6.8 mi) north of Horseshoe Bay. Heading east, immediately make a left on Crosscreek Road. On the far side of Harvey Creek, go right on Centre Road, left on Bayview Road, left on Mountain Drive, and left on Sunset Drive. If the small parking area at Sunset's north end is full (99 per cent guaranteed), find a spot on Mountain Drive or lower down. Beware of the many no-parking signs.

18
BRUNSWICK MOUNTAIN

Distance: 14 km (8.7 mi)
Time: 8.5 hours (round trip)
Elevation gain: 1,560 m (5,120 ft)
High point: 1,788 m (5,870 ft)

Quality: ★★★
Difficulty: ◆◆
Maps: NTS 92-G/6 North Vancouver, Trail
Ventures BC North Shore
Trailhead: 49°28'15" N, 123°14'05" W

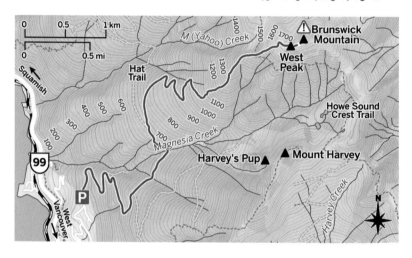

NAMED AFTER a late-1700s British naval warship turned prison boat, Bruns-wick Mountain is the highest of the North Shore peaks. It shares the same Lions Bay trailhead as neighbouring Mount Harvey (Hike 17), which com-memorates the gunship's captain, and the Twin Sisters, also known as The Lions. Like those objectives, Brunswick stands in Squamish Nation territory and calls for an insanely arduous ascent. No pain, no elevation gain.

From the Sunset Drive gate (230 m/755 ft), the logging road climbs ruth-lessly into Lions Bay's drinking watershed. Keep right at the first fork, then hang a left at the next junction (49°28'16" N, 123°13'33" W), signed for Bruns-wick Mountain. Heading north on an overgrown road, the Brunswick trail eases up on the grade and crosses Magnesia Creek—likely your last chance to refill water bottles.

After an hour or more of hiking, go right at the next fork. (Left is for the Hat Trail, which approaches Tunnel Bluff [Hike 19] and Hat Mountain.) Now it's time to face the punishing wooded slopes of Brunswick. The old road rises stiffly, giving way to a path and then dispensing with switchbacks. Eventu-ally, reach a high four-way junction (1,520 m/4,990 ft) with the Howe Sound

Deeks Lakes from Brunswick Mountain's west peak.

Crest Trail, in the middle of its 29 km (18 mi) journey from Cypress Bowl to Highway 99, south of Porteau Cove (Xwáẃchayay to the Squamish).

Don't break out the (melted) chocolate-covered blueberries yet. The path straight ahead is rocky, even steeper, and sometimes faint. Finally, gain a saddle on the west ridge and the fringe of Cypress Provincial Park. Go right for the easy (without rain, snow, or ice) scramble to the west peak. Most hikers are content to stop here. Admire Davidson's penstemon blooming from cracks in the rock.

Only experienced parties should go any farther. To claim the true summit (49°29′16″ N, 123°12′05″ W), continue east along the south side of the ridge. Drop down to a loose gully and clamber over a mountaintop helipad. A final crux of exposed scrambling deposits you on top. Your panoramic prizes: Deeks Lakes, Mount Hanover, the Sisters (Ch'ich'iyúy), Mount Harvey (Hike 17), and Howe Sound (Atl'Kitsem) close at hand, with Tetrahedron Peak, the Tantalus Range, Mount Garibaldi, and The Black Tusk (Hike 31) in the distance. Return the way you came.

GETTING THERE
Transit: TransLink Bus 259 (Lions Bay) to the Highway 99 underpass or Community Shuttle C12 (Brunswick) to Crosscreek Road. Walk 2 km (1.2 mi) to the Sunset Drive trailhead.
Vehicle: On Highway 99 (Sea to Sky Highway), take the Lions Bay Avenue exit, 11 km (6.8 mi) north of Horseshoe Bay. Heading east, immediately make a left on Crosscreek Road. On the far side of Harvey Creek, go right on Centre Road, left on Bayview Road, left on Mountain Drive, and left on Sunset Drive. If the small parking area at Sunset's north end is full (99 per cent guaranteed), find a spot on Mountain Drive or lower down. Beware of the many no-parking signs.

19
TUNNEL BLUFF

Distance: 9 km (5.6 mi)
Time: 5 hours (round trip)
Elevation gain: 640 m (2,100 ft)
High point: 700 m (2,270 ft)

Quality: ★★★
Difficulty: ■
Maps: NTS 92-G/6 North Vancouver
Trailhead: 49°29'06" N, 123°14'52" W

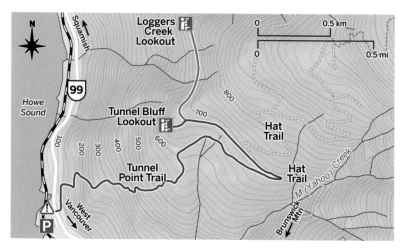

AFTER SAILING into Howe Sound in 1792, Captain George Vancouver assessed it as a "dreary and comfortless region." Indeed, the British naval officer wrote that the fjord's shores constituted "the base of the stupendous snowy barrier, thinly wooded, and rising from the sea abruptly to the clouds; from whose frigid summit, the dissolving snow in foaming torrents rushed down the sides and chasms of its rugged surface, exhibiting altogether a sublime, though gloomy spectacle, which animated nature seemed to have deserted."

So it's safe to say Vancouver wouldn't have enjoyed a shoulder-season jaunt to Tunnel Bluff—his loss—in Squamish Nation territory. Sweeping views of Howe Sound (Atl'Kitsem) are the raison d'être for this hike. The most treacherous parts of this outing are the start and the finish. That's because the trailhead lies across the fast-moving Sea to Sky Highway from the Tunnel Point rest area's off-ramp. Plus, with the curve in the road, visibility is poorer on the return.

The Tunnel Point Trail quickly gets down to business, following yellow markers up into the forest. A succession of viewpoints facing Howe Sound or the north face of Mount Harvey (Hike 17) offer ample opportunity for breaks.

View of Howe Sound (Atl'Kitsem) from the Tunnel Bluff Lookout.

Fixed ropes assist with steep bits. Eventually, you emerge on a pleasant old logging road, and the grade eases.

At the first junction, 2 hours in, head left on the Hat Trail. (Right leads to the Brunswick Mountain trail [Hike 18] and Lions Bay.) Then it's left again on the trail to Tunnel Bluff Lookout. (The Hat Trail continues toward Hat Mountain, northwest of Brunswick.)

Soon a "Lookout" sign directs you left yet again. Your clifftop destination overlooks several landforms put in context by the Squamish Lil'wat Cultural Centre's interpretative panels at Tunnel Point. Take a long lunch and savour the far-from-gloomy scene: Horseshoe Bay (Ch'axáy), Bowyer Island (Lhákw'tich), Bowen Island (Nex̱wlélex̱wem; Hike 80), Gambier Island (Chá7elkwnech), Seagull Rocks (Kwiyitkm), and Anvil Island (Lhaxwm). Return the way you came.

LONGER OPTION

At the "Lookout" sign, go straight to follow the rough route to Loggers Creek Lookout (15 minutes one way) before making your way to Tunnel Bluff. Sure, this farther viewpoint is nothing special, but it's still a worthy extension on a repeat visit.

GETTING THERE

Vehicle: The Tunnel Point rest area is found on the southbound side of Highway 99 (Sea to Sky Highway), 15 km (9 mi) north of Horseshoe Bay. Northbound drivers should U-turn via the Porteau Road/Deeks Lake Trail exit, 9 km (5.6 mi) past Lions Bay.

20
SEA TO SUMMIT TRAIL

Distance: 8 km (5 mi)
Time: 4 hours (up)
Elevation gain: 850 m (2,790 ft)
High point: 885 m (2,900 ft)

Quality: ★★
Difficulty: ■
Maps: NTS 92-G/11 Squamish, Hiking
GuideMaps Squamish
Trailhead: 49°40'17" N, 123°09'38" W

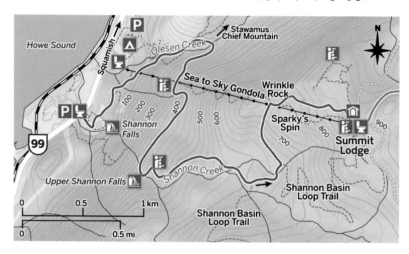

WHEN THE Sea to Sky Gondola was proposed, many outdoor recreationists (including this author) were justifiably upset. After all, the commercial development tore a narrow strip out of Stawamus Chief Provincial Park. However, since the gondola opened in 2014, hikers have flocked to its growing trail network and superlative viewing platforms. The Sea to Summit Trail, a more scenic alternative to the overcrowded and viewless Grouse Grind (Hike 9), is the major draw.

Marked by 400 green diamonds, the Sea to Summit Trail starts at the gondola base and piggybacks on B.C. Parks trails before forging its own path to the wooded ridge northwest of Mount Habrich. Unfortunately, parking is limited to 3 hours at the base. So our hike begins in Shannon Falls Provincial Park, across the Sea to Sky Highway from the gondola's Darrell Bay overflow parking lot. Following the gondola signs takes you to the Lower Shannon Falls Trail, which merges with the Sea to Summit (keep right) en route to Stawamus Chief Provincial Park.

Just before crossing Olesen Creek, you might notice a climbers' path to the right that provides access to the Olesen Creek Wall. Across the bridge, the Sea to Summit joins the Chief Peaks Trail (go right at marker 16) and stair-climbs

Squamish Harbour from the top of the Upper Shannon Falls Trail.

to the Upper Shannon Falls Trail junction (marker 68). Straight leads to the three peaks of Squamish's famous granodiorite monolith, but turn right, following the once-sleepy trail across Olesen Creek again, under the gondola, past two viewpoints, and up some steep and slippery bits to Upper Shannon Falls.

You might hear a Steller's jay's "chook-chook-chook" as you lunch and admire Howe Sound (Atl'Kitsem) and Stawamus Chief Mountain (Siyám Smánit; Hike 22)—in the heart of Squamish Nation territory—from the bluff 15 minutes past the falls. Leaving the Upper Shannon Falls Trail behind, the newer portion of the Sea to Summit presses on through pleasant forest. At its 5 km (3.1 mi) mark, the Sea to Summit goes left on a shady logging road and then left again. (Both rights are for the Shannon Basin Loop Trail.)

Just after the Sea to Summit's 6 km (3.7 mi) mark, the trail ducks under the gondola and reaches a fork at the base of aptly named Wrinkle Rock. Keep left for the Upper Sea to Summit Trail, only 1 km (0.6 mi) from the top. (Right is for the steeper, single-track Sparky's Spin, which follows the gondola line up.)

After drinking craft beer at the lodge, most hikers opt for the easy way down—ponying up for a 10-minute gondola download. (The other option is to hike down the way you came up.) Before you depart, take time to stroll across the suspension bridge and savour the stunning view of Sky Pilot Mountain. Thankfully, the upper terminal area is a no-fly zone for drones.

LONGER OPTION

Aim higher by continuing onto Al's Habrich Ridge Trail (Hike 21), which ascends from the upper terminal plaza to Neverland Lake.

GETTING THERE

Transit: Better Environmentally Sound Transportation's Parkbus offers coach service on select summer weekends to the Shannon Falls parking lot from downtown Vancouver.

Vehicle: On Highway 99 (Sea to Sky Highway), 2 km (1.2 mi) south of downtown Squamish, turn west on Darrell Bay Road (opposite Shannon Falls Provincial Park entrance) to find the Sea to Sky Gondola's overflow parking lot.

21
AL'S HABRICH RIDGE TRAIL

Distance: 7.5 km (4.7 mi)
Time: 4.5 hours (round trip)
Elevation gain: 350 m (1,150 ft)
High point: 1,235 m (4,050 ft)

Quality: ★★★
Difficulty: ■
Maps: NTS 92-G/11 Squamish, Hiking GuideMaps Squamish
Trailhead: 49°40'17" N, 123°07'48" W

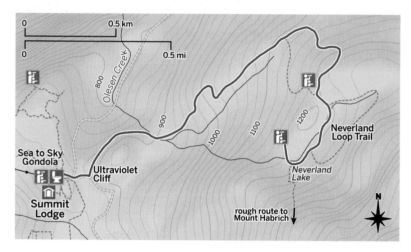

FORMERLY CALLED Eagle Head by climbers, Mount Habrich is a distinctive rock horn rising southeast of Squamish. Habrich Ridge, in Squamish Nation territory, is the wooded high ground extending northwest of the peak and the destination of the Sea to Sky Gondola. Therefore, Al's Habrich Ridge Trail must be preceded by a hike on the Sea to Summit Trail (Hike 20) in Stawamus Chief Provincial Park or a ride on the gondola.

From the map board at the upper gondola plaza, go east on the backcountry access road, pass Ultraviolet Cliff (home to Haley's Vomit and other rock climbs), and keep left on the gravel road. Uphill from a water tank, Al's Habrich Ridge Trail leaves to the left. Follow brown numbered diamonds (1 to 44) into the woods and cross Olesen Creek. Fixed ropes assist with fun scrambly bits.

Gaining elevation over rocky ground earns you a bird's-eye view of Stawamus Chief Mountain (Siýám̓ Smánit; Hike 22). Eventually, the trail ducks back into the forest en route to an open bluff. Overlooking Howe Sound (Atl'Kitsem) and the Squamish River, this spot is a suitable turn-around for some hikers.

Stawamus Chief Mountain (Siỷám̓ Smánit) from Al's Habrich Ridge Trail.

From there, the trail loses a bit of altitude as it travels over moist ground to reach Neverland Lake. This is the end of the marked trail. Cross the charming pond's outlet to find a path to a rocky viewpoint ideal for lunch. Enjoy the elevated vantage of Squamish Harbour, the Stawamus Chief, and the top of the gondola before heading back down.

Back in 2012, development of the gondola resulted in the removal of 2.4 ha (5.9 acres) from Stawamus Chief Provincial Park. The strip of land was redesignated as a protected area. The gondola's top terminal (a no-drone zone) and network of radiating trails lie on provincial land. Dogs are only allowed to download on the gondola (with a ticket). Make sure to check the gondola's closing time.

GETTING THERE

Transit: Parkbus offers coach service on select summer weekends to the Shannon Falls parking lot from downtown Vancouver.

Vehicle: On Highway 99 (Sea to Sky Highway), 2 km (1.2 mi) south of downtown Squamish, turn west on Darrell Bay Road (opposite Shannon Falls Provincial Park entrance) to find the Sea to Sky Gondola's overflow parking lot.

22
STAWAMUS CHIEF MOUNTAIN

Distance: 14 km (8.7 mi)
Time: 5 hours (circuit)
Elevation gain: 625 m (2,050 ft)
High point: 702 m (2,300 ft)

Quality: ★★★★
Difficulty: ■
Maps: NTS 92-G/11 Squamish, Hiking
GuideMaps Squamish
Trailhead: 49°40'43" N, 123°09'16" W

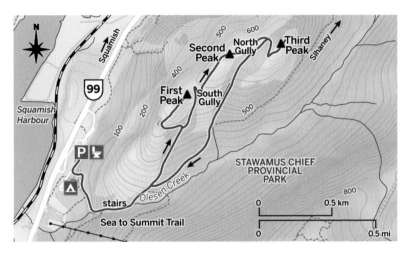

KNOWN AS Siy̓ám̓ Smánit in the S̲k̲wx̲wú7mesh language, Stawamus Chief Mountain is a landmark sacred to the Squamish Nation. The Ice Age–sculpted granodiorite monolith is also an international rock-climbing destination. For hikers, its backside offers a leg-burning stair climb, fun scrambling (and some exposure), three summits, and soaring views. Plus it's doable most of the year.

Start by strolling south through the campground to the trailhead. The steep Chief Peaks Trail kicks off with lots of stairs. Soon the Sea to Summit Trail (Hike 20) joins from the right via a wooden bridge over Olesen Creek and the Lower Shannon Falls Trail. With all the Sea to Sky Gondola hikers mixed in, the next section is extra busy.

After the Sea to Summit Trail leaves to the right via the Upper Shannon Falls Trail, you arrive at a major fork. Choose the left trail, signed for the first and second peaks. Before long, the trail splits again. Go left and ascend well-worn switchbacks to the bare rock (slippery when wet) of the crowded First Peak (610 m/2,000 ft).

Retrace your steps to the previous fork, turn left (north), and proceed to the top of the South Gully. Ascend a ledge with a fixed chain, traverse a cleft

Stawamus Chief Mountain (Siyám Smánit) from Mount Crumpit.

covered by logs, and climb a short ladder (expect a traffic jam) to the also-bustling Second Peak (655 m/2,150 ft). Savour the sight of the Squamish River estuary below and Mount Garibaldi (Nch'kay') to the north, from the prettiest of the three peaks.

Follow markers northeast to the North Gully. Stay left at the junction with the third backside trail. Push on, skirting the great precipice, through the woods, and to a ledge. A U-turn leads to a narrow ridge of rock and the quieter Third Peak (49°41'10" N, 123°08'06" W). For a fast, challenging descent, return to the last junction and plunge down the rough North Gully trail. Turn right (south) when you meet the path to Slhaney, an adjacent peak, and return to the trailhead. Campfires are prohibited in the park.

SHORTER OPTION

If you have to pick one summit, make it the Second Peak. The Stawamus Chief's centre summit offers the best views and most enjoyable scrambling. Descend via the North Gully for a 2-hour round trip.

GETTING THERE

Transit: Parkbus offers coach service on select summer weekends to the Shannon Falls parking lot from downtown Vancouver.
Vehicle: On Highway 99 (Sea to Sky Highway) in Squamish, just north of Shannon Falls Provincial Park and the Sea to Sky Gondola, turn east into Stawamus Chief Provincial Park. Take the first right at the roundabout to reach the day-use parking area adjacent to the campground.

23
WATERSPRITE LAKE

Distance: 17 km (10.6 mi)
Time: 7 hours (round trip)
Elevation gain: 668 m (2,190 ft)
High point: 1,479 m (4,852 ft)

Quality: ★★★★
Difficulty: ■
Maps: NTS 92-G/10 Pitt River, 92-G/15
Mamquam Mountain
Trailhead: 49°45'08" N, 122°56'03" W

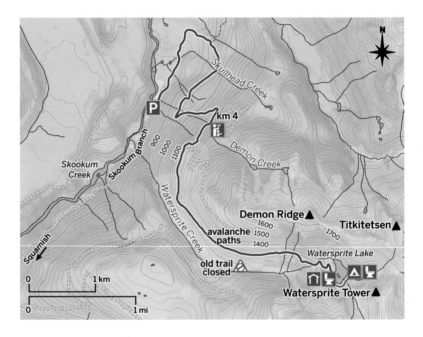

WATERSPRITE LAKE is a stunning turquoise tarn surrounded by rugged peaks in Squamish Nation territory. Its popularity has soared in recent years, as evidenced by the steady stream of photos (yoga poses, anyone?) on social media.

In 2016, the B.C. Mountaineering Club (BCMC) built the new Watersprite Lake Trail and closed the old, deteriorating route. From the gate by the Skookum Creek intake dam, head up to the trailhead kiosk and hike northeast over gravel to a deactivated logging road. Cross Demon and Skullhead Creeks on bridges. In 20 minutes, the path leads uphill before turning right on another logging road at the 1.8 km (1.1 mi) mark. Follow the orange diamonds south and then east in the regenerating clear-cut, with bridges once again over Skullhead and Demon Creeks.

After 1 hour of hiking, swing back south and pass the 4 km (2.5 mi) signpost at an elevation of 1,074 m (3,524 ft). Shortly after, a landslide area offers the best vantage yet of Diamond Head, Mount Garibaldi (Nch'kay' in the S<u>k</u>w<u>x</u>wú7mesh language), Opal Cone, Pyramid Mountain, and Mamquam Mountain in Garibaldi Provincial Park. A log lies across Demon Creek, but you can cross it below on boulders. Stay right at the Demon Ridge fork (49°44'51" N, 122°55'39" W) and negotiate a rockslide.

Watersprite Tower looms over Watersprite Lake.

The trail curves eastward through fireweed—with views of Sky Pilot Mountain, the Tantalus Range (Tsewílx), and Slhaney (Stawamus Chief Mountain's northeastern companion) overlooking the mouth of the Squamish River—to head up the Watersprite Creek valley in more challenging fashion. Three hours in, begin an ascending traverse of the boulder-covered avalanche slopes below Demon Ridge. Next, the path goes through bushes and under Douglas firs blanketed in witch's hair. Keep an eye out for the orange shelves of chicken of the woods fungi on tree trunks.

Just after the 8 km (5 mi) mark, switch to river left via a bridge over Watersprite Creek. Finally, the steepening trail goes up a boulder field. Spy the BCMC's locked, reservation-only, no-dogs Watersprite Lake Cabin, built in 2017, atop a bluff. Pass the hut turnoff (49°43'53" N, 122°53'50" W) and outhouse en route to the shore of fantastical Watersprite Lake. Return the way you came.

LONGER OPTION

Traverse boulders on the south shore to reach the designated camping area and outhouse on the east side of Watersprite Lake. The summits of Titkitetsen and Watersprite Tower (1,810 m/5,938 ft) loom over the enchanting cirque. Campfires are prohibited. Please use the outhouses and Leave No Trace practices. No one likes the sight or smell of toilet-paper flowers.

GETTING THERE

Vehicle: On Highway 99 (Sea to Sky Highway), just north of Stawamus Chief Provincial Park in Squamish, head east on potholed Mamquam River Forest Service Road. Stay left at the Stawamus/Indian River FSR fork. Twelve km (7.5 mi) up, go left onto the Mamquam River (Mámxwem) bridge. Keep right at the Ring Creek Main fork to cross the Skookum Creek bridge. Turn left at the Skookum Creek power plant, 13 km (8 mi) up, and follow steep and water-barred Skookum Branch (4WD recommended, but doable with high-clearance 2WD) northeast for 6.5 km (4 mi) to the parking area.

24
MOUNT CRUMPIT

Distance: 8 km (5 mi)
Time: 4 hours (loop)
Elevation gain: 270 m (885 ft)
High point: 325 m (1,065 ft)

Quality: ★★★
Difficulty: ■
Maps: NTS 92-G/11 Squamish, SORCA Squamish
Trailhead: 49°42'29" N, 123°06'56" W

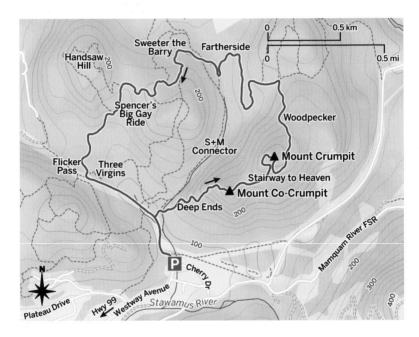

THOSE IN search of the Grinch may want to focus on the maze of mountain-bike trails in delightful Crumpit Woods. Don't be disappointed by the fact that Squamish's Mount Crumpit is only a third as tall as its 3,000 ft (900 m) namesake in the classic Christmas tale by Dr. Seuss, or by the lack of singing down in Whoville (Valleycliffe, in this case). A shoulder-season hike to the "tiptop" earns you striking views of Slhaney and Stawamus Chief Mountain (Siyám Smánit; Hike 22), in the heart of Squamish Nation territory.

It's easy to get lost in these mixed woods, so don't set off without the Squamish Off-Road Cycling Association's trail map. Note: On trail signs, *Crumpit* is often spelled "Crumpet," like the yummy griddle cakes. Starting at the map board at the corner of Westway Avenue and Cherry Drive, walk northwest, cross a bridge, and turn left on the muddy Flicker Pass road, which bisects

Crumpit Woods. Signs alert you to the importance of keeping dogs out of frog-breeding ponds.

Several minutes in, go right on S+M Connector and quickly right again on Deep Ends. Follow the steep and scrambly trials-motorbike trail up Mount Co-Crumpit. In a half-hour, a viewpoint with a

Wooden bench on Mount Co-Crumpit.

bench is off to the right. The minor summit is 10 minutes farther.

Continue east, ascending Stairway to Heaven to Mount Crumpit, ignoring AA Hill to the left and a bypass to the right. A rocky perch rewards with a unique perspective of the Chief and Squamish Harbour. The path dips before meeting a Northface sign, 1.5 hours (2 km/1.2 mi) in. Just off to the left is the unremarkable summit (49°42′51″ N, 123°06′21″ W); the right fork compensates with a lovely lunch spot.

From there, drop down a slippery-when-wet ramp and stick with the Woodpecker trail. (Listen for downy woodpeckers.) If you detour right for viewpoints, return to Woodpecker or risk losing your way. A half-hour from the summit, turn left on Fartherside. Keep left at The RAAA, then go right to stay on Fartherside at the Lacking Head T-junction. Cross a creek with skunk cabbage to reach S+M Connector and S+M proper (49°43′09″ N, 123°06′40″ W), where you choose the latter and turn right.

A quick right and left takes you to Sweeter the Barry. Then it's right on a connector to Spencer's Big Gay Ride and Hairy Bomber, and left to take Spencer's. The trail contours below Handsaw Hill, splitting into two paths that rejoin. (The Tamiami motorbike trail, which heads up the hill, is tricky to navigate.) Keep right at Three Virgins to be spit out onto the Flicker Pass road.

Descend southeast over puddles and boardwalk, along the proposed route of FortisBC's Eagle Mountain–Woodfibre Gas Pipeline, which would serve the controversial Woodfibre LNG project on Howe Sound (Atl'Kitsem). Exit right to return to the trailhead and Ravens Plateau subdivision.

GETTING THERE

Transit: Squamish Transit Bus 3 (Valleycliffe) to Spruce Drive at Westway Avenue. Walk 1 km (0.6 mi) east on Westway to Cherry Drive.

Vehicle: From Highway 99 (Sea to Sky Highway), just north of Stawamus Chief Provincial Park in Squamish, head east on Clarke Drive. Immediately turn left to stay on Clarke. Go right on Guilford Drive and then left on Westway Avenue, driving 2 km (1.2 mi) to find street parking near the trailhead at Cherry Drive.

25
ELFIN LAKES

Distance: 22 km (14 mi)
Time: 7 hours (round trip)
Elevation gain: 685 m (2,250 ft)
High point: 1,600 m (5,250 ft)

Quality: ★★★★
Difficulty: ■
Maps: NTS 92-G/14, 92-G/15; Clark
Geomatics 102 Garibaldi Park
Trailhead: 49°45'01" N, 123°03'11" W

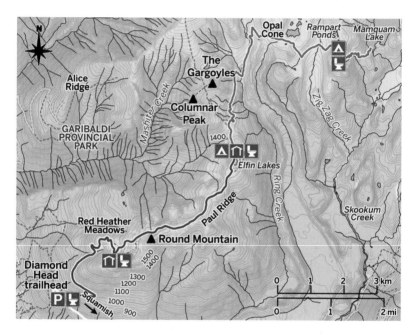

THERE'S NO way around it. The beginning of Garibaldi Provincial Park's Elfin Lakes Trail is a chore. However, everything changes for the better at Red Heather Meadows. Ground squirrels chatter and whisky jacks eye your snacks. (Don't feed the wildlife.) From Paul Ridge, Atwell Peak, the formidable south summit of stratovolcanic Mount Garibaldi (Nch'kay' to the Squamish Nation), commands the northern scene. To the south, Sky Pilot Mountain and its jaggy companions loom like eerie gargoyles.

From the busy Diamond Head trailhead (914 m/3,000 ft), this classic hike kicks off with a trudge up a gravel road, broken by a vista of Stawamus Chief Mountain (Siý̓ám̓ Smánit; Hike 22) and a waterfall. In 5 km (3.1 mi), breach timberline to reach the Red Heather day-use shelter (49°45'45" N, 123°02'17" W), where snow camping is allowed in winter. Past the outhouse, hikers fork left and mountain bikers right, then rejoin a bit farther northwest.

Mount Garibaldi (Nch'kay') and Diamond Head from Paul Ridge at dusk.

Gain height on Paul Ridge and contour along its meadowy northern slopes. (Marked with orange poles, the winter route for snowshoers and ski tourers sticks to the crest and just south to avoid cornices and avalanche paths.) The trail passes beneath inconspicuous Round Mountain (1,644 m/ 5,390 ft), the lava-dome summit of Paul Ridge.

Finally, descend to Elfin Lakes—the first for swimming, the second for drinking water—11 km (6.8 mi) from the trailhead. The Elfin Lakes shelter (49°47′21″ N, 122°59′16″ W) and the 35-site campground require reservations all year. (Backcountry camping permits are also required year-round for overnight stays in the park.) Spectacular views of The Saddle between Columnar Peak and The Gargoyles (Hike 26), Mount Garibaldi and the Garibaldi Névé, and Pyramid Mountain and Mamquam Mountain reward your efforts. Savour these sights before retracing your steps.

This is black bear country. Dogs and campfires are prohibited.

LONGER OPTION

Mamquam Lake is a remote hiking destination 11 km (6.8 mi) northeast of Elfin Lakes. The strenuous route crosses avalanche slopes, drops to Ring Creek, and bypasses Opal Cone (1,725 m/5,660 ft), the volcanic crater responsible for the 10,000-year-old Ring Creek lava flow. Camping is allowed at Rampart Ponds, which has twelve tent platforms, 1 km (0.6 mi) before Mamquam Lake. Elevation change: 570 m (1,870 ft).

GETTING THERE

Vehicle: On Highway 99 (Sea to Sky Highway), 4 km (2.5 mi) north of downtown Squamish, turn east on Mamquam Road, which goes from paved to rough gravel (2WD). Take a left, 6 km (3.7 mi) from the highway. Pull into the Diamond Head parking lot at 16 km (10 mi). Snow tires and chains required in winter. Warning: Vehicle break-ins have been reported here.

26
THE GARGOYLES

Distance: 27 km (17 mi)
Time: 9 hours (round trip)
Elevation gain: 905 m (2,970 ft)
High point: 1,820 m (5,970 ft)

Quality: ★★★★
Difficulty: ◆
Maps: NTS 92-G/14, 92-G/15; Clark
Geomatics 102 Garibaldi Park
Trailhead: 49°45'01" N, 123°03'11" W

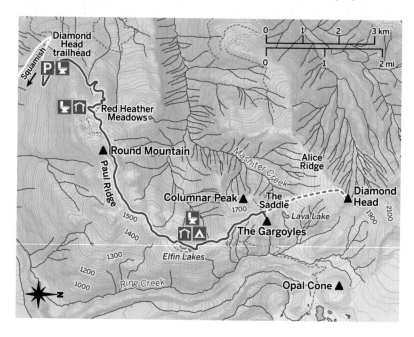

IT'S SURE hard to turn around at Elfin Lakes (Hike 25), in Garibaldi Provincial Park, with so much glaciovolcanic splendour ahead. Expending the extra time and effort to gain higher ground has its scenic rewards.

From the Diamond Head trailhead (914 m/3,000 ft), set off on the Elfin Lakes Trail. In 5 km (3.1 mi), reach the day-use shelter at Red Heather Meadows (49°45'45" N, 123°02'17" W). The trail splits past the outhouse into the summer and winter routes. Gain elevation on Paul Ridge and contour along its meadowy northern slopes, passing beneath Round Mountain.

Descend to Elfin Lakes, site of the historical Diamond Head Chalet, 11 km (6.8 mi) from the parking lot. The Elfin Lakes shelter (49°47'21" N, 122°59'16" W) and the 35-site campground require reservations all year. (Backcountry camping permits are also required year-round for overnight stays in the park.)

The Gargoyles and Atwell Peak (Nch'kay') from Elfin Lakes in autumn.

At a junction past the shelter, go left for the Saddle Trail. Hike north through heather, over scree, and up the increasingly steep slope to the low point on The Saddle joining Columnar Peak (1,826 m/5,990 ft) and The Gargoyles (1,823 m/5,980 ft; 49°48'21" N, 122°59'52" W), 2.5 km (1.6 mi) from the lakes. Columnar Peak is a scramble to the left.

To admire The Gargoyles, turn right and follow the ridge up to the nearest high point. Use caution on the loose rock. Look out over these volcanic rock pillars, once mapped as Lava Peaks, as well as Mount Garibaldi (Nch'kay' to the Squamish Nation), the Garibaldi Névé, Ring Creek, Opal Cone, and the rest of the dramatic fire-and-ice landscape. Drop back down to Elfin Lakes and retrace your steps to the trailhead.

LONGER OPTION

For Elfin Lakes campers, it's worth pushing on beyond The Saddle to intriguing Diamond Head (2,056 m/6,745 ft; 49°49'33" N, 123°00'27" W). Often called "Little Diamond Head" in deference to Atwell Peak, the imposing south summit of Mount Garibaldi, this pyramid of rubble points to the much larger size of the Garibaldi stratovolcano in the past.

Diamond Head sits at the south end of a loose ridge extending from Atwell and forms the apex of Alice Ridge (formerly Cheekye Ridge). It's 2 km (1.2 mi) north of The Saddle via a fading but self-evident route passing to the west of Lava Lake.

GETTING THERE

Vehicle: On Highway 99 (Sea to Sky Highway), 4 km (2.5 mi) north of downtown Squamish, turn east on Mamquam Road, which goes from paved to rough gravel (2WD). Take a left, 6 km (3.7 mi) from the highway. Pull into the Diamond Head parking lot at 16 km (10 mi). Snow tires and chains required in winter. Warning: Vehicle break-ins have been reported here.

27
TANTALUS VIEW LOOKOUT

Distance: 10.5 km (6.5 mi)
Time: 3.5 hours (loop)
Elevation gain: 155 m (510 ft)
High point: 385 m (1,260 ft)

Quality: ★★★
Difficulty: ●
Maps: NTS 92-G/14 Cheakamus River,
SORCA Squamish
Trailhead: 49°49'20" N, 123°08'01" W

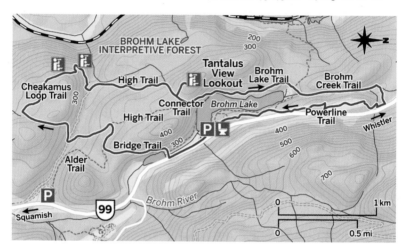

EVEN IF you make frequent trips to Whistler, there's a good chance you've driven by Brohm Lake Interpretive Forest numerous times without giving it a second thought. However, Brohm Lake, which lies in the district of Squamish and the territory of the Squamish Nation, is definitely worth a stop, especially if you're looking for a quick and easy fall hike or a refreshing dip in summer.

Administered by the B.C. Ministry of Forests, Lands, Natural Resource Operations, and Rural Development, the interpretative forest contains 10 km (6.2 mi) of trails in its 400 ha (990 acres). A walk in these very pleasant woods (dogs should be leashed) can earn you fine views of the imposing peaks and glaciers of the Tantalus Range (Tsewílx̱ in the Sḵwx̱wú7mesh language).

Begin a clockwise circuit by heading south on the Brohm Lake Trail and crossing a bridge over a wetland. (Did you know that wetlands are important carbon sinks? The preservation and restoration of forested swamps, grassy marshes, and peaty bogs and fens is key to addressing the climate crisis, as well as protecting biodiversity and water quality.)

Keep left to follow the Bridge Trail into the forest, stay right at the Alder Trail junction, and turn left when you hit the High Trail. Find the Cheakamus

Old fire lookout in Brohm Lake Interpretive Forest.

Loop Trail on the other side of a horse road. Two delightful viewpoints on this 2 km (1.2 mi) trail reward your mild efforts. Alpha Mountain (Ḵiyáẏaḵep), Mount Dione, and Mount Tantalus dominate the scenery.

Go left on the High Trail and left again on the short and steep Tantalus View Trail to reach popular Tantalus View Lookout, the day's high point. After visiting the historic fire lookout and savouring the views, it's back down to the High Trail, where you go left (north). Two more lefts, on the Connector Trail and Brohm Lake Trail, lead you to the north end of the lake. Stay right at a junction with the Thompson Trail. Then go left on the Brohm Creek Trail, right on the Powerline Trail, and left on the Brohm Lake Trail to return to the parking lot.

To learn more about Sḵwx̱wú7mesh place names, check out *squamishatlas. com.* The interactive map is curated by Kwi Awt Stelmexw, a non-profit that works to strengthen the heritage, language, culture, and art of the Squamish people.

GETTING THERE
Vehicle: On Highway 99 (Sea to Sky Highway) in Squamish, 5 km north of the Alice Lake Provincial Park entrance, turn east into the Brohm Lake parking lot.

28
GARIBALDI LAKE

Distance: 20 km (12.4 mi)
Time: 7 hours (lollipop)
Elevation gain: 1,080 m (3,500 ft)
High point: 1,650 m (5,400 ft)

Quality: ★★★★
Difficulty: ■
Maps: NTS 92-G/14 Cheakamus River,
Clark Geomatics 102 Garibaldi Park
Trailhead: 49°57'28" N, 123°07'13" W

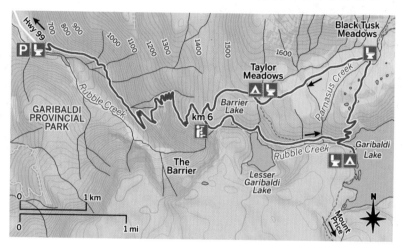

DURING THE Pleistocene epoch, a volcano that would later be named Clinker Peak erupted in what is now Garibaldi Provincial Park. Dacite lava flowed north, creating an ice-contact dam 450 m (1,500 ft) tall across a glaciated valley. Water ponded behind The Barrier, as this cliff is now known, forming beautiful Garibaldi Lake—a favoured destination of Lower Mainland hikers.

From the trailhead at Rubble Creek (Spú7ets' to the Squamish Nation, Spó7ez to the Lil'wat Nation), the path to Garibaldi Lake climbs 770 m (2,530 ft) as it switchbacks more than twenty times to a junction (49°56' 55" N, 123°05'13" W) at 6 km (3.7 mi). Take the right fork for Garibaldi Lake. (Left heads to the Taylor Meadows campground.) Another right brings you to a viewpoint of The Barrier and the Tantalus Range.

Continue on the Garibaldi Lake trail for 3 km (1.9 mi), passing small Barrier Lake and larger Lesser Garibaldi Lake. The latter is a spectacular sight (on snowshoes) when it's partially frozen in spring. Ignore a path on the left to Taylor Meadows and arrive at Garibaldi Lake (1,472 m/4,829 ft). Turn right (left goes to Black Tusk Meadows), cross the glacial lake's outlet, and follow the shore to the Garibaldi Lake campground (49°56'41" N, 123°03'18" W).

Facilities include 50 tent sites, 4 day-use shelters, and 4 pit toilets. If you

lunch outside, friendly whisky jacks will probably visit. (Don't feed the wildlife.) The Battleship Islands are close at hand, while The Black Tusk (T'ekt'akmúy̓in tl'a In7íńy̓áxa7en to the Squamish, Q'elqámtensa ti Skenknápa to the Lil'wat; Hike 31), Panorama Ridge (Hike 30), Castle Towers Mountain, The

Looking across Garibaldi Lake to the Sphinx Glacier.

Sphinx (at the head of the receding Sphinx Glacier), and Guard Mountain rise across the turquoise water. Mount Price (Hike 29) and Clinker Peak loom to the south.

When satiated, return to the outlet and turn right (north) to take the trail to Black Tusk Meadows, where the wildflowers hit peak bloom in July and August. Look out for arctic lupine and red paintbrush, and for black bears, Columbian black-tailed deer, and ruffed grouse. Stay on the main path, and don't trample the sensitive subalpine meadows. Turn left at Outhouse Junction to pass through the Taylor Meadows campground (40 tent sites, 2 day-use shelters, and 2 pit toilets), return to the Taylor Meadows–Garibaldi Lake junction, and descend the switchbacks to the parking lot.

B.C. Parks requires camping reservations for Garibaldi Lake and Taylor Meadows year-round. Dogs, fires, guns, and mushroom- and flower-picking are banned in the park. Motorized vehicles and aircraft takeoffs and landings are similarly restricted.

SHORTER OPTION

The Barrier viewpoint (2.5 hours up) is an adequate early-season destination, when snowshoes or touring skis are required to make it all the way to Garibaldi Lake. Geologists predict the rockfall-prone lava dam will eventually suffer a catastrophic failure. Accordingly, camping is prohibited in the Rubble Creek Landslide Hazard Area below The Barrier—food for thought during the 4-hour round trip (12 km/7.5 mi).

GETTING THERE

Transit: Better Environmentally Sound Transportation's Parkbus offers coach service on select summer weekends to the Garibaldi Lake parking lot from downtown Vancouver.

Vehicle: Turn east off Highway 99 (Sea to Sky Highway) between Rubble Creek and Daisy Lake, 30 km (19 mi) north of Squamish and 20 km (12 mi) south of Whistler. Follow the paved road (not snowplowed in winter) for 2.5 km (1.6 mi) to the Garibaldi Lake parking lot. Warning: Vehicle break-ins have been reported here.

29
MOUNT PRICE

Distance: 27 km (17 mi)
Time: 11 hours (round trip)
Elevation gain: 1,480 m (4,855 ft)
High point: 2,052 m (6,730 ft)

Quality: ★★★★★
Difficulty: ◆◆
Maps: NTS 92-G/14 Cheakamus River,
Clark Geomatics 102 Garibaldi Park
Trailhead: 49°57'28" N, 123°07'13" W

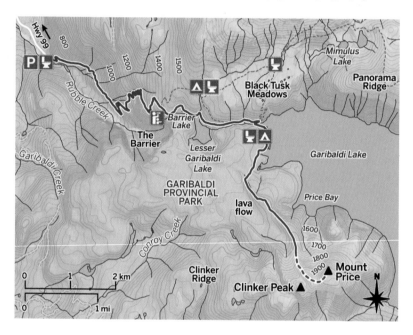

LOOKING SOUTH from the Garibaldi Lake campground (Hike 28), an enticing triple summit catches the eye. The left and highest peak is Mount Price, a stratovolcano that dates back 1.2 million years. The centre and right summits are remnants of a volcanic crater, Clinker Peak, which last erupted 10,000 years ago. An ice-marginal lava flow from the latter created the dacite Barrier that impounds Garibaldi Lake. Although the approach is not on B.C. Parks maps, experienced hikers with solid route-finding skills can gain these summits.

From the parking lot at Rubble Creek (Spú7ets' to the Squamish Nation, Spó7ez to the Lil'wat Nation), the switchbacking path climbs 770 m (2,530 ft) to a junction at 6 km (3.7 mi). Take the right fork to continue on the Garibaldi Lake trail for 3 km (1.9 mi). Detour right for the viewpoint of The Barrier, then pass Barrier Lake and Lesser Garibaldi Lake. Upon arriving at Garibaldi Lake (1,472 m/4,829 ft), turn right, cross the outlet, and follow the shore past the

Mount Price and Clinker Peak from Garibaldi Lake.

campground (49°56′41″ N, 123°03′18″ W; reservations and permits required year-round).

Finding and staying on the route to Mount Price can be a challenge. Be bear aware! Past the ranger station and dock, look for a path leaving to the right. Early on, the flagged route returns to the lakeshore, before heading inland to go south along Clinker Peak's Barrier lava flow. There are boulders to negotiate. Eventually, reach open terrain north of the peaks. Please practice Leave No Trace techniques.

Aim for the middle bump—the summit of Clinker Peak (1,987 m/ 6,520 ft)—and pass to the left of it. Drop east to the Price-Clinker col and take the final steps to the top of Mount Price (49°55′03″ N, 123°02′08″ W), formerly called Red Mountain for obvious reasons. Scrambling is not required—just scree and snow plodding.

This otherworldly vantage point, across Garibaldi Lake from The Black Tusk (T'ḵt'aḵmúy̓in tl'a In7iny̓áx̱a7en to the Squamish, Q'elqámtensa ti Skenknápa to the Lil'wat; Hike 31) and Panorama Ridge (Hike 30), affords a closer look at two spectacular volcanoes to the south. On the other side of the Culliton Creek valley, Mount Garibaldi (Nch'kay' to the Squamish) and its west peak, Dalton Dome, tower over the Warren Glacier. Nearby, The Table is a textbook example of a tuya; the flat-topped edifice is attributed to an early Holocene eruption under the Cordilleran Ice Sheet. With a dozen or so volcanic vents in the vicinity, geologists call this area the Garibaldi Lake Volcanic Field, part of the larger Garibaldi Volcanic Belt and Cascade Volcanic Arc. Retrace your steps to the lake and parking lot.

GETTING THERE

Transit: Parkbus offers coach service on select summer weekends to the Garibaldi Lake parking lot from downtown Vancouver.

Vehicle: Turn east off Highway 99 (Sea to Sky Highway) between Rubble Creek and Daisy Lake, 30 km (19 mi) north of Squamish and 20 km (12 mi) south of Whistler. Follow the paved road (not snowplowed in winter) for 2.5 km (1.6 mi) to the Garibaldi Lake parking lot. Warning: Vehicle break-ins have been reported here.

30
PANORAMA RIDGE

Distance: 29.5 km (18.3 mi)
Time: 10.5 hours (round trip)
Elevation gain: 1,555 m (5,100 ft)
High point: 2,126 m (6,975 ft)

Quality: ★★★★★
Difficulty: ◆
Maps: NTS 92-G/14 Cheakamus River, Clark Geomatics 102 Garibaldi Park
Trailhead: 49°57'28" N, 123°07'13" W

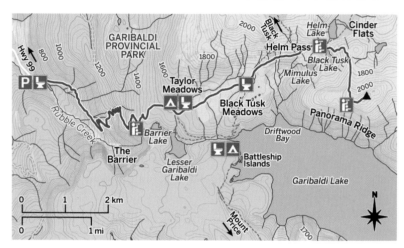

SHRINKING GLACIERS around the world are one sign of the global climate shift caused by human activity. Regular visitors to the Garibaldi Lake area of Garibaldi Provincial Park are familiar with the plight of the Sphinx Glacier. This ice mass has visibly receded over the past century, revealing millennia-old tree stumps on the ground below. Panorama Ridge is an ideal vantage point from which to survey the glacier and ponder the local environmental consequences of a warming world.

From the trailhead at Rubble Creek (Spú7ets' to the Squamish Nation, Spó7ez to the Lil'wat Nation), the switchbacking path climbs 770 m (2,530 ft) to a junction at 6 km (3.7 mi). Take the left fork to hike 1.5 km (0.9 mi) to the Taylor Meadows campground, which offers 40 tent sites, 2 day-use shelters, pit toilets, food caches, and drinking water from Taylor Creek. (Right is the longer route via Garibaldi Lake [Hike 28].)

Push on to dreamy Black Tusk Meadows, meeting a path coming up from Garibaldi Lake. Here the annual wildflower show takes place in July or August. Please respect the sensitive subalpine meadows by staying on the eroding trail, which in recent years has benefited from repairs by Friends of Garibaldi

Panorama Ridge and Mimulus Lake from Black Tusk Meadows.

Park Society volunteers. Keep an eye out for bears. Continue east, passing the turnoff for The Black Tusk (T'eḵt'aḵmúy̓in tl'a In7iṅy̓áx̱a7en to the Squamish, Q'elqámtensa ti Skenknápa to the Lil'wat; Hike 31) on your left, to arrive at a junction in Helm Pass.

Head south—enjoying the elevated perspective of Black Tusk Lake and Mimulus Lake, as well as outcrops of 100-million-year-old seabed strata—and ascend scree and snow to the viewpoint atop Panorama Ridge in 3 km (1.9 mi). The summit (49°57′15″ N, 123°00′51″ W) lies nearby to the east. Stars of the unspoiled 360-degree view include several volcanoes—The Black Tusk, Cinder Cone, Glacier Pikes, Mount Garibaldi (Nch'kay' to the Squamish), The Table, Mount Price (Hike 29), and Clinker Peak—and, of course, beautifully blue Garibaldi Lake. Retrace your inward route on the return.

B.C. Parks requires camping reservations and permits for Taylor Meadows and Garibaldi Lake year-round. Dogs, fires, guns, and mushroom- and flower-picking are prohibited in Garibaldi, established as B.C.'s fourth provincial park in 1927.

SHORTER OPTION

Experience the full splendour of Black Tusk Meadows with Helm Pass as your destination. Look northeast to Helm Lake and the Cinder Flats, with hoary marmots for company. It's a 23 km (14.3 mi) return trip.

GETTING THERE

Transit: Parkbus offers coach service on select summer weekends to the Garibaldi Lake parking lot from downtown Vancouver.

Vehicle: Turn east off Highway 99 (Sea to Sky Highway) between Rubble Creek and Daisy Lake, 30 km (19 mi) north of Squamish and 20 km (12 mi) south of Whistler. Follow the paved road (not snowplowed in winter) for 2.5 km (1.6 mi) to the Garibaldi Lake parking lot. Warning: Vehicle break-ins have been reported here.

31
THE BLACK TUSK

Distance: 29 km (18 mi)
Time: 10.5 hours (round trip)
Elevation gain: 1,740 m (5,710 ft)
High point: 2,310 m (7,580 ft)

Quality: ★★★★★
Difficulty: ◆◆
Maps: NTS 92-G/14 Cheakamus River, Clark Geomatics 102 Garibaldi Park
Trailhead: 49°57'28" N, 123°07'13" W

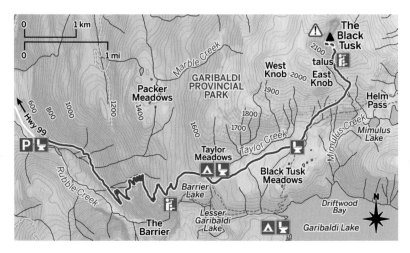

MEMBERS OF the B.C. Mountaineering Club named Garibaldi Provincial Park's distinctive lava plug "The Black Tusk" back in 1912, but the beloved peak has long borne other toponyms. To the Squamish Nation, the stratovolcano is T'ekt'akmúyin tl'a In7ińyáxa7en (Landing Place of the Thunderbird). The Lil'wat Nation refers to it as Q'elqámtensa ti Skenknápa (Place Where the Thunder Rests). The strenuous ascent earns you breathtaking views of the glaciovolcanic wonderland surrounding turquoise Garibaldi Lake.

From the trailhead at Rubble Creek (Spú7ets' to the Squamish, Spó7ez to the Lil'wat), the path climbs 770 m (2,530 ft) as it switchbacks more than twenty times to the junction at 6 km (3.7 mi). Take the left fork to hike 1.5 km (0.9 mi) to Taylor Meadows campground. (Right is the longer route via Garibaldi Lake [Hike 28].) Featuring 40 tent sites, 2 day-use shelters, pit toilets, food caches, and drinking water from Taylor Creek, it's an attractive base for an overnighter.

Leaving the Taylor Meadows boardwalk behind, the trail continues into paradisiacal Black Tusk Meadows, meeting the path coming up from Garibaldi Lake. Reaching peak bloom in July and August, the wildflowers include arctic lupine, red paintbrush, and Sitka valerian. Sightings of black bears,

The Black Tusk (T'ekt'akmúyin tl'a In7iŋýáxa7en/Q'elqámtensa ti Skenknápa).

hoary marmots, Columbian black-tailed deer, ruffed grouse, and whisky jacks are common. Respect the subalpine meadows by sticking to the eroding trail. Keeping left in the meadows, you soon arrive at the Black Tusk turnoff. Turn left and ascend the steep trail and talus for 4.4 km (2.7 mi) to the Black Tusk viewpoint. (Hikers unprepared for scrambling, stop here.) Press on to the windblown saddle southeast of your objective, then traverse west below the columnar jointed wall to the final wide chimney (helmets advised). Many hikers are satisfied by seeing the base of the chimney, which is lined with loose rock, foolhardy to climb when wet, and prone to traffic jams.

To tackle the Class 3 route, climb up the chimney crux and keep right to find a narrow gully. Emerge higher up the gully, which ends precipitously, following the boot-beaten path right and then left up the talus to the south summit (49°58′31″ N, 123°02′34″ W). The slightly higher north summit lies across a formidable gap and is inaccessible to scramblers. Survey the scene: Castle Towers Mountain, Panorama Ridge (Hike 30), and Mount Price (Hike 29), as well as majestic Mount Garibaldi (Nch'kay' to the Squamish) further south.

Take care to retrace your ascent route on the descent. B.C. Parks requires camping reservations and permits for Taylor Meadows and Garibaldi Lake year-round. Dogs, fires, and mushroom- and flower-picking are prohibited.

SHORTER OPTION
Turn around at the Black Tusk viewpoint for a scramble-free 28 km (17.4 mi) round trip.

GETTING THERE
Transit: Parkbus offers coach service on select summer weekends to the Garibaldi Lake parking lot from downtown Vancouver.
Vehicle: Turn east off Highway 99 (Sea to Sky Highway) between Rubble Creek and Daisy Lake, 30 km (19 mi) north of Squamish and 20 km (12 mi) south of Whistler. Follow the paved road (not snowplowed in winter) for 2.5 km (1.6 mi) to the Garibaldi Lake parking lot. Warning: Vehicle break-ins have been reported here.

32
BREW LAKE

Distance: 8 km (5 mi)
Time: 6 hours (round trip)
Elevation gain: 700 m (2,300 ft)
High point: 1,430 m (4,700 ft)

Quality: ★★★
Difficulty: ◆
Maps: NTS 92-J/3 Brandywine Falls,
Clark Geomatics 103 Callaghan Valley
Trailhead: 50°02'11" N, 123°08'57" W

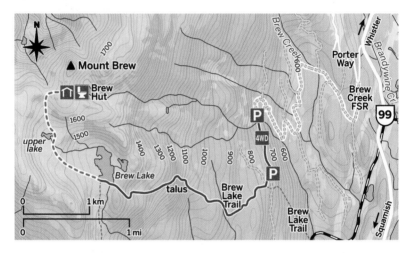

BREW LAKE is a lovely, secluded tarn in Squamish Nation territory that's most familiar to ski tourers with the University of British Columbia's Varsity Outdoor Club, which maintains a hut nearby. Founded in the early 1900s, the VOC has published a journal since 1958 and is the namesake of Veeocee Mountain (next to the Ubyssey Glacier and the triple-peaked Lecture Cutters) in Garibaldi Provincial Park.

From the Brew Creek FSR bridge, head south on the gravel bed, passing a yellow 5 km (3.1 mi) distance marker for the road. Keep right at a fork to find the trailhead in a clear-cut. The marked route quickly intercepts the Brew Lake Trail, which comes up from its old trailhead along the Canadian National Railway (formerly B.C. Rail) tracks. Turn right and head uphill in the trees. (There are big yellow diamonds in this area, but it's easy to miss this turnoff on the descent.)

The trail is rugged, steep, and overgrown in parts, but well marked with tapes, old metal, and cairns. Look out for bright orange chicken of the woods mushrooms in the forest. Your path wanders eastward, climbing steep talus slopes, encountering plenty of wild blueberries, negotiating bluffs,

Wet day at Brew Lake.

and crossing subalpine meadows. Look back for views of The Black Tusk (T'ek̲t'ak̲múy̲in tl'a In7iń̲y̲áx̲a7en to the Squamish Nation, Q'elqámtensa ti Skenknápa to the Lil'wat; Hike 31), The Barrier (Hike 28), Daisy Lake, and Squamish en route.

After 3 hours, arrive at the rocky south shore of Brew Lake (50°01′41″ N, 123°10′48″ W), lying in a gentle bowl below Mount Brew. This spot is also accessible via an alternative route from Roe Creek FSR. After lunch, return the way you came.

LONGER OPTION

Both the Brew Hut (1,685 m/5,530 ft; 50°02′24″ N, 123°11′28″ W) and Mount Brew (1,757 m/5,765 ft; 50°02′37″ N, 123°11′19″ W) are off-trail rambles from Brew Lake. The hut—the third built in this location by the VOC—lies northwest of the lake. Non-VOC guests are asked to make a donation. The epic backcountry journey along the Squamish-Cheakamus divide from Brew Lake to Brandywine Meadows (Hike 33) is known as the Alcoholic Traverse, involves scrambling and route-finding, and takes most parties three days to complete.

GETTING THERE

Vehicle: On Highway 99 (Sea to Sky Highway), 1 km (0.6 mi) north of Brandywine Falls Provincial Park and 15 km (9 mi) south of Whistler Village, head west on Brew Creek Forest Service Road. Quickly take the gravel road left where the pavement goes right as Porter Way. Stay on the mainline (2WD) as it swings right, aiming northwest and then south. Ignore spurs on both sides, including branches 200, 100, and D. The road zigzags and then steeply climbs northwest to a junction with Brew Creek North (50°02′21″ N, 123°08′53″ W). Go left and swing south. Park before the bridge. (4WD vehicles can drive a bit farther.)

33
BRANDYWINE MOUNTAIN

Distance: 10 km (6.2 mi)
Time: 5.5 hours (round trip)
Elevation gain: 860 m (2,820 ft)
High point: 2,213 m (7,260 ft)

Quality: ★★★★★
Difficulty: ◆◆
Maps: NTS 92-J/3 Brandywine Falls,
Clark Geomatics 103 Callaghan Valley
Trailhead: 50°05'22" N, 123°10'51" W

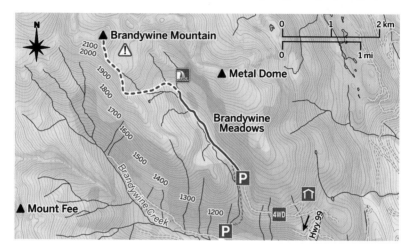

EVERYWHERE YOU look, there's evidence of glaciation in the Coast Mountains. Arêtes, cirques, fjords, horns, paternoster lakes, tarns, and U-shaped valleys are just some of the landforms shaped by glacial erosion, while moraines arise from sediment deposited by glacial ice. At Brandywine Meadows, you'll explore a hanging valley. Once home to a tributary glacier, its floor is higher than the deeper valley, carved out by a larger glacier, into which it runs.

From the upper trailhead, the new Brandywine Meadows Trail switch-backs north and crosses a few small creeks. After a mere 15 minutes, you arrive in the colourful meadows and the old, longer trail from the lower trailhead joins from the left (1,440 m/4,720 ft; 50°05'39" N, 123°11'15" W). Please protect the sensitive subalpine flora by keeping to the raised gravel path that meanders up the valley. Leave No Trace practices are essential in this environment.

The sights include a high floodplain, pretty streams pouring down both sides of the valley, and Brandywine Mountain looking impressive ahead. Eventually, the gravel ends and the trail merges with an old path coming from the right (east). Wildflowers, glacial erratics, and a headwall waterfall

Descending Brandywine Mountain, with Mount Fee at upper right.

catch the eye. Looking back, the hanging valley beautifully frames a trio of peaks in Garibaldi Provincial Park: Castle Towers Mountain, The Black Tusk (T'ekt'akmúyin tl'a In7íńyáxa7en to the Squamish Nation, Q'elqámtensa ti Skenknápa to the Lil'wat Nation; Hike 31), and Mount Garibaldi (Nch'kay' to the Squamish).

Brandywine Mountain (50°06'52" N, 123°13'16" W) beckons scramblers at the head of the valley. The challenging route climbs west up steep heather, talus, and snow (ice axes are advisable) to a shoulder at the end of the south ridge. A dirt track and a sequence of snow and boulders lead north to the summit cairn (2 hours up from the meadows). Stay off the glacier and cornices to the right. Drink up the volcanic views: Mount Fee's ominous twin towers, the unclimbed Vulcan's Thumb, Pyroclastic Peak, and Mount Cayley. Head down the same way you came up.

SHORTER OPTION

Stick to Brandywine Meadows for an easy, 2-hour stroll with little elevation gain. The wildflowers are sensational. Round trip: up to 6 km (3.7 mi). Frigid creek crossings may provide impetus to turn around. Take your time heading back and soak up the view. Visit in fall for a less buggy, though muddy, outing.

Although the Brandywine Meadows Trail is for non-motorized use, the area is very popular with snowmobilers in winter. On the drive down, a cat-ski cabin lies just up a fork to the left (north), which also provides access to Metal Dome, a subsidiary peak of Brandywine Mountain.

GETTING THERE

Vehicle: Turn west off Highway 99 (Sea to Sky Highway) onto Callaghan Valley Road, 3 km (1.9 mi) north of Brandywine Provincial Park and 10 km (6.2 mi) south of Whistler. In 900 m (0.6 mi), go left on Brandywine Creek Forest Service Road and drive the rough gravel surface to a signed junction. Take the right fork (high-clearance 4WD) and follow signs for the Brandywine Meadows Trail for 5 km (3.1 mi) to arrive at the upper trailhead. (The left fork reaches the lower parking lot [50°04'41" N, 123°11'08"W] in 2 km/1.2 mi and is 2WD until the final hill before the trailhead.)

34
CONFLICT LAKE

Distance: 12 km (7.5 mi)
Time: 4 hours (lollipop)
Elevation gain: 182 m (595 ft)
High point: 1,372 m (4,500 ft)

Quality: ★★★★
Difficulty: ■
Maps: NTS 92-J/3 Brandywine Falls,
Clark Geomatics 103 Callaghan Valley
Trailhead: 50°11'27" N, 123°10'56" W

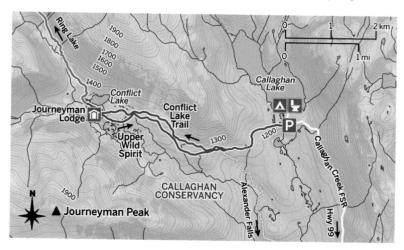

THE SQUAMISH Nation has designated five wild spirit places (*Kwa kwayx welh-aynexws*)—areas of cultural and spiritual importance that are to remain wilderness and be off-limits to industrial development. One of them is the Páyakéntsut Wild Spirit Place in the Callaghan Valley, which also lies in Lil'wat Nation territory and is home to old-growth forests.

From its unsigned trailhead in Callaghan Lake Provincial Park, the Conflict Lake Trail goes west into Páyakéntsut and the Callaghan Conservancy and up the Solitude Valley. To begin, follow the Parkway cross-country ski track (part of the Callaghan Country Nordic ski area) over a log bridge in the woods. Orange tapes lead hikers right on a rooty path with planks over brooks and muddy sections.

A half-hour or 1.8 km (1.1 mi) in, after a pond with lily pads, there's a signed fork (50°11'07" N, 123°12'06" W). Right is for Conflict and Ring Lakes. (Left links up with a service road that goes to Alexander Falls, which is worth a stop on the drive out.) As you continue up-valley, conifers give way to heather, allowing glimpses of Journeyman Peak to the south. Skirt thickets at the base of the wooded ridge leading to Hidden Peak, 1 hour in.

Pond along the Conflict Lake Trail.

The trail descends to cross a creek and wander through lonely subalpine meadows. Dark-eyed juncos flit among wildflowers such as arctic lupine, red paintbrush, and subalpine daisy. Ponds in the foreground make for postcard mountain scenes. Upon reaching Journeyman Lodge (closed in summer), turn right and follow the meadows path down to Conflict Lake, arriving at its west shore (50°11′39″ N, 123°14′38″ W) after 2 hours of hiking.

Retracing your steps through the meadows is the more scenic return route. Nevertheless, a quicker alternative is to walk east from the lodge on the service road, which doubles as the Upper Wild Spirit trail in winter. Leave the road 3.7 km (2.3 mi) from the lake and go left on a trail signed for Callaghan Lake. Moments later, rejoin the Conflict Lake Trail at the fork 1.8 km (1.1 mi) from your start.

The area around Callaghan Lake and Conflict Lake is closed to winter motorized use between November and May.

LONGER OPTION
Ring Lake lies in a cirque 4 km (2.5 mi) northwest of Conflict Lake and 300 m (985 ft) higher. It's a 20 km (12.4 mi) round trip from the trailhead.

GETTING THERE
Vehicle: Turn west off Highway 99 (Sea to Sky Highway) onto Callaghan Valley Road, 3 km (1.9 mi) north of Brandywine Provincial Park and 10 km (6.2 mi) south of Whistler. In 8 km (5 mi), pass Alexander Falls Recreation Site and go left on Callaghan Creek Forest Service Road (high-clearance 2WD), which has cross-ditches and becomes a cross-country ski trail in winter. Take a left fork and enter Callaghan Creek Provincial Park to find the trailhead on the left just before the Callaghan Lake campground.

35
CRATER RIM TRAIL

Distance: 10.5 km (6.5 mi)
Time: 5.5 hours (loop)
Elevation gain: 360 m (1,180 ft)
High point: 912 m (2,992 ft)

Quality: ★★★
Difficulty: ■
Maps: NTS 92-J/3 Brandywine Falls, WORCA Whistler
Trailhead: 50°05'11" N, 123°02'10" W

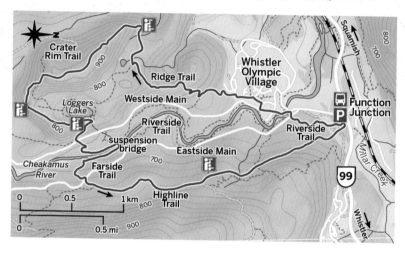

YOU CAN travel to Oregon to circumambulate a picture-postcard lake nestled in a volcanic crater. Or, you can make a day trip to Whistler Interpretive Forest. Created in 1980 and now part of Cheakamus Community Forest—overseen by the Lil'wat Nation, Squamish Nation, and Resort Municipality of Whistler—the interpretive forest supports continued logging while preserving remnants of old-growth under an ecosystem-based management approach. It's also home to a miniature version of famed Crater Lake.

Although it's one of the lesser-known hikes in Whistler, the Crater Rim Trail is highly enjoyable and just the ticket for shoulder season. A loop allows you to survey Loggers Lake, which sits in a 10,000-year-old crater, from all sides. From the north end of the parking lot, cross the Valley Trail and head south, reading interpretive panels about the forest, on the multi-use Riverside Trail. Cross the Eastside Main logging road and then the Cheakamus River via the Westside Main bridge. Stay with Westside Main for two blocks, then go right on a brief pathway leading to Whitewater Drive, where you turn left.

Welcome to Cheakamus Crossing, an instant neighbourhood created out of 2010's Whistler Olympic and Paralympic Village and largely reserved for local residents. Take a left on Mount Fee Road and go right on Cloudburst Drive. The Ridge Trail heads into the trees behind the bus stop on your left, giving you a peek at the West Bowl of Whistler Mountain as it rises. At the signed start of the Crater Rim Trail, turn right and leave the mountain bikers

The Crater Rim Trail overlooks Loggers Lake.

behind. The trail dips slightly and then ascends talus, switchbacking up to a lookout that delivers lovely views of Tricouni Peak, Mount Fee, and Brandywine Mountain (Hike 33) to the west and Empetrum Peak and The Black Tusk (Tʼekt'akmúy̓in tl'a In7iń̓y̓áxa7en to the Squamish, Q'elqámtensa ti Skenknápa to the Lil'wat; Hike 31) to the south.

Following orange and brown markers through the marvellous forest of the Crater Rim crest, you'll notice plenty of witch's hair lichen adorning the conifers. Indigenous uses of this green epiphyte include medicine and clothing. You might spot a red-breasted sapsucker, a woodpecker that drills sap wells in tree bark. After descending a ridge with a minor viewpoint at its south end, you cross paths with the Ridge Trail again. Go left and then right to stay on the Crater Rim as it curves north. (At a second minor viewpoint, ignore a trail to the left that leads prematurely to Loggers Lake.) Just past the viewpoint overlooking Loggers Lake, take a moment to drop down on a trail to the lakeshore.

Back on the main trail, turn right on the logging road and descend to a gate, cross Westside Main, and rejoin the Riverside Trail, going left (downstream) alongside the Cheakamus River. Once over MacLaurin's Crossing suspension bridge (watch for whitewater kayakers), turn right (upstream) on the Farside Trail and follow the river until the trail curves up to the road. Cross Eastside Main to go north on the Highline Trail. Stay left and head downhill when the Highline spits you onto a 4×4 road. (Admire Mount Fee from a viewpoint off to the left.) Walk down the gravel road, cross the paved Valley Trail, and return to the parking lot.

GETTING THERE

Transit: Whistler Transit Bus 20 (Cheakamus) to Cheakamus River Road at Highway 99.

Vehicle: On Highway 99 (Sea to Sky Highway), 8 km south of Whistler Village, turn east onto Cheakamus River Road (opposite Function Junction). Immediately turn left to enter the Whistler Interpretive Forest parking lot.

36
HALF NOTE TRAIL

Distance: 6 km (3.7 mi)
Time: 2.5 hours (down)
Elevation loss: 333 m (1,091 ft)
High point: 2,182 m (7,160 ft)

Quality: ★★★★
Difficulty: ◆
Maps: NTS 92-J/2 Whistler, Green Trails
92J1S Whistler
Trailhead: 50°03'30" N, 122°57'27" W

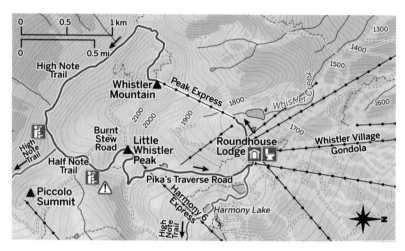

PURISTS WON'T touch this hike with a 10-foot trekking pole. For one thing, there's no free public access on foot to Whistler Mountain's alpine; hikers generally ride a gondola and chairlift to the top and walk down. Furthermore, Whistler Blackcomb's development of lift-serviced trails that breach Garibaldi Provincial Park is yet another example of the creeping commercialization of B.C. parks. Nevertheless, the superlative Coast Mountains scenery of the High Note Trail, which this outing samples, is guaranteed to elicit oohs and ahhs.

To reach the trailhead, take the Whistler Village Gondola to the Roundhouse Lodge (1,850 m/6,069 ft), stroll down the Peak Express Traverse (0.6 km/0.4 mi), and board the Peak Express chairlift to the summit lookout.

As of 2017, the High Note Trail starts at the fork in the road just down from the mountaintop terminal. (Previously, the trailhead was found behind the big inuksuk.) Bear right on the dirt road plunging down the back side of the mountain. A few minutes later, turn right (west) and drop down a steep path with a fixed chain for one bit. Cross the ski-area boundary and Top of the World mountain-bike trail after 20 minutes of hiking, and enter the wilds of Garibaldi Provincial Park.

Castle Towers Mountain, as seen from the High Note Trail.

Views of Castle Towers Mountain and The Black Tusk (T'ek̲t'ak̲múy̲in tl'a In7iń̲y̲áx̲a7en to the Squamish Nation, Q'elqámtensa ti Skenknápa to the Lil'wat Nation; Hike 31) amaze. So do the loud calls of the hoary marmots that gave Whistler Mountain (formerly London Mountain) its name. The High Note traverses southeast across steep wildflower meadows and creeks en route to the Cheakamus Lake Lookout, 1 hour in. Dark-eyed juncos and the Cheakamus River, far below in the Squamish Nation's Kwáyatsut Wild Spirit Place, provide the soundtrack.

Ten minutes later at a junction (50°02'57" N, 122°56'52" W), go left on the Half Note Trail. Follow green hiker signs, negotiate snow and boulders, and cross Burnt Stew Road (Hike 37) to reach Overlord Lookout. Stay clear of the cliff to the right as the trail climbs to Little Whistler Peak (2,115 m/ 6,939 ft). Turn right at Harmony Hut and pick up Pika's Traverse Road to the left of the Harmony 6 Express chairlift. The snow-walled road leads down to the Roundhouse Lodge and your gondola ride back to Whistler Village.

Camping, dogs, fires, and smoking are prohibited at Whistler Blackcomb, as are drones (without authorization). Guns and mushroom- and flower-picking are also banned in Garibaldi Provincial Park.

LONGER OPTION

For a 4-hour hike, stick with the High Note Trail (9.4 km/5.8 mi) all the way down. Follow the Harmony Lake Loop and Spearhead Loop back to the Roundhouse Lodge.

GETTING THERE

Transit: Whistler Transit Bus 5, 6, 7, 8, 20, 21, 30, or 32, or Pemberton Valley Transit Bus 99 (Pemberton Commuter) to Gondola Exchange.

Vehicle: On Highway 99 (Sea to Sky Highway) in Whistler, turn east on Village Gate Boulevard and then left on Blackcomb Way to find the Whistler Village day lots.

37
FLUTE SUMMIT

Distance: 9 km (5.6 mi)
Time: 4 hours (down)
Elevation loss: 455 m (1,490 ft)
High point: 2,182 m (7,160 ft)

Quality: ★★★★
Difficulty: ■
Maps: NTS 92-J/2 Whistler, Green Trails
92J1S Whistler
Trailhead: 50°03'31" N, 122°57'26" W

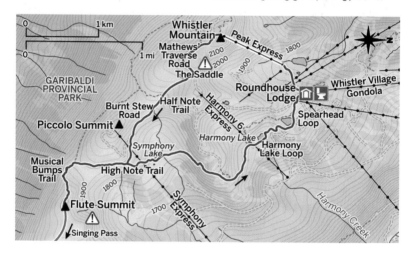

WITH VEHICLE access to the old Singing Pass trailhead—5 km (3.1 mi) up from Whistler Village—cut off since the 1990s due to an earth slump and commercial interests, many hikers opt to pay for lift-serviced admission to the Musical Bumps. The alpine scenery reaches a crescendo atop the trio of woodwind-themed summits, southeast of Whistler Mountain. In 2017, the Federation of Mountain Clubs of B.C. proposed a new trailhead and parking lot on the north side of Fitzsimmons Creek to restore public access to Garibaldi Provincial Park via the Singing Pass Trail.

To reach Flute Summit the Whistler Blackcomb way, ride the Whistler Village Gondola to the Roundhouse Lodge (1,850 m/6,069 ft), walk down the Peak Express Traverse (0.6 km/0.4 mi), and board the Peak Express chairlift to the summit lookout.

Just down from the mountaintop terminal, take the left fork for Mathews' Traverse Road. (Stop it with the inuksuit, people.) Pause to watch mountain bikers dropping into Top of the World. At The Saddle, before Little Whistler Peak, turn right onto the steep and loose—or snow-buried—Burnt Stew Road. Cross the Half Note Trail (Hike 36) and take the right fork to contour below Piccolo Summit.

Hoary marmot along the High Note Trail.

Bear left on a path through the boulders (50°02'54" N, 122°56'19" W), pass under the Symphony Express above Tower 19, and arrive at a T-junction with the High Note Trail after 50 minutes of hiking. Go right (south) and follow the mellow path through rock and heather terrain to the Flute-Piccolo col. Leave High Note, and head east (left) and up the Musical Bumps Trail to tick off Flute Summit (50°02'23" N, 122°55'34" W) at 2,012 m (6,600 ft), 1.5 hours in. Continue beyond the ski area to the provincial park boundary for stellar views of the Spearhead and Fitzsimmons Ranges (a 35 km/22 mi ski traverse where the Spearhead Huts Society has three new huts in the works). Beware of cornices.

To return to the Roundhouse Lodge, retrace your steps to the T-junction with the Burnt Stew connector, and stick with High Note as it drops to Symphony Lake and rises to Harmony Ridge. (Enjoy the subalpine flower show in July and August.) Where High Note ends under the Harmony 6 Express, bear right for Harmony Lake Loop and left on the lakeside boardwalk to pop out on Spearhead Loop, steps from the Roundhouse and your gondola ride down to Whistler Village.

Owned by Colorado-based Vail Resorts, Whistler Blackcomb operates in a controlled recreation area on provincial land and in the territories of the Squamish and Lil'wat First Nations. Camping, dogs, fires, and smoking are no-nos, as are drones.

LONGER OPTION

Take note of the gondola's posted hours. If time allows, leave the ski area behind and continue on the Musical Bumps Trail to Oboe Summit (1,956 m/6,417 ft)—and perhaps even farther to Singing Pass—before retracing your steps.

GETTING THERE

Transit: Whistler Transit Bus 5, 6, 7, 8, 20, 21, 30, or 32, or Pemberton Valley Transit Bus 99 (Pemberton Commuter) to Gondola Exchange.
Vehicle: On Highway 99 (Sea to Sky Highway) in Whistler, turn east on Village Gate Boulevard and then left on Blackcomb Way to find the Whistler Village day lots.

38
BLACKCOMB BURN

Distance: 5.2 km (3.2 mi)
Time: 2.5 hours (up)
Elevation gain: 1,175 m (3,855 ft)
High point: 1,860 m (6,102 ft)

Quality: ★★★
Difficulty: ◆
Maps: NTS 92-J/2 Whistler
Trailhead: 50°06'55" N, 122°56'51" W

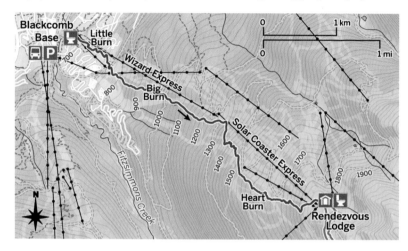

WHISTLER'S BLACKCOMB Burn is the newbie in the triumvirate of lift-serviced ascent trails in the southernmost Coast Mountains. Fully opened in 2017, the three segments that compose the Burn collectively boast 38 per cent more elevation gain than Squamish's Sea to Summit Trail (Hike 20) and North Vancouver's Grouse Grind (Hike 9). Throw in the fact that Whistler Blackcomb engineered the Burn to provide a virtually continuous uphill climb, and you have an appealing summer workout for hikers, trail runners, and fitness freaks.

The first section, Little Burn, starts between the Wizard Express and Magic Chair lifts at a base elevation of 685 m (2,247 ft). The mellow gravel path, shared with mountain bikers, leads into pleasant woods between ski runs, emerging in 0.8 km (0.5 mi) at Base 2, 74 m (243 ft) higher.

Gaining 494 m (1,621 ft) over 2.2 km (1.4 mi), Big Burn (hiking only) is the most scenic section. It steepens, following a riparian zone and transitioning from montane to alpine snow forest with Douglas fir, western hemlock, western red cedar, and yellow cedar trees that are hundreds of years old. Wildlife sightings include Douglas squirrels and pileated woodpeckers. Going up and across the Upper Mainline ski run, take a breather to savour the valley view and colourful wildflowers, including arctic lupine, red paintbrush, subalpine daisy, and tiger lily.

Heart Burn begins at the Wizard–Solar Coaster Express mid-station, visits the Magic Castle kids' play area, and switchbacks up the Bark Sandwich glade run. After gaining 607 m (1,991 ft) over 3.1 km (1.9 mi), the trail terminates at the Rendezvous Lodge (50°05'45" N, 122°54'05" W), where you can ride the Solar Coaster and Wizard chairlifts back to the base. (Make sure to buy a download ticket in advance.)

Stairs are scarce on the rainy-day-friendly Blackcomb Burn. Fixed chains and ropes near the start and end help with potentially slippery bits. For you quantified selves, the Burn adds more than 11,000 steps and 300 floors climbed to your day.

Foggy morning on the Heart Burn Trail.

Owned by Colorado-based Vail Resorts since 2016, Whistler Blackcomb operates in a controlled recreation area on provincial land and in the territories of the Squamish and Lil'wat First Nations. Camping, dogs, fires, and smoking are prohibited, as are drones (without authorization).

LONGER OPTION

Not ready to stop feeling the burn? Check the lift system's posted hours. Then keep your lactate levels up by following the Alpine Walk and cutting across the Sunburn ski run on the Overlord Trail to Blackcomb Lake and/or Decker Tarn (Hike 39) and back.

GETTING THERE

Transit: Whistler Transit Bus 5, 6, 7, 8, 20, 21, 30, or 32, or Pemberton Valley Transit Bus 99 (Pemberton Commuter) to Gondola Exchange. Walk east on Blackcomb Way for 500 m (0.3 mi) to Blackcomb base in the Upper Village.
Vehicle: On Highway 99 (Sea to Sky Highway) in Whistler, turn east on Village Gate Boulevard and then left on Blackcomb Way to find the Whistler Village day lots. Walk east to Blackcomb base.

39
DECKER TARN

Distance: 9 km (5.6 mi)
Time: 3.5 hours (double lollipop)
Elevation gain: 236 m (775 ft)
High point: 2,051 m (6,730 ft)

Quality: ★★★★
Difficulty: ■
Maps: NTS 92-J/2 Whistler
Trailhead: 50°05'45" N, 122°53'59" W

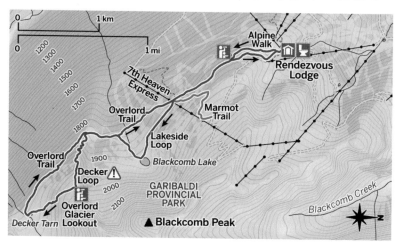

EVER WONDER why Blackcomb Glacier Provincial Park exists? It's a legacy of the B.C. government's moves over the years to delete land from Garibaldi Provincial Park for the benefit of the two ski areas that now compose Whistler Blackcomb. Food for thought as you hike across stellar subalpine terrain currently or formerly protected by Garibaldi's Class A park boundary.

That being said, the resort offers a superb mini-selection of summer trails in the 7th Heaven zone below Blackcomb Peak. Access entails booting it up the Blackcomb Burn (Hike 38) and/or coughing up for a lift ticket. The trailhead lies near the Rendezvous Lodge (1,860 m/6,102 ft)—by the Peak 2 Peak Gondola and Solar Coaster Express terminals—and overlooks the legendary Couloir Extreme and Blackcomb Bowl.

With Blackcomb Lake, Decker Tarn, or both as your goal, follow selfie-seeking sightseers up and immediately right on the gravel Alpine Walk. In 10 minutes, the Fitzsimmons Lookout grants a beautiful view of the Musical Bumps (Hike 37) and Whistler Mountain. At the next right, leave the tourist loop and head southeast on the Overlord Trail, traversing bouldery meadows with hoary marmots for company and losing some elevation.

Under the 7th Heaven Express, bear left for the Lakeside Loop (1.3 km/ 0.8 mi), which quickly ascends to Blackcomb Lake (1,918 m/6,293 ft) in

Decker Mountain rises behind Decker Tarn.

its cirque at the foot of Blackcomb Peak. Cross the outflow, descend the muddy path, and turn left to rejoin the Overlord Trail. Several minutes later (50°04'40" N, 122°53'07" W), take the left fork for the more challenging Decker Loop (1.8 km/1.1 mi).

Switchback up a ridge—avoiding a cornice to your left—to the windy Overlord Glacier Lookout, the day's high point. Look back at forbidding Blackcomb Peak and south to Fissile Peak and the Fitzsimmons Range. After crossing a snowy boulder field, the trail plunges to your ultimate destination. After 2 hours of hiking, reach milky Decker Tarn (50°04'05" N, 122°52'20" W) at 1,925 m (6,310 ft). Decker Mountain, close at hand, is a potential target for scramblers.

Cross the tarn's boulder dam and recross the outflow creek to begin the mellow return via the Overlord Trail (3.7 km/2.3 mi). See how many wildflowers you can identify in the lovely meadows: fan-leaved cinquefoil, leafy aster, red paintbrush, spreading phlox, western pasqueflower (the fruit of which reminds one of the Truffula trees in Dr. Seuss's *The Lorax*), etc. At the Alpine Walk, head right to complete the tourist loop and return to the base via the chairlifts.

Whistler Blackcomb lies in the territories of the Squamish and Lil'wat First Nations. Camping, dogs, fires, and smoking are prohibited, as are drones.

LONGER OPTION

To extend your hike, follow the aptly named Marmot Trail (1.2 km/0.7 mi) to the treeline and back on your return. It heads uphill from the Overlord Trail, just west of the 7th Heaven Express.

GETTING THERE

Transit: Whistler Transit Bus 5, 6, 7, 8, 20, 21, 30, or 32, or Pemberton Valley Transit Bus 99 (Pemberton Commuter) to Gondola Exchange. Walk east on Blackcomb Way for 500 m (0.3 mi) to Blackcomb base in the Upper Village.
Vehicle: On Highway 99 (Sea to Sky Highway) in Whistler, turn east on Village Gate Boulevard and then left on Blackcomb Way to find the Whistler Village day lots. Walk east to Blackcomb base.

40
RAINBOW PASS

Distance: 18.5 km (11.5 mi)
Time: 7 hours (round trip)
Elevation gain: 890 m (2,900 ft)
High point: 1,520 m (5,000 ft)

Quality: ★★★★
Difficulty: ■
Maps: NTS 92-J/2 Whistler, 92-J/3 Brandywine Falls; Green Trails 92J1S Whistler
Trailhead: 50°07'49" N, 122°59'09" W

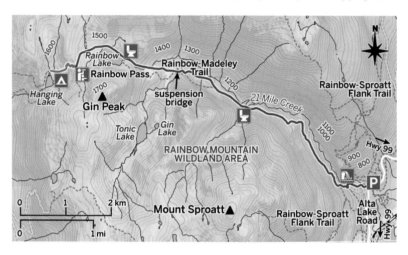

THE RAINBOW-MADELEY Trail is an overnight backpacking route linking Whistler's Westside and the Callaghan Valley, in the territories of the Squamish and Lil'wat First Nations. Day hiking the eastern section between Alta Lake Road and Rainbow Lake is popular, especially during wildflower season. This trip takes you into the Rainbow Mountain Wildland Area and the municipal watershed supplying 45 per cent of Whistler's drinking water. Accordingly, camping and swimming are banned at Rainbow Lake, and the watershed is a no-go zone for dogs, snowmobiles, and other motorized vehicles.

From the start, the trail stays south of 21 Mile Creek as it steadily climbs from the forest to the subalpine over 5 km (3.1 mi). Early on, you pass a short side trail to Rainbow Falls and come to a gravel road and water-supply building. Follow the road—ignoring turnoffs for the Whip Me Snip Me mountain-bike path and the multi-use Rainbow-Sproatt Flank Trail—until it ends at a bike rack. Continue on the footpath, crossing streams and muddy sections on bridges and boardwalks. The suspension bridge over the creek fed by Gin and Tonic Lakes has its decking removed for winter.

After crossing to the north side of 21 Mile Creek, it's time for the final steep push to the outhouse and Rainbow Lake, 8 km (5 mi) from the trailhead.

View of Rainbow Mountain and Rainbow Lake from Rainbow Pass.

Go ahead and pause to admire the pretty tarn sitting in its bowl between Rainbow Mountain and Gin Peak at an elevation of 1,460 m (4,790 ft), but don't call it quits here. Keep going to Rainbow Pass for superlative views of Metal Dome, Brandywine Mountain (Hike 33), Mount Cayley, and Powder Mountain to the west and a satisfying look back at its namesake mountain and lake. Retrace your steps to the trailhead.

LONGER OPTION

If you want to cool off with a swim, Hanging Lake lies 1 km (0.6 mi) west of Rainbow Pass—and outside the municipal watershed. You can camp there too. Say hi to the whisky jacks.

GETTING THERE

Vehicle: On Highway 99 (Sea to Sky Highway), 5 km (3.1 mi) south of Whistler Village, turn west on Alta Lake Road. Drive 6 km (3.7 mi) and park by the Rainbow Trail sign on the left.

41
SKYWALK SOUTH

Distance: 18 km (11.2 mi)
Time: 6 hours (lollipop)
Elevation gain: 1,060 m (3,480 ft)
High point: 1,790 m (5,870 ft)

Quality: ★★★★
Difficulty: ◆
Maps: NTS 92-J/2 Whistler, 92-J/3 Brandywine Falls
Trailhead: 50°08'40" N, 122°58'23" W

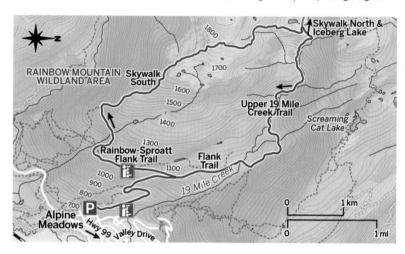

THE FORCE was strong with the Alpine Club of Canada's Whistler section in 2014, when volunteers completed the stellar Skywalk hiking trail network on the east side of Rainbow Mountain. It's best explored in two loops—Skywalk South and Skywalk North (Hike 42)—which enter the Rainbow Mountain Wildland Area, in the territories of the Squamish and Lil'wat First Nations. Skywalk South is the shorter of the two, but no less rewarding.

From the community watershed gate (no dogs allowed) at the top of Alpine Way in Alpine Meadows, ascend the gravel road, ignoring two leftward spurs. At the Rick's Roost sign, detour right for the first viewpoint of the day. About 45 minutes from the trailhead, turn left on the Rainbow-Sproatt Flank Trail, soon scoring a big Whistler Valley view at a paragliding launch site featuring a treetop windsock. Shortly thereafter, Skywalk South begins on the right (50°08'37" N, 122°59'13" W).

Marked by yellow flagging, the superbly built trail (not for bikes or horses) climbs northwest, steepening as it passes over rocky outcrops. After 1 hour on Skywalk South, the forest thins and snags are abundant. Soon, colourful meadows of arctic lupine, mountain arnica, Sitka valerian, and subalpine

Wildfire smoke obscures the view from a tarn on Skywalk South.

daisy are predominant, and the glaciated crown of Rainbow Mountain comes into view. Passing a pond and crossing a brook, the trail gains elevation over increasingly rocky terrain.

Beside a gorgeous tarn, 4 km (2.5 mi) up Skywalk South, the trail takes a right turn. Skirting the next tarn is tricky when steep snow hugs the shore and overhangs the water. Reach the high point, and follow cairns and orange squares through the wild, boulder-covered landscape.

Up next is the most difficult section of the clockwise loop: the thrilling descent to the 19 Mile Creek basin. Hands and route-finding skills are called into service as the trail hurtles down steep, bouldery slopes—treacherous with lingering snow. After crossing creeks above two waterfalls, the path eases up somewhat, following a smooth ridge with tarns to a junction with Skywalk North and the Upper 19 Mile Creek Trail (50°10′39″ N, 123°01′01″ W), 4.5 hours from the start.

Go right to descend the latter trail for 4 km (2.5 mi). Spurs on the left lead to waterfalls. Turn right on the Flank Trail, cross the 19 Mile Creek bridge, and make a left on the Rick's Roost road to return to the trailhead.

LONGER OPTION

From the top of the Upper 19 Mile Creek Trail, detour 1 km (0.6 mi) up Skywalk North to visit out-of-this-world Iceberg Lake before looping back to Alpine Way.

GETTING THERE

Transit: Whistler Transit Bus 30 (Emerald via Alpine) to Drifter Way at Alpine Way. Walk west for 350 m (0.2 mi) to the top of Alpine.

Vehicle: From Highway 99 (Sea to Sky Highway), 4 km (2.5 mi) north of Whistler Village, head west on Alpine Way for 1 km (0.6 mi). Park below the cul-de-sac at the top.

42
SKYWALK NORTH

Distance: 20 km (12.4 mi)
Time: 8.5 hours (lollipop)
Elevation gain: 1,050 m (3,445 ft)
High point: 1,784 m (5,850 ft)

Quality: ★★★★
Difficulty: ■
Maps: NTS 92-J/2 Whistler, 92-J/3 Brandywine Falls
Trailhead: 50°09'16" N, 122°58'05" W

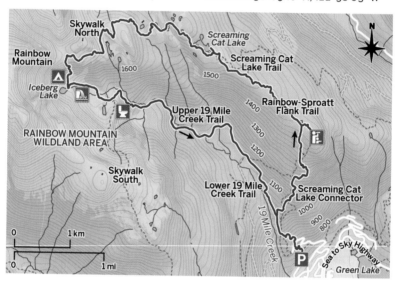

MANY HIKERS venturing into Whistler's Skywalk trail network make a beeline to Iceberg Lake. However, this worthy destination is better experienced as the centrepiece of a grand loop—Skywalk North. Longer than Skywalk South (Hike 41), Skywalk North pays off with more quality time in subalpine meadows. Both trails enter the Rainbow Mountain Wildland Area, in the territories of the Squamish and Lil'wat First Nations.

From the top of Mountain View Drive in Alpine Meadows, strike off on the Lower 19 Mile Creek Trail, paying close attention to faded blue signs and orange markers. Within the first 10 minutes, quickly turn left to rise under the trees, cross a mountain-bike trail, bear right on a telephone line right-of-way, go left on a gravel road, and take a trail leaving to the right. Shortly thereafter, a big yellow sign keeps hikers on the right track.

A half-hour in, a viewpoint overlooks Green Lake. Cross a downhill bike path and turn right on a steep gravel road with yellow flagging. Go left at a T-junction, 1.2 km (0.7 mi) from the start, and immediately right for the 1.4 km (0.9 mi) Screaming Cat Lake Connector. You might scare up a ruffed grouse. After 1.5 hours of hiking, head right and uphill on the Rainbow-Sproatt Flank Trail. The signed Valley Lookout is worth a detour to the right; the 360-degree view includes Rainbow Mountain and The Black Tusk (T'ekt'akmúyin tl'a In7ińyáxa7en to the Squamish, Q'elqámtensa ti Skenknápa to the Lil'wat; Hike 31).

Iceberg Lake is the scenic climax of Skywalk North.

Leave Flank and go left on the Screaming Cat Lake Trail, 3 hours in. Just before Screaming Cat Lake itself, a left fork marks the start of Skywalk North (50°11′06″ N, 122°59′28″ W). The trail runs along the lakeshore, then ascends to glorious subalpine meadows, ponds, and brooks. Higher up, with glaciated Rainbow Mountain before you, cairns lead the way across rocky slopes and snow patches. Fixed chains help with a couple of slippery spots.

From the high point, survey the Coast Mountains—from Mount Currie (Ts'zil to the Lil'wat; Hike 43) to Wedge Mountain, the Spearhead Range, and the Fitzsimmons Range. The fun descent to spectacular Iceberg Lake (50°10′45″ N, 123°01′38″ W) is muddy and steep, with a fixed rope on one bit. Cross a boulder moraine to reach the lake outlet (don't ford it) and tent sites, 12.5 km (7.8 mi) from the start.

Continuing the counterclockwise loop, descend the rocky path, with a waterfall to your right, to lush meadows and a junction. Right is for Skywalk South, but go left on the Upper 19 Mile Creek Trail for 4 km (2.5 mi). Leftward spurs lead to waterfalls. Following signs for Mountain View Drive, turn left on the Flank Trail and then right on the Lower 19 Mile Creek Trail a few minutes later. Keep right until you meet the Screaming Cat Lake Connector. Back on familiar ground, stick with Lower 19 Mile to the trailhead.

SHORTER OPTION

Turn around at Screaming Cat Lake—preferably after a dip—for an out-and-back hike of 13.5 km (8.4 mi).

GETTING THERE

Transit: Whistler Transit Bus 30 (Emerald via Alpine) to Mountain View Drive at Valley Drive. Walk west for 700 m (0.4 mi) to the top of Mountain View.

Vehicle: From Highway 99 (Sea to Sky Highway), 4 km (2.5 mi) north of Whistler Village, turn west on Meadow Lane and immediately right on Parkwood Drive. Go left on Mountain View Drive, reaching the cul-de-sac at the top in 1 km (0.6 mi).

43
MOUNT CURRIE TRAIL

Distance: 13 km (8.1 mi)
Time: 7.5 hours (round trip)
Elevation gain: 1,240 m (4,070 ft)
High point: 1,600 m (5,250 ft)

Quality: ★★
Difficulty: ◆
Maps: NTS 92-J/2 Whistler, 92-J/7 Pemberton
Trailhead: 50°14'17" N, 122°51'15" W

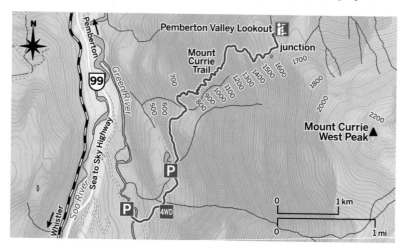

KNOWN AS Ts'zil in the Ucwalmicwts language of the Lil'wat Nation, imposing Mount Currie (2,591 m/8,500 ft) towers above the Pemberton Valley. Therefore, tackling the Mount Currie Trail might impress your friends, even though the hike described here gets you only halfway to the summit. Be prepared for lots of switchbacks and boulder fields, and carry sufficient water.

From the Green River bridge, head east and north on the steep logging road for 30 minutes (1.4 km/0.9 mi) to find the official trailhead on the right (530 m/1,740 ft; 50°14'44" N, 122°50'42" W). Built by the Pemberton Valley Trails Association, the Mount Currie Trail trades the clear-cut for the forest and gently ascends north, paralleling a wetland, negotiating a rockslide, and crossing another cutblock.

Following 45 minutes of taking it easy, the fine trail turns uphill and relentlessly but pleasantly switchbacks northeast, with only the occasional cairn or flagging. Three hours in, a painted orange arrow directs you across a rockslide below a cliff. Soon the grade lessens.

After almost 4 hours of hiking, come to a lake and a signed junction (1,500 m/4,920 m). To the right, the Mount Currie Trail carries on climbing

Boulder fields abound on the Mount Currie Trail.

to meadows and campsites. However, turn left for our objective, the Pemberton Valley Lookout (50°15′53″ N, 122°49′19″ W). This is an adequate turn-around point, unless you really haven't seen enough elevation gain yet. With thoughts of dinner, reverse your ascent route for the switchbacking, bouldery descent.

GETTING THERE

Vehicle: On Highway 99 (Sea to Sky Highway), 21 km (13 mi) north of Whistler Village and 9 km (5.6 mi) south of Pemberton, turn east at the Green River Motocross Park and Pemberton Speedway. Drive south on the logging road (2WD), passing the racetracks, and park before the Green River bridge. (4WD vehicles may be able to go a bit farther, though there are big water bars.)

44
TENQUILLE LAKE

Distance: 12.5 km (7.8 mi)
Time: 4 hours (round trip)
Elevation gain: 450 m (1,480 ft)
High point: 1,710 m (5,610 ft)

Quality: ★★★★
Difficulty: ■
Maps: NTS 92-J/10 Birkenhead Lake
Trailhead: 50°32'21"N, 123°00'01" W

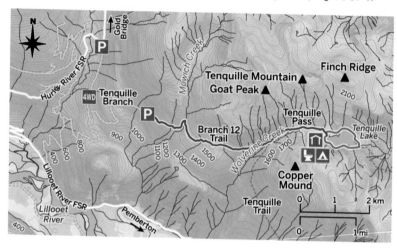

THE LIL'WAT Nation has designated five *Nt'ákmen* (Our Way) areas in its territory. These zones are meant to preserve wilderness and protect places for Lil'wat people to harvest traditional resources and continue cultural practices. The Qwelimak Nt'ákmen Area is home to transformer routes, legends, rock art, culturally modified trees, and village and burial sites. Located in the Upper Birkenhead River watershed, Qwelimak includes beautiful Tenquille Lake, which is flanked by enticing mountains to the north and south.

For hikers, the Branch 12 Trail (motorized vehicles prohibited) is the easiest way in. From the buggy trailhead, the well-established but barely marked path climbs and then undulates eastward. Cross Mowich Creek and steadily gain elevation in the woods above Wolverine Creek to a junction (50°32'02" N, 122°57'10" W) at 4.5 km (2.8 mi). Go left, merging with the longer and steeper Tenquille Trail from the Lillooet River, which is popular with mountain bikers.

A glorious subalpine meadow stroll awaits at Tenquille Pass (warning: high avalanche danger in winter and spring). There are plenty of Dr. Seuss Who-flowers (western pasqueflower), and planks cover muddy bits.

The trail descends to Tenquille Lake Cabin (50°32'12" N, 122°55'47" W)—maintained by the Pemberton Wildlife Association, a hunting and fishing group—2 hours in. A snow survey station and the beautiful blue-green lake

Tenquille Mountain rises above Tenquille Pass.

(1,661 m/5,450 ft) are steps away. Scramblers have no shortage of objectives here: Goat Peak, Tenquille Mountain, and Finch Ridge to the north; Copper Mound, Mount McLeod (Crown Mountain), and Mount Barbour to the south. Retrace your steps on your return.

Industrial development, water-power projects, agriculture, and intensive tourism are banned at Tenquille Lake and throughout the *Nt'ákmen*. Tenquille Lake is also part of the Tenquille-Owl Recreation Area, managed by Recreation Sites and Trails B.C. Respect this land; practice Leave No Trace.

LONGER OPTION
A 2.6 km (1.6 mi) loop around Tenquille Lake leads to campsites. Fires must be confined to established metal rings. Beyond is a 25 km (15.5 mi) multi-day backpacking route to Chain Lakes and Owl Creek that will test your navigation skills.

GETTING THERE
Vehicle: In Pemberton, turn north off Highway 99 (Sea to Sky Highway) onto Portage Road. Go left at a roundabout, then turn right from Birch Street onto Pemberton Meadows Road. In 23.5 km (14.6 mi), head right on the unpaved Lillooet River Forest Service Road and, 8.5 km (5.3 mi) later, right on Hurley River FSR (rough 2WD). At 20 km (12.4 mi) past the Lillooet River bridge, go right on Tenquille Branch (high-clearance 4WD) for 5.2 km (3.2 mi). Branch 12 continues left and uphill at a Tenquille Lake sign, 2 km (1.2 mi) in. Drive to the end.

45
CAMEL PASS

Distance: 17.5 km (11 mi)
Time: 7.5 hours (round trip)
Elevation gain: 1,090 m (3,580 ft)
High point: 2,130 m (6,990 ft)

Quality: ★★★★
Difficulty: ■
Maps: NTS 92-J/15 Bralorne, Trail Ventures BC Southern Chilcotin Mountains
Trailhead: 50°55'48" N, 122°47'31" W

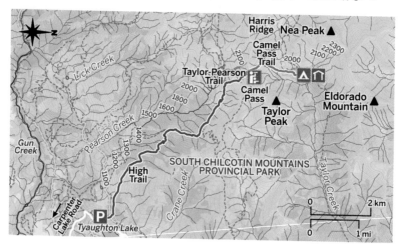

A FORAY on the High Trail is guaranteed to whet your appetite for hiking in the colourful, multi-use paradise known as South Chilcotin Mountains Provincial Park, in St'át'imc territory. Along the way, you'll encounter mountain bikers, horseback riders, trail runners, dirt bikers, and ATV drivers—and step in plenty of horse poop.

From the parking area (1,040 m/3,410 ft), go north on the gravel road. Immediately fork right then left to start the High Trail. Stick with the old mining road as it heads northwest, steadily gains elevation, encounters clear-cuts, crosses streams, and passes a provincial park boundary marker.

After 6 km (3.7 mi), turn left at a signed junction (1,790 m/5,870 ft; 50°57'30" N, 122°49'54" W). Say goodbye to the motorized folks and hello to lovely single track and the wildflower meadows and ore-stained mountains of the Pearson Creek basin.

In 1.6 km (1 mi), turn right on the Taylor-Pearson Trail in the subalpine meadows. Keep an eye out for spruce grouse. Ascend northwest and up a dirt track to otherworldly Camel Pass (50°58'20" N, 122°51'30" W). Spot The Camel? The Chilcotin Ranges surround you, Harris Ridge and Taylor Peak

View of Nea Peak from Camel Pass.

are nearby high points, and Nea Peak rises across the Taylor Creek basin. Return the way you came.

Tim and Claudia O'Hearn's *Southern Chilcotin Mountains Guidebook* (Trail Ventures B.C., 2015) is packed with details about this fascinating area. Dogs must be leashed. Bikes yield to hikers; both make way for horses.

LONGER OPTION

To spend a night in the Taylor Creek basin, descend north for 2 km (1.2 mi), keeping right for the Camel Pass Trail, to find campsites around Taylor Cabin (1,875 m/6,150 ft; 50°59′14″ N, 122°51′30″ W). Northwest of the dilapidated "Taylor Basin Resort," Nea Peak (2,490 m/8,170 ft; 50°59′51″ N, 122°52′44″ W) is an easy scramble via its south ridge (2 hours up). The basin lies outside of the park, in the Taylor Creek Mining and Tourism Area, formerly part of the Spruce Lake Protected Area.

GETTING THERE

Vehicle: In Pemberton, turn north off Highway 99 (Sea to Sky Highway) onto Portage Road. Go left at a roundabout, then turn right from Birch Street onto Pemberton Meadows Road. In 23.5 km (14.6 mi), head right on the unpaved Lillooet River Forest Service Road and, 8.5 km (5.3 mi) later, right on Hurley River FSR (rough 2WD). At the Hurley's north end, go right on Gun Lake Road South and continue onto Carpenter Lake Road (Lillooet-Pioneer Road 40) for 11.5 km (7.1 mi). (Road 40 can also be accessed via Highway 99 at Lillooet.) Turn north on Tyaughton Lake Road. In 5.5 km (3.4 mi), head left on the Gun Creek logging road (just before Hornal Road and Tyaughton Lake). Find a huge parking area on the left.

46
COOL CREEK CANYON

Distance: 2 km (1.2 mi)
Time: 2 hours (loop)
Elevation gain: 320 m (1,050 ft)
High point: 710 m (2,330 ft)

Quality: ★★★★
Difficulty: ■
Maps: NTS 92-J/7 Pemberton
Trailhead: 50°25'29"N, 122°41'37" W

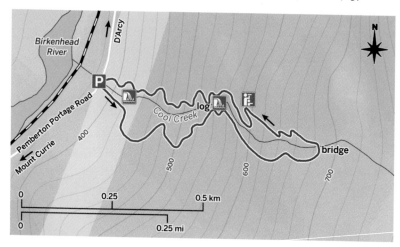

COOL CREEK Canyon is every bit as wicked as it sounds. Whitewater plunges over a series of cascades in this narrow gorge on the western fringe of Mount Gardiner, part of the Place Glacier Group. The canyon lies in the Qwelimak Nt'ákmen (Our Way) Area, designated by the Lil'wat Nation as a wilderness preserve in the Upper Birkenhead River watershed.

For a fun little counterclockwise loop, start at the map board on river left. Built with funds from the Squamish-Lillooet Regional District, the single track climbs steeply up the south side of the canyon in forest. Wooden barriers keep hikers away from the precipice at several waterfall viewpoints.

In 20 minutes, the unmarked path switchbacks away from a boulder field on the right and arrives at a spot where a log lies across the rushing water. The trail continues up the ridge of rock that confines the creek to the canyon—not advisable for young children or those with acrophobia—soon offering views of the Birkenhead River below and the wooded mountains across the valley. Take your time and savour the roar and the breeze.

An hour in, a wooden bridge donated by the Pemberton Valley Trail Association marks the top of the trail (50°25'23" N, 122°41'07" W). The north-side descent rewards with a different perspective on the waterfalls you saw on the way up.

Picnic spot overlooking the Birkenhead River.

A side trail to the right leads to a picnic table contributed by the Birken Recreational and Cultural Society. From the fantastic overlook, multi-summited Mount Currie (Ts'zil in the Ucwalmicwts language of the Lil'wat; Hike 43) strikes an imposing figure to the south. When you hit Pemberton Portage Road, turn left to return to the trailhead.

GETTING THERE

Vehicle: East of Pemberton, leave Highway 99 (Sea to Sky Highway) at Mount Currie and head north on Main Street, which continues as Pemberton Portage Road en route to D'Arcy. Thirteen km (8.1 mi) north of Mount Currie, find the trailhead at a small pullout on the right side of the road.

47
TWIN LAKES

Distance: 16 km (10 mi)
Time: 7.5 hours (round trip)
Elevation gain: 965 m (3,170 ft)
High point: 2,215 m (7,270 ft)

Quality: ★★★★★
Difficulty: ◆
Maps: NTS 92-J/8 Duffey Lake, 92-J/9 Shalalth
Trailhead: 50°28'57" N, 122°22'23" W

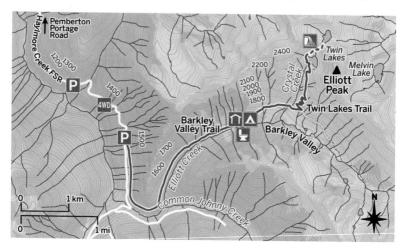

A **STUNNING** pair of tarns drained by Crystal Creek in the Cayoosh Range, Twin Lakes lie in high bowls worthy of Middle-earth fantasy. Potential sightings of alpine icebergs only add to the dramatic scene.

Coming up Haylmore Creek FSR, the Barkley Valley Trail leaves to the left at a green map board (1,250 m/4,100 ft). The old mining road turned ATV track heads south in the trees, then curves northwest, staying north of Common Johnny Creek. After an hour of steadily plodding uphill, spy Elliott Creek below to the right and glimpse the eye-popping montane landscape ahead. Soon, edible thistle and red paintbrush colour the meadows and daunting switchbacks higher up enter the view. Welcome to paradise—or Lawlaton, as the Barkley Valley is known to the N'Quatqua First Nation.

At 5 km (3.1 mi) up, reach a junction (1,580 m/5,180 ft; 50°29'15" N, 122°20'17" W). To the right is a campsite and ramshackle shelter built by the Cayoosh Recreation Club. A pit toilet is nearby. Go left on the Twin Lakes Trail, with 3 km (1.9 km) to your destination. Cross Crystal Creek and stay left on the double track where an overgrown branch goes right (1,740 m/5,710 ft) and continues up the wondrous Barkley Valley. Ascend the switchbacks you

Sunrise over the Cayoosh Range, as seen from above Upper Twin Lake.

spotted earlier—perhaps the most scenic ever—to the "End of trail" sign (2,100 m/6,900 ft), which warns of steep and snowy terrain to come.

Just 10 minutes on rocky single track delivers you to aquamarine Lower Twin Lake. Up the hanging valley, a series of waterfalls connects the tarns. Behind you, the Joffre Group and Cayoosh Mountain loom. Cross the outlet and pick up a rough path above the left lakeshore.

Follow indistinct tracks, with hoary marmots galore, up the final rise to Upper Twin Lake (50°30'07" N, 122°18'53" W). Moss campion grows on the talus. Attractive ridges line the bowl. Routes up Crystal Peak and Elliott Peak are described in Matt Gunn's *Scrambles in Southwest British Columbia* (Cairn Publishing, 2005). From the gap at the far end of the upper lake, you can peer down the Melvin Creek drainage. There are spots suitable for tenting at both lakes; please practise minimum-impact camping. Once you've explored, retrace your steps.

GETTING THERE

Vehicle: East of Pemberton, leave Highway 99 (Sea to Sky Highway) at Mount Currie and head north on Main Street, which continues as Pemberton Portage Road en route to D'Arcy. Thirty-four km (21 mi) north of Mount Currie, pass the Birkenhead Lake Provincial Park turnoff and go right on Devine Street, which swings left after the railway tracks. At pavement's end, turn right on Haylmore Creek Forest Service Road. Follow the mainline over Haylmore Creek and up switchbacks. After the 5 km marker, keep right at a fork. High-clearance 4WD vehicles might make it all the way to the Barkley Valley trailhead, 13 km (8 mi) up the logging road. (Boulders and washouts may stop 2WD vehicles 7 km/4.3 mi short, adding to the approach time.)

48
JOFFRE LAKES

Distance: 9.5 km (5.9 mi)
Time: 4 hours (round trip)
Elevation gain: 360 m (1,180 ft)
High point: 1,570 m (5,150 ft)

Quality: ★★★★★
Difficulty: ●
Maps: NTS 92-J/8 Duffey Lake, Trail Ventures BC Stein to Joffre
Trailhead: 50°22'10" N, 122°29'55" W

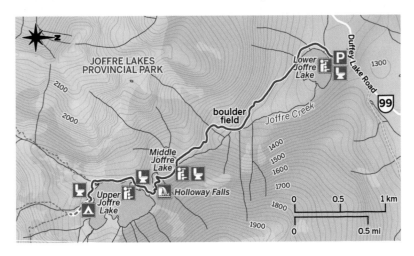

WHILE SOLITUDE is in short supply at picture-perfect Joffre Lakes, alpine splendour is certainly not. A very early start is required to secure a legal parking spot and beat the hordes of day trippers.

Just south of the trailhead, the Joffre Lakes Trail forks. The left spur terminates quickly at Lower Joffre Lake (1,213 m/3,980 ft). Right continues on to the middle and upper of these paternoster lakes, 3 km (1.9 mi) and 4 km (2.5 mi) up, respectively.

With the all-ages, international crowd and tourist-grade trail—made markedly easier in recent years—Joffre Lakes Provincial Park has the feel of a national park. Gravel now carries hikers over a once-tricky boulder field, and stairs tackle steep sections. At deep-blue Middle Joffre Lake (1,490 m/ 4,890 ft), you may see a queue for photo ops on an Instagram-famous log.

The last push is more challenging. Holloway Falls, a staircase waterfall, is an impressive sight. After 1.5 hours on foot, many hikers turn around at the boulder viewpoint on Upper Joffre Lake (1,564 m/5,130 ft). Continue around the west shore to the campground (50°20'39" N, 122°28'38" W), which lies below Mount Matier and the Matier Glacier. Retrace your steps on your return.

Lunch spot on the moraine above Upper Joffre Lake.

Designated as a provincial recreation area in 1988, Joffre Lakes gained Class A park status in 1996. Dogs are banned, drones require B.C. Parks' permission, fires are prohibited year-round, and tenting is allowed only at the Upper Joffre Lake site. (A backcountry camping permit is required between June and September.) Outhouses are located at the trailhead and middle and upper lakes. Signs near the trailhead advise hikers to "Leave No Trace," "Pack it in, pack it out," and stay on the path to protect fragile vegetation. Nevertheless, discarded energy bar and chocolate bar wrappers as well as wine and water bottles, plus graffiti, were spotted on one visit.

The park lies in the territories of the Lil'wat and N'Quatqua First Nations. In 1911, chiefs representing those and fourteen other St'át'imc bands signed the landmark Declaration of the Lillooet Tribe: "We are aware the B.C. government claims our Country, like all other Indian territories in B.C.; but we deny their right to it. We never gave it nor sold it to them."

LONGER OPTION

Southeast of the campground, head up the moraine for 15 minutes to lunch above Upper Joffre Lake with dark-eyed juncos for company. Joffre Peak and Slalok Mountain loom over the cirque, while Cayoosh Mountain rises across Cayoosh Pass. Higher terrain, exposed to icefall, is for experienced mountaineers only. Several years ago, an avalanche swept through the original campground at Upper Joffre Lake in late summer (no one was hurt); note that this area is particularly prone to avalanches in winter and spring.

GETTING THERE

Transit: Better Environmentally Sound Transportation's Parkbus offers coach service on summer weekends to the Joffre Lakes parking lot from downtown Vancouver.

Vehicle: From Pemberton, go east on Highway 99 (Duffey Lake Road). At Mount Currie, turn right and stay on Highway 99 for 23 km (14.3 mi). The Joffre Lakes parking lot is on the right. Shoulder parking on Highway 99 is prohibited.

49
MOUNT ROHR

Distance: 12 km (7.5 mi)
Time: 8 hours (round trip)
Elevation gain: 1,030 m (3,380 ft)
High point: 2,423 m (7,950 ft)

Quality: ★★★★★
Difficulty: ◆◆
Maps: NTS 92-J/8 Duffey Lake, John
Baldwin Duffey Lake
Trailhead: 50°24'18" N, 122°27'44" W

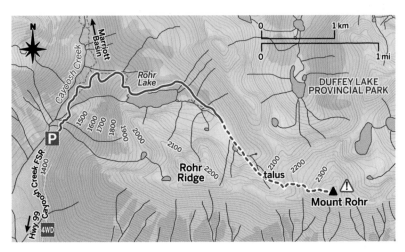

IN WINTER, the alpine terrain surrounding Rohr Lake and Marriott Meadows in the Cayoosh Range offers excellent ski touring. These glacier-carved valleys, north of Joffre Lakes (Hike 48), are also spectacular for summer hiking and scrambling.

From the avalanche-terrain warning sign at the top of Cayoosh Creek Forest Service Road, head northeast under cover of forest, spotting salmonberries and crossing several creeks. Reach a major junction in 20 minutes (50°24'37" N, 122°27'30" W). Left is signed for "Aspen," but take the right fork for Rohr Lake.

The steep trail switchbacks east through blueberries to a lovely subalpine bowl filled with fluffy white Chamisso's cottongrass. Follow the muddy path up the right side of a boulder field. Listen for the whistling of an American pika. Traverse left at a waterfall and ascend to the shore of beautiful blue Rohr Lake (50°24'35" N, 122°26'54" W), 1.5 hours from the trailhead.

Mount Rohr lies 2.5 hours beyond the lake, requires solid route-finding skills, and should be left to experienced parties. From the lakeshore, follow meadow paths and cairns up-valley, passing to the left of tarns and picking

View of Rohr Lake and the Marriott Basin from Mount Rohr.

your way through boulders. At the head of the valley, ascend slopes of talus and fireweed east toward your objective. Stay away from cornices.

Once on the west ridge, a quick bit of easy scrambling leads to a succession of false summits and finally the top, with its cairn and summit register (50°23′52″ N, 122°24′32″ W). From this lofty perch on the edge of Duffey Lake Provincial Park, the glorious panorama includes the Anniversary Glacier (Hike 50) and Joffre Group to the south and Cayoosh Mountain, Mount Marriott, and Marriott Basin to the west. Retrace your steps to the start.

SHORTER OPTION

Rohr Lake is more than ample reward for a 3-hour round trip involving a distance of 4 km (2.5 mi) and elevation gain of 410 m (1,345 ft). There are lakeside tent sites, and Rohr Ridge looms across the chilly water, which hosts rainbow trout and invites swimming.

The lake lies in the territories of the Lil'wat and N'Quatqua First Nations. It's part of the Nlháxten Nt'ákmen (Our Way) Area, designated by the Lil'wat as off-limits to industrial development, in the Cayoosh Creek basin.

GETTING THERE

Vehicle: From Pemberton, go east on Highway 99 (Duffey Lake Road). At Mount Currie, turn right and stay on Highway 99 for 26.5 km (16.5 mi). Turn left on the unsigned Cayoosh Creek Forest Service Road, just before the sand shed. With 4WD and high clearance, drive north as far as 2.3 km (1.4 mi), keeping left, to the trailhead at road's end. (Those with 2WD or concerned about their vehicle's exterior paint should park near the bottom or on the roadside by the sand shed and walk the remainder.)

50
ANNIVERSARY GLACIER

Distance: 9 km (5.6 mi)
Time: 5.5 hours (round trip)
Elevation gain: 450 m (1,480 ft)
High point: 1,660 m (5,450 ft)

Quality: ★★★★
Difficulty: ■
Maps: NTS 92-J/8 Duffey Lake, Trail Ventures BC Stein to Joffre
Trailhead: 50°22'52" N, 122°24'45" W

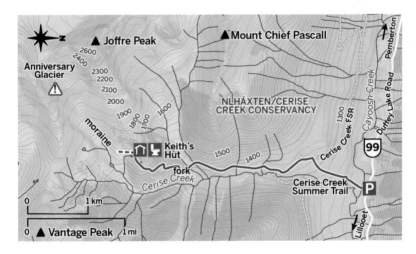

AT TRENDY Joffre Lakes (Hike 48), one's eyes are drawn upward to the treacherous Matier Glacier, which is grinding away at Joffre Peak and Mount Matier. Just over the col, and out of view, lies the Anniversary Glacier, a well-loved ski-touring spot in winter and hiking destination in summer.

From Highway 99, a path descends south to a log bridge over Cayoosh Creek (1,210 m/3,970 ft). Keep right for the signed Cerise Creek Summer Trail, henceforth staying west of Cerise Creek's main stem. In 20 minutes, turn left on the overgrown Cerise Creek Forest Service Road. Soon a rock arrow directs you onto a right fork (50°22'05" N, 122°24'56" W). Head through a clear-cut, with Mount Howard, Mount Matier, and Joffre Peak before you, to the end of the logging road where the marked trail resumes.

Continue south in the forest, with bridges over streams. From the corduroy trail through a soggy meadow, Joffre Peak's northeast face is a breathtaking sight. Back in the trees, reach a signed fork: left for "Glacier," right for "Hut." Choose the latter (steep) path and negotiate a boulder field. Looking back, spy Mount Rohr (Hike 49) to the north.

Just after a small pond, arrive at Keith's Hut (1,650 m/5,410 ft; 50°20' 48" N, 122°25'08" W), built in 1988 to commemorate a mountaineer who

Vantage Peak reflected in a pond near Keith's Hut.

died on Mount Logan. Guests should make a donation to the Keith Flavelle Memorial Hut Society. Expect whisky jacks to drop in.

Continue to the subalpine meadows beyond the cedar log cabin, past a larger pond and a small drinking-water tank, and up to the crest of the steep and loose lateral moraine of the Anniversary Glacier for a thrilling perspective (3 hours up). Vantage Peak, Mount Matier, and Joffre Peak tower over the till-covered cirque, which holds a small milky tarn. (Don't venture onto the ice without proper equipment and experience.) Retrace your steps to the highway.

This basin is protected by Nlháxten/Cerise Creek Conservancy, adjacent to Joffre Lakes Provincial Park. It's also part of the larger Nlháxten (Cayoosh) Nt'ákmen (Our Way) Area designated by the Lil'wat Nation. The area is valued by the Lil'wat for vision questing, plant gathering, and hunting, as well as for its culturally modified trees and rock art.

GETTING THERE

Vehicle: From Pemberton, go east on Highway 99 (Duffey Lake Road). At Mount Currie, turn right to stay on Highway 99. Park in an unsigned pullout on the right, 3 km (1.9 mi) past the sand shed at Cayoosh Pass.

51
LAKEVIEW TRAIL

Distance: 11 km (6.8 mi)
Time: 3 hours (loop)
Elevation gain: 150 m (490 ft)
High point: 275 m (900 ft)

Quality: ★
Difficulty: ●
Maps: NTS 92-G/7 Port Coquitlam, Canadian Map Makers Coquitlam Port Moody
Trailhead: 49°20'24" N, 122°51'33" W

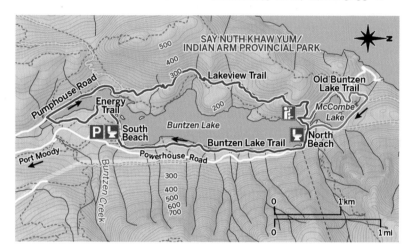

A **LOOP** around Buntzen Lake in Anmore is just the thing for the unambitious days of shoulder season. However, it's no fun to stick to the lakeshore path the whole way. Taking the Lakeview Trail on the west side of Lake Beautiful, as the B.C. Hydro reservoir was once known, adds some ups and downs and will make you break a sweat. It's a suitable option for kids and rainy days.

From the South Beach parking area, kick off the clockwise loop by wandering over to the boat launch on Buntzen Lake (123 m/400 ft). Go southwest on the interpretative Energy Trail and keep right to take the Buntzen Lake Trail over the floating bridge at the south end of the lake. Hang a right on Pumphouse Road and continue north to find the start of the Lakeview Trail (6 km/3.7 mi) on the left.

The Lakeview Trail flirts with the power line corridor that runs to the hydroelectric powerhouse on Indian Arm, before disappearing into the lush forest on the eastern slopes of Buntzen Ridge. As the trail rises and falls, there are steep sections to negotiate. A lovely viewpoint near the trail's north terminus offers a look across Buntzen Lake to impressive Swan Falls on Eagle Ridge (Hike 52).

Buntzen Lake, as seen from South Beach.

Turn right on the Old Buntzen Lake Trail and left on the contemporary Buntzen Lake Trail to cross the suspension bridge (49°21′57″ N, 122°51′31″ W) over the narrows at the lake's north end. Head south to visit North Beach, pass the tunnel carrying water from Coquitlam Lake, and follow the Buntzen Lake Trail along the eastern shore back to South Beach.

The Lakeview Trail is shared with horses and mountain bikes. This loop straddles the Buntzen Lake Recreation Area and Say Nuth Khaw Yum/ Indian Arm Provincial Park and lies in the territories of the Tsleil-Waututh, Musqueam, Squamish, and Stó:lō First Nations. Camping, drones, guns, and open fires are prohibited at Buntzen Lake, and dogs must be on-leash. B.C. Hydro closes the entrance gate for the day once the parking lots are full.

LONGER OPTION

For an extended outing, skip the suspension bridge and stroll around McCombe Lake (Trout Lake), the north arm of Buntzen Lake. Continue north on the Old Buntzen Lake Trail to the water intake and dam, and follow Powerhouse Road around to the east side of the lake to rejoin the main loop.

GETTING THERE

Transit: TransLink Bus 182 (Belcarra) to Anmore Grocery. Walk 1.8 km (1.1 mi) to South Beach. In summer, Bus 179 (Buntzen Lake) provides service to South Beach.

Vehicle: From its junction with Highway 7 (Lougheed Highway) in Coquitlam, head west on Barnet Highway (formerly Highway 7A), then north on Johnson Street. Turn left on David Avenue, right on Forest Park Way, and left on Aspenwood Drive, which becomes East Road. Go right on Sunnyside Road and continue to the South Beach parking area. Note the posted closing time.

52
MOUNT BEAUTIFUL

Distance: 20 km (12.4 mi)
Time: 8 hours (loop)
Elevation gain: 1,130 m (3,710 ft)
High point: 1,259 m (4,130 ft)

Quality: ★
Difficulty: ◆
Maps: NTS 92-G/7 Port Coquitlam, Canadian Map Makers Coquitlam Port Moody
Trailhead: 49°20'10" N, 122°51'21" W

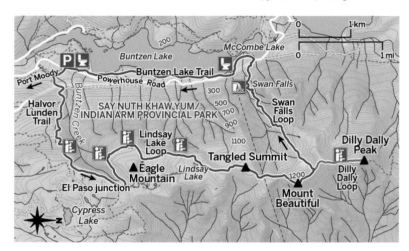

MOUNT BEAUTIFUL is one of several bumps on Eagle Ridge, the woodsy divide between Buntzen Lake and Coquitlam Lake in Anmore. This gruelling counterclockwise loop is located within Say Nuth Khaw Yum/Indian Arm Provincial Park, B.C. Hydro's Buntzen Lake Recreation Area, and the territories of the Tsleil-Waututh, Kwikwetlem, Musqueam, Squamish, and Stó:lō First Nations.

Find the trailhead just north of the Powerhouse Road gate. Head east on the Lindsay Lake Loop portion of the Halvor Lunden Trail, named after the illustrious trail builder who died in 2008. Your path merges with the Academy Trail momentarily, passes under a power line, and goes left and then right. Follow orange blazes up Eagle Ridge, on which you keep left at all junctions. Stop to catch your breath at Polytrichum Lookout. As the grade eases, the trail is flanked by a regenerating clear-cut on the right and the Buntzen Creek gorge to the left.

At El Paso junction, choose viewpoints over lakes by forking left. Swing around the west side of Eagle Mountain to visit Spahat Ridge, The Pulpit, and towering old-growth trees. The viewpoints and lower lakes routes reunite at

Lindsay Lake (1,150 m/3,770 ft). Continue north on the undulating Swan Falls Loop, where route-finding may be especially challenging in snow.

Negotiate Dead Tree Pass, Tangled Summit (1,218 m/3,995 ft; 49°22'02" N, 122°49'48" W), Hemlock Pass, and Spirit Pass en route to the adequate summit of Mount Beautiful, also known

Eagle Ridge rises east of Buntzen Lake.

as Eagle Peak (5 hours up; 49°22'35" N, 122°49'35" W). The far-reaching views extend from Coquitlam Mountain, in the Coquitlam Watershed, to Mount Garibaldi (Nch'kay' to the Squamish Nation) and Mount Baker in the distance. Press on northward to a saddle, where a super-steep trail goes left and down to Swan Falls and the north end of Buntzen Lake (123 m/400 ft), once called Lake Beautiful. At the bottom, turn left on Powerhouse Road and allow the easy Buntzen Lake Trail to lead you along the eastern shore to South Beach.

Camping, drones, guns, and open fires are banned at Buntzen Lake, and dogs must be leashed. The entrance gate closes for the day once the parking lots are full. B.C. Hydro feeds water from Coquitlam Lake into Buntzen Lake via a tunnel under Eagle Ridge and down to a powerhouse on Indian Arm.

LONGER OPTION

At the Swan Falls junction, north of Mount Beautiful, go right to visit 117 Lookout and ascend the rough route to remote Dilly Dally Peak (1,272 m/4,170 ft) before turning around.

GETTING THERE

Transit: TransLink Bus 182 (Belcarra) to Anmore Grocery. Walk 1.8 km (1.1 mi) to South Beach. In summer, Bus 179 (Buntzen Lake) provides service to South Beach.

Vehicle: From its junction with Highway 7 (Lougheed Highway) in Coquitlam, head west on Barnet Highway (formerly Highway 7A), then north on Johnson Street. Turn left on David Avenue, right on Forest Park Way, and left on Aspenwood Drive, which becomes East Road. Go right on Sunnyside Road. Drive past gated Powerhouse Road just before arriving at the South Beach parking area. Note the posted closing time.

53
COQUITLAM LAKE VIEW TRAIL

Distance: 13 km (8.1 mi)
Time: 5.5 hours (circuit)
Elevation gain: 600 m (1,970 ft)
High point: 920 m (3,020 ft)

Quality: ★★
Difficulty: ■
Maps: NTS 92-G/7 Port Coquitlam, Canadian Map Makers Coquitlam Port Moody
Trailhead: 49°18'49" N, 122°44'57" W

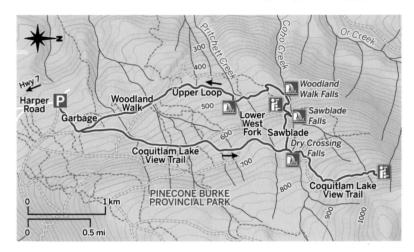

COQUITLAM'S BURKE Mountain area features a variety of delectable hikes that pair well with rainy days and shoulder season. Let's call this one the falls bagger's special: Sawblade Falls is the entrée, Dry Crossing Falls is the appetizer, and Woodland Walk Falls is the dessert. This triple serving of waterfalls is found in Pinecone Burke Provincial Park, established in 1995.

Left of the Harper Road gate, head northeast into the woods on the Garbage mountain-bike path. (Bike trail etiquette: Hike in single file, step aside to let bikers pass, and be respectful.) Emerging on a gravel road, pick the right uphill fork. Cross a power line corridor and follow Coquitlam Lake View Trail signs north. Take another right fork but stay left at the following junction. Where the trail crosses Coho Creek, Dry Crossing Falls fans out over a rock incline.

At the next junction, go right and then keep left to stick with the rerouted Coquitlam Lake View Trail. Vistas of the reservoir are served at trail's end (49°21'03″ N, 122°44'15″ W). Backtrack to Dry Crossing Falls.

A few minutes south of the waterfall, find the discreet entrance to the Sawblade bike path on the west side of the trail (49°20'25″ N, 122°44'28″ W).

Welcome to the Sawblade Trail.

In the trees, look for a track leading to the right and the seriously sharp Sawblade trailhead sign. Have fun plunging through the forest to the top of the Coquitlam Lake View Trail's Lower West Fork. Detour upstream to devour Sawblade Falls, the most impressive waterfall on today's menu.

Head south on the Lower West Fork momentarily, following tapes off to the right. In short order, take the right fork to reach a viewpoint. Don't turn around; a steep path drops north to the top of the Woodland Walk. Admire Woodland Walk Falls and an old-growth Douglas fir before checking out a humongous western red cedar stump just down the trail. Farther south, take the left fork for the Woodland Walk's Upper Loop.

Turn left on a power line road and cross a bridge over Pritchett Creek. (Consider the bonus cascade here the digestif.) Follow the Woodland Walk off the road to the right and back to the Coquitlam Lake View Trail junction from earlier. Take a right on Garbage to return to Harper Road.

Burke Mountain lies in the territories of the Katzie, Kwikwetlem, and Stó:lō First Nations. Learn more about the area in Lyle Litzenberger's *Burke and Widgeon: A Hiker's Guide* (Pebblestone Publishing, 2013). In 2008, a public outcry shot down a proposal to remove land from northern Pinecone Burke for a power line. The Wilderness Committee and Burke Mountain Naturalists, among others, deserve our thanks for protecting this "wilderness backyard."

GETTING THERE

Vehicle: From Highway 7 (Lougheed Highway) in Port Coquitlam, head north on Coast Meridian Road for 5 km (3 mi). Enter Coquitlam and turn right on Harper Road. Drive 2 km (1.2 mi) to find the inconspicuous Pinecone Burke Provincial Park gate on the right, outside of the noisy gun range. Park on the opposite shoulder.

54
HIGH KNOLL

Distance: 7.5 km (4.7 mi)
Time: 3 hours (lollipop)
Elevation gain: 165 m (540 ft)
High point: 169 m (554 ft)

Quality: ★★★
Difficulty: ●
Maps: NTS 92-G/7 Port Coquitlam, Canadian Map Makers Coquitlam Port Moody
Trailhead: 49°17'48" N, 122°42'00" W

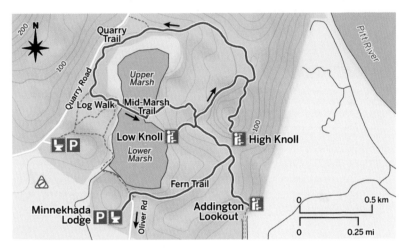

COQUITLAM'S MINNEKHADA Regional Park is a family-friendly jewel that's little known outside of the Tri-Cities. If you hike to High Knoll, this Metro Vancouver park will make you work up a sweat.

Start this pleasant jaunt by heading east on the Fern Trail. After mandatory side trips to Addington Lookout (right) and Low Knoll (left), turn right at the next two junctions to ascend the High Knoll Trail. The day's high point affords you an outstanding perch overlooking the Pitt River and Lower Marsh.

Backtrack to the last intersection and continue north (right) to loop around the Upper Marsh, staying left on the Quarry Trail. Turn left on the Log Walk and follow the Mid-Marsh Trail over the scenic dike dividing the marshes. Go right at the tri-junction to revisit the Fern Trail en route to the trailhead.

Opened in 1981, Minnekhada Regional Park lies in the heart of Katzie First Nation territory. Indeed, Sheridan Hill, just across the Pitt River, is key to the Katzie creation story. "Swaneset and his people, from whom the Katzie descend, were created at Sheridan Hill—they were the original and only human inhabitants of the land," the First Nation recalled in a 2015 statement opposing a mining proposal.

High Knoll overlooks the Pitt River.

The Minnekhada Lodge dates back to the 1930s, and Minnekhada Farm is closed to the public. Dedicated volunteers with the Minnekhada Park Association work to preserve the park's environment and its historical aspects. In addition, the Pacific Parklands Foundation raises funds for enhancement projects across the regional park system.

In summertime, the park is open 7 a.m. to 10 p.m. Bear sightings are common, and dogs must be leashed. Metro Vancouver regional parks have a Canine Code of Conduct. To stop dogs from causing damage, keep them out of ponds, streams, wetlands, and shorelines. Dog walkers are also requested to yield the right-of-way to other hikers.

GETTING THERE

Transit: TransLink Bus 173 (Cedar) or 174 (Rocklin) to Victoria Drive at Rocklin Street. Cycle east for 3.5 km (2.2 mi) on Victoria Drive, Cedar Drive, and Oliver Road to Minnekhada Lodge.

Vehicle: From Highway 7 (Lougheed Highway) in Port Coquitlam, turn north on Lougheed-Meridian Connector and left on Coast Meridian Road (which traces a historic Dominion Land Survey line). Go right on Prairie Avenue and then left on Cedar Drive, which enters Coquitlam and becomes Oliver Road. Turn left at the gate to arrive at the Minnekhada Lodge parking area.

55
ALOUETTE MOUNTAIN

Distance: 22 km (14 mi)
Time: 9 hours (round trip)
Elevation gain: 1,110 m (3,640 ft)
High point: 1,361 m (4,465 ft)

Quality: ★★★
Difficulty: ■
Maps: NTS 92-G/7 Port Coquitlam,
92-G/8 Stave Lake
Trailhead: 49°16'22" N, 122°32'06" W

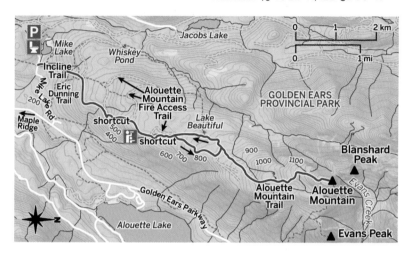

FROM THE west, Alouette Mountain appears to be a wooded, viewless ridge of little interest on the fringe of the Mount Blanshard massif, which is capped by Golden Ears (Hike 57). Well, don't judge a mountain by its far-off visage. The million-dollar views from the stadium-sized summit plateau are a revelation.

Previously known as Battery Mountain, Alouette lies immediately south of dramatic Blanshard Peak (aka Blanshard Needle) and west of Evans Peak (Hike 56) in Maple Ridge, Golden Ears Provincial Park, and Katzie First Nation territory. Although Alouette can be accessed more speedily via the rough Evans Peak route, the classic approach follows its long, mellow south ridge.

From Mike Lake Road, set off north on the steep Incline Trail (1.2 km/ 0.7 mi), which was historically used by loggers to "skyline" timber down to the lake. (Did you remember to leave a trip plan with a reliable person?) Continue on to the winding Alouette Mountain Fire Access Trail, an old rail bed, enjoying the pleasant grade and shady second-growth. (Ignore the Eric Dunning Trail on the right.) Keep right at the next four junctions to take advantage of two shortcut trails, visit a viewpoint, and forest bathe amid old-growth trees.

Angel wings near Lake Beautiful.

The fire-access road ends at an emergency helipad. Go left onto the Alouette Mountain Trail for 4 km (2.5 mi) to finally arrive on the wide-open summit, with its large cairn and spectacular vantages (4.5 hours up; 49°20′ 19″ N, 122°29′47″ W). To the north, imposing Blanshard and Edge Peaks frame Golden Ears. Mount Robie Reid and Mount Judge Howay stand out to the northeast.

On the way back, go right on the side loop to Lake Beautiful (officially named Beautiful Lake) for some added variety. The lovely old-growth and colourful fungi along this stretch are invigorating. The lake is closed to camping, due to the sensitive environment.

GETTING THERE

Vehicle: Dewdney Trunk Road mainly runs parallel to, but also intersects, Highway 7 (Lougheed Highway) in Maple Ridge and Mission. In Maple Ridge, turn north onto 232 Street from Dewdney Trunk. At the traffic circle, go right on Fern Crescent, which becomes Golden Ears Parkway. Take the Mike Lake turnoff on the left. Fork left on Mike Lake Road and park by the Incline Trail or lake. Golden Ears Provincial Park's main gate is closed 11 p.m. to 7 a.m. from April to mid-October and 5:30 p.m. (ugh) to 8 a.m. from mid-October to March.

56
EVANS PEAK

Distance: 9 km (5.6 mi)
Time: 5 hours (round trip)
Elevation gain: 950 m (3,120 ft)
High point: 1,132 m (3,714 ft)

Quality: ★★★★
Difficulty: ◆
Maps: NTS 92-G/8 Stave Lake
Trailhead: 49°19'38" N, 122°27'47" W

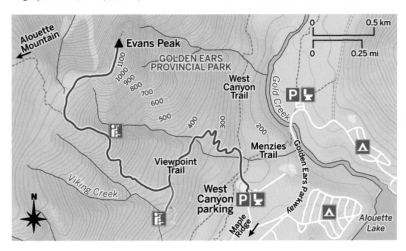

THIS QUICK route to Evans Peak, which has benefited from the volunteer work of the Ridge Meadows Outdoor Club, isn't found on the official Golden Ears Provincial Park map. And although this outing is not suitable for novices, young children, or dogs, the airy summit ridge is an excellent day trip for experienced hikers. It's also a fine option for restless car campers staying at the Alouette, Gold Creek, and North Beach campgrounds.

After a few minutes on the well-trafficked West Canyon Trail, make a left turn onto the Viewpoint Trail. Just past the 1.5 km (0.9 mi) marker, a sign on the right identifies the start of the Evans Peak Trail (49°19'41" N, 122°28'21" W) as well as an alternate route to Alouette Mountain (Hike 55).

Now the sweating (and spiderweb eating) begins. Unrelentingly steep, the forest path is rough but well defined and marked. A viewpoint 1.5 hours in offers peeks at your imposing-looking objective and Alouette Lake. At 2 hours, reach a signed fork: left for Alouette Mountain, right for Evans Peak.

Before the final push, you earn a breather following the crest of a wooded ridge. Then the steepness goes up another level. Exercise caution as the route comes uncomfortably close to drop-offs. A fixed line helps with scrambling up one bit.

Cloudy day on Evans Peak.

The rocky summit, crowned by a small tree, comes 2.5 hours in (49°20′ 17″ N, 122°28′41″ W). Scrambling north along the ridge is an exhilarating reward. To the southeast, Alouette Lake looms. Waterfalls plunge and snow caves (accessed via the Evans Valley Trail) lie at the foot of Edge Peak to the northwest.

The going is much quicker on the descent. Hiking poles will save your knees. Evans Peak is named for a father and son who vanished in 1966 while on a hike in the valley below. A plaque near the summit commemorates them.

Golden Ears Provincial Park, carved out of Garibaldi Provincial Park in 1967, lies in the heart of Katzie First Nation territory. Fires are banned in the backcountry.

SHORTER OPTION

Leaving Evans Peak for another day, stay on the easy Viewpoint Trail for less-impressive vistas of Alouette Lake and Viking Creek. It's just 2 km (1.2 mi) one way.

GETTING THERE

Transit: Better Environmentally Sound Transportation's Parkbus plans once-a-month coach service in summer (starting in 2018) to the Gold Creek parking lot from downtown Vancouver. Walk south on Golden Ears Parkway, cross the Gold Creek bridge, and go right on the Menzies Trail to join the West Canyon Trail.

Vehicle: Dewdney Trunk Road mainly runs parallel to, but also intersects, Highway 7 (Lougheed Highway) in Maple Ridge and Mission. In Maple Ridge, turn north onto 232 Street from Dewdney Trunk. At the traffic circle, go right on Fern Crescent, which becomes Golden Ears Parkway. Watch for the West Canyon Trail turnoff on the left and pull into the parking lot. Golden Ears Provincial Park's main gate is closed 11 p.m. to 7 a.m. from April to mid-October and 5:30 p.m. (ugh) to 8 a.m. from mid-October to March.

57
GOLDEN EARS

Distance: 25 km (15.5 mi)
Time: 11 hours (round trip)
Elevation gain: 1,530 m (5,020 ft)
High point: 1,716 m (5,630 ft)

Quality: ★★★★
Difficulty: ◆◆
Maps: NTS 92-G/7 Port Coquitlam, 92-G/8 Stave Lake
Trailhead: 49°19'38" N, 122°27'47" W

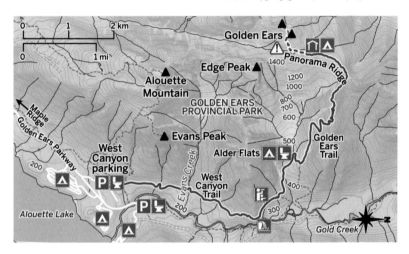

ONCE DUBBED the Golden Eyries by colonists, the Golden Ears are the distinctive twin summits of Mount Blanshard, the rugged massif encompassing Edge Peak and Blanshard Peak to the south and recognizable from much of Metro Vancouver. An ascent can be done in a very long day or, more happily, with a night or two at Alder Flats or Panorama Ridge.

Set off north on the relatively gentle West Canyon Trail, passing turnoffs for the Viewpoint Trail and Lower Falls. Take a breather at the Gold Creek Lookout. Stay left at the East-West Canyon Connector (Hike 58) junction to reach the buggy backcountry campsite at Alder Flats (480 m/1,600 ft; 49°21'49" N, 122°28'19" W) in 5.7 km (3.5 mi). Water can be scarce past this point.

Up next: the merciless switchbacks of the Golden Ears Trail. Heading northwest to the wooded east spur of Panorama Ridge, there's a lookout and stairs. Follow the ridge southwest—with Pitt Lake below to your right—through meadows and rock. At 5.8 km (3.6 mi) from Alder Flats, you arrive at the Panorama Ridge shelter (emergency use only) and campsite (49°22'00" N, 122°30'05" W).

Golden Ears from the summit of Alouette Mountain.

The final, challenging 1 km (0.6 mi) lies before you. Backcountry experience, avalanche awareness, and route-finding skills are essential, and ice axes are advisable. Beware of sudden whiteouts. Ascend steep snow to a dip on the east ridge of the North Ear. Once on the rock and heather of the ridge, turn west for the Class 2 scramble to the summit (49°21'46" N, 122°30'27" W). Soak in the Pacific Ranges panorama: Widgeon Peak, Mount Judge Howay, Mount Robie Reid, and Edge Peak. Descend the way you came.

Golden Ears Provincial Park lies in the heart of Katzie First Nation territory. Permits are required for camping, fires are banned, and dogs are discouraged in the backcountry. Take only photographs, leave only footprints.

LONGER OPTION
The lower, less-visited South Ear (1,701 m/5,580 ft) is an easy enough scramble from the North Ear. Regaining the main summit, however, can prove more challenging due to the steep, rocky slope.

GETTING THERE
Transit: Parkbus plans once-a-month coach service in summer (starting in 2018) to the Gold Creek parking lot from downtown Vancouver. Walk south on Golden Ears Parkway, cross the Gold Creek bridge, and go right on the Menzies Trail to join the West Canyon Trail.

Vehicle: Dewdney Trunk Road runs mainly parallel to, but also intersects, Highway 7 (Lougheed Highway) in Maple Ridge and Mission. In Maple Ridge, turn north onto 232 Street from Dewdney Trunk. At the traffic circle, go right on Fern Crescent, which becomes Golden Ears Parkway. Watch for the West Canyon Trail turnoff on the left and pull into the parking lot. Golden Ears Provincial Park's main gate is closed 11 p.m. to 7 a.m. from April to mid-October and 5:30 p.m. (ugh) to 8 a.m. from mid-October to March.

58
GOLD CREEK

Distance: 14 km (8.7 mi)
Time: 4.5 hours (circuit)
Elevation gain: 340 m (1,100 ft)
High point: 480 m (1,600 ft)

Quality: ★★
Difficulty: ■
Maps: NTS 92-G/8 Stave Lake
Trailhead: 49°20'03" N, 122°27'25" W

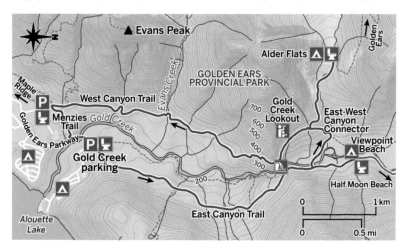

IN 2015, B.C. Parks built a new bridge over Gold Creek, connecting the East Canyon and West Canyon Trails and, thereby, creating an attractive loop for hikers and trail runners in Golden Ears Provincial Park. The shoulder-season hike described here includes detours to visit the scenic backcountry campsites at Viewpoint Beach and Alder Flats.

The East Canyon Trail starts at the northeast corner of the Gold Creek parking lot. Within minutes, take the left fork and go left again where the trail merges with an old logging road. Head north on the horse and mountain-bike trail—crossing numerous creeks, and flanked by salmonberry brambles, mossy conifers, and thick stumps—for a half-hour to the Lower Falls junction. Stay with the road as it descends to Gold Creek and intersects the East-West Canyon Connector, 1 hour (4 km/2.5 mi) in.

To the left, the Gold Creek footbridge rests on an old concrete pier that supported a logging bridge until the 1960s. Before crossing, however, follow the East Canyon Trail upstream for 10 minutes to an outhouse (spot a salamander?) and Viewpoint Beach (49°21'57" N, 122°27'21" W), where the scene includes the double summits of Edge Peak and Golden Ears on Mount Blanshard.

Gold Creek bridge on the East-West Canyon Connector.

Back at the bridge, go west on the East-West Canyon Connector (1 km/0.6 mi), passing the Hiker's Beach turnoff and rising to the West Canyon Trail junction. Turn right on the watery, rooty (and snowy in spring) path. Metal planks have replaced the slippery wooden boardwalks. Arrive at often-buggy Alder Flats (49°21′49″ N, 122°28′19″ W) a half-hour later.

Saving the Golden Ears Trail (Hike 57) for a longer day, retrace your steps to the previous junction and turn right to continue south on the West Canyon Trail. The path crosses two debris channels en route to the Gold Creek Lookout, which overlooks the bridge from earlier. Pass a Lower Falls turnoff, Evans Creek, the unsigned Evans Valley Trail (maintained by the Ridge Meadows Outdoor Club), and the Viewpoint Trail. Turn left on the Menzies Trail and walk among vine maples to Golden Ears Parkway. Cross the bridge to return to the Gold Creek parking lot.

Golden Ears Provincial Park lies in the heart of Katzie First Nation territory. Backcountry fires are banned. Pack out eggshells, orange peels, and other trash.

LONGER OPTION

The East Canyon Trail continues upstream to Half Moon Beach. A rough trail heads through the floodplain to a ford on Gold Creek. From the west bank, a path climbs to remote Hector Ferguson Lake for a very long day.

GETTING THERE

Transit: Parkbus plans once-a-month coach service in summer (starting in 2018) to the Gold Creek parking lot from downtown Vancouver.

Vehicle: Dewdney Trunk Road mainly runs parallel to, but also intersects, Highway 7 (Lougheed Highway) in Maple Ridge and Mission. In Maple Ridge, turn north onto 232 Street from Dewdney Trunk. At the traffic circle, go right on Fern Crescent, which becomes Golden Ears Parkway. The parkway ends at the Gold Creek parking lot and East Canyon trailhead. Golden Ears Provincial Park's main gate is closed 11 p.m. to 7 a.m. from April to mid-October and 5:30 p.m. (ugh) to 8 a.m. from mid-October to March.

59
MOUNT ST. BENEDICT

Distance: 11 km (6.8 mi)
Time: 6.5 hours (round trip)
Elevation gain: 1,020 m (3,350 ft)
High point: 1,278 m (4,190 ft)

Quality: ★
Difficulty: ■
Maps: NTS 92-G/8 Stave Lake
Trailhead: 49°17'48" N, 122°13'58" W

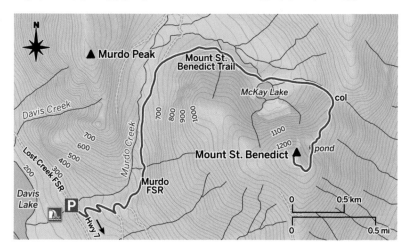

NAMED BY the Catholic monks of Westminster Abbey in Mission, Mount St. Benedict rises east of Stave Lake in Kwantlen First Nation territory. The trail to this modest peak begins in Davis Lake Provincial Park, established in 1963 but wanting in signage, ecological restoration, and a management plan.

From Lost Creek Forest Service Road, head east on the lower section of the Mount St. Benedict Trail, switchbacking up to Murdo FSR within 30 minutes. Go left and keep left at the next two logging road junctions, staying south of Murdo Creek. After almost an hour on the road, the upper section of the provincially designated recreation trail leaves to the right (49°18'33" N, 122°13'15" W).

Ascend east through second-growth forest for another half-hour to McKay Lake (49°18'26" N, 122°12'27" W). Sitting at the foot of cliffs and talus below Mount St. Benedict's crown, the lovely lake is the scenic highlight of this outing.

Pushing on, climb the super-steep, muddy, and slippery path to the col between McKay Peak and Mount St. Benedict. (Hiking poles will prove helpful here.) Follow the ridge south to a subalpine pond east of the top, which is closer than it appears. The trail swings west to gain the summit (49°18'04" N, 122°12'13" W) from the south.

Summit view from Mount St. Benedict.

Sadly, the surrounding landscape is heavily scarred by clear-cuts, logging roads, and power lines. To the east, wooded Mount Crickmer lies across Stave Lake. Prominent peaks in view include Golden Ears (Hike 57), Mount Robie Reid, Mount Judge Howay, and Mount Baker (Kweq' Smánit to the Nooksack Tribe). After lunch, retrace your steps to Lost Creek FSR. Before you take off, check out McDonald Falls, just downstream of the Murdo Creek bridge.

GETTING THERE

Vehicle: From Highway 7 (Lougheed Highway), just east of Hatzic in Mission, go north on Sylvester Road for 15 km (9.3 mi). Passing the turnoff for Cascade Falls Regional Park, continue onto Lost Creek Forest Service Road (2WD). After 2 km (1.2 mi) on gravel, the trailhead is on the right, immediately south of the Murdo Creek bridge.

60
CAMPBELL LAKE

Distance: 10 km (6.2 mi)
Time: 6 hours (round trip)
Elevation gain: 679 m (2,230 ft)
High point: 695 m (2,280 ft)

Quality: ★
Difficulty: ■
Maps: NTS 92-H/5 Harrison Lake
Trailhead: 49°17'46" N, 121°47'06" W

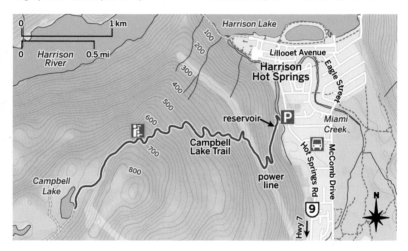

THE CELEBRITY of North Vancouver's Grouse Grind has spawned a number of copycats around the region: the Seymour Grind, Abby Grind, Dewdney Grind, etc. The Campbell Lake Trail is Harrison Hot Spring's version of a steep and satisfying workout trail, on the northeast flank of Mount Agassiz in the territories of the Sts'ailes and Stó:lō peoples.

After consulting the map board at the trailhead, go west through the gate. Immediately turn right on a gravel road, which climbs steeply to the village water reservoir. Head south into the woods on the now mossy, cobbly, water-bearing road, with the hum of Highway 9 to your left and the sight of numerous outcrops among the cedars on your right. After switchbacking, you follow a power line right-of-way north.

Returning to tree cover after an hour of hiking, the pleasant trail switchbacks west, indicated by orange diamonds and arrows, pink flagging tape, and rotting wooden stairs. There's a creek crossing, the 2 km (1.2 mi) marker, and then a sketchy log bridge, 2 hours in. The rooty, muddy path ascends slopes littered with moss-covered boulders and deadfall, passing the 3 km (1.9 mi) sign en route to the lookout (683 m/2,240 ft; 49°17'41" N, 121°48'25" W) that's the scenic crescendo of this outing. After 3 hours and 4 km (2.5 mi) on

Mount Agassiz is the home of the Harrison Grind.

the trail, you've earned a fine view of Echo Island in the freshwater fjord of Harrison Lake (Qualts to the Sts'ailes, Peqwpa:qotel to the Stó:lō).

Backtrack a few steps to continue on the undulating trail to your ultimate destination. Cross a boulder-filled gully, descend slippery steps, and follow an old, puddly road to the east shore of Campbell Lake, 30 minutes beyond the lookout. As you retrace your steps to the trailhead, keep your eyes peeled for white trillium, a perennial herb with a distinctive three-petaled flower. By hike's end, you'll have climbed and then descended the equivalent of 170 or so floors of a building.

SHORTER OPTION
The Harrison Grind portion of the trail tops out at the lookout over Harrison Lake. The 5-hour, 8 km (5 mi) round trip is a decent option for days of rain or hail, or when car camping at Sasquatch Provincial Park. It's popular with families and dogs.

GETTING THERE
Transit: Agassiz-Harrison Transit Bus 11 (Harrison Hot Springs) to Hot Springs Road at Pine Street. Walk north on Hot Springs Road for 500 m (0.3 mi).
Vehicle: From Trans-Canada Highway 1 (Exit 135), east of Chilliwack—or Highway 7 (Lougheed Highway), west of Agassiz—head north on Highway 9 (Agassiz-Rosedale Highway/Hot Springs Road) to Harrison Hot Springs. At Balsam Avenue, 2 km (1.2 mi) north of the village limits, turn west into the trailhead parking area or find street parking nearby.

61
BEAR MOUNTAIN

Distance: 18 km (11 mi)
Time: 7 hours (round trip)
Elevation gain: 1,000 m (3,280 ft)
High point: 1,036 m (3,400 ft)

Quality: ★
Difficulty: ■
Maps: NTS 92-H/5 Harrison Lake
Trailhead: 49°19'58" N, 121°45'02" W

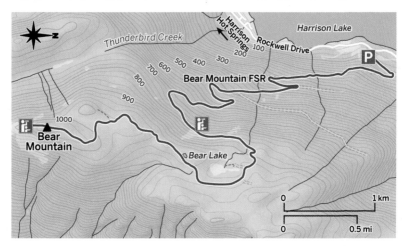

KICKING BACK on the beach at Harrison Hot Springs, in the territories of the Sts'ailes and Stó:lō peoples, you'll see Bear Mountain—the wooded hill visible due east. If you plod all the way up it, your reward is one of the best vantages of the Fraser Valley. Enough motivation to trade sand for second-growth forest?

From the gate, the aging logging road maintains a fairly constant, moderate uphill grade. (Ignore any old mining company warnings to keep off public land. Bear Mountain has been the site of gold exploration activity, including diamond drilling and soil sampling, since the 1970s.) Stick with the mainline at junctions, assisted by occasional flagging. Enjoy a small waterfall, a view of Echo Island in Harrison Lake (Qualts to the Sts'ailes, Peqwpa:qotel to the Stó:lō), scattered wildflowers, and walking through spiderwebs, as you ascend the well-shaded road.

You reach a signed junction after 2.5 hours of slogging. Right descends to Bear Lake. Take the left fork to keep climbing on the road, which becomes more trail-like and overgrown. A half-hour past the lake junction, the road dwindles. Look for a marked path heading off to the left. Follow it downward and then as it rises to amble along a wooded ridge. Four hours in, descend to

Bear Mountain lies across the Fraser River (Stó:lō) from Cheam Peak (Lhílheqey).

a lookout (49°17′56″ N, 121°44′28″ W) just south of the tree-covered summit. Finally, you escape the forest and get smacked with an eyeful of the Fraser Valley and Cascade Mountains (from the Coast Mountains, no less).

With its brilliant wildflowers and incredible views, this paragliding launch site is a surprisingly satisfying destination. Cheam Peak (Lhílheqey to the Stó:lō; Hike 63), Lady Peak (Sqwema:y), and the other impressive summits of Cheam Ridge loom across the Fraser River (Stó:lō). Davidson's penstemon and red paintbrush brighten the foreground, while a wooden helipad provides the perfect setting for a picnic. On a sunny day, you may wish to stay and relax awhile before retracing your steps on the descent. Water is scarce on this route, so make sure to carry enough liquids with you.

GETTING THERE

Vehicle: From Trans-Canada Highway 1 (Exit 135), east of Chilliwack—or Highway 7 (Lougheed Highway), west of Agassiz—head north on Highway 9 (Agassiz-Rosedale Highway/Hot Springs Road) to Harrison Hot Springs. Go right on Lillooet Road, which becomes Rockwell Drive, and continue 5 km (3 mi) east along Harrison Lake. Turn right on an easy-to-miss gravel road. Pass a couple of driveways and park below the gate at the bottom of Bear Mountain Forest Service Road.

62
TEAPOT HILL

Distance: 13 km (8.1 mi)
Time: 5 hours (circuit)
Elevation gain: 255 m (840 ft)
High point: 310 m (1,020 ft)

Quality: ★★
Difficulty: ●
Maps: NTS 92-H/4 Chilliwack, Trail Ventures BC Chilliwack West
Trailhead: 49°03'19" N, 121°58'16" W

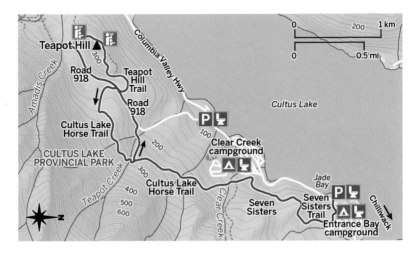

WITH ITS ceramic scenery, Teapot Hill sure lives up to its name. Spotting the porcelain hidden in nooks and crannies along the trail is cupfuls of fun for kids and adults alike. Add in a spoonful of the old-growth Seven Sisters, and you've got an all-season outing that's sweet enough for the whole family. Both points of interest are found in Cultus Lake Provincial Park, which lies outside Chilliwack in the territory of the Soowahlie First Nation.

From the Jade Bay boat launch, cross the Columbia Valley Highway and enter the Entrance Bay campground. Keep right to find the start of the Seven Sisters Trail between campsites 7 and 9, and dive into the mossy forest. Reach the Seven Sisters in 1.7 km (1.1 mi). Do the short and steep loop trail to find out how few of the old-growth Douglas fir giants are still standing.

Continue south on the Seven Sisters Trail. As you near the Clear Creek campground, turn left on a brief connector path. Go right on the Cultus Lake Horse Trail, then right again at the next fork (signed for Teapot Hill). Hang a left on Road 918 to get on the Teapot Hill Trail, which soon leaves right.

Heading uphill in the trees, keep your eyes peeled for the colourful teapots, some intact and others broken. A viewpoint overlooks Cultus Lake,

One of many teapots in Cultus Lake Provincial Park.

whose name is derived from a Chinook Wawa word meaning "worthless." (A trade language long spoken by Indigenous peoples of the Pacific Northwest and later adopted by European colonizers, Chinook Wawa has seen revitalization efforts in recent years. In 2012, the Confederated Tribes of Grand Ronde in Oregon published a dictionary of the intertribal and interethnic lingua franca.)

The Teapot Hill Trail ends at a fenced lookout near the summit (2 hours up; 49°01′50″ N, 121°59′44″ W) with vistas of the Columbia Valley and Vedder Mountain. Descend the way you came to the intersection at the bottom of the hill, where you turn right to continue southwest on Road 918 and enjoy a bit more of the woods. Turn around at the Road 918–Watt Creek intersection. On the way back to the trailhead, keep right at two junctions to stay on the Horse Trail. Now on familiar ground, retrace your steps to Jade Bay.

GETTING THERE

Vehicle: On Trans-Canada Highway 1 in Abbotsford, take Exit 104. Head east on No. 3 Road. Turn right on Tolmie Road and left on No. 3 Road. Go left on Yarrow Central Road, which becomes Vedder Mountain Road. Turn right on Cultus Lake Road, which continues south as Columbia Valley Highway. Enter Cultus Lake Provincial Park and turn right into the Jade Bay boat launch parking lot. More parking is available at the Entrance Bay picnic ground.

63
CHEAM PEAK

Distance: 9 km (5.6 mi)
Time: 4 hours (round trip)
Elevation gain: 690 m (2,260 ft)
High point: 2,104 m (6,902 ft)

Quality: ★★★★★
Difficulty: ■
Maps: NTS 92-H/4 Chilliwack, Trail Ventures BC Chilliwack East
Trailhead: 49°10'06" N, 121°41'39" W

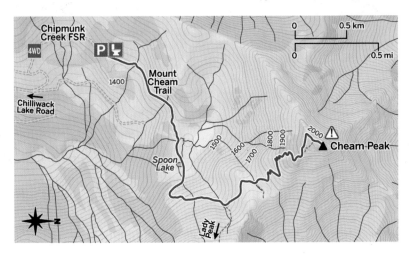

AT THE Cheam Peak trailhead and outhouse, the west face of impressive Lady Peak (2,178 m/7,145 ft) draws your gaze upwards. From bottom to top, the scenery on this bustling trail is solid gold. Although kids and dogs are a common sight, this hike may not be suitable for all, due to the steepness and some exposure at the top.

Cheam Peak is known as Lhílheqey (the wife of Mount Baker and mother of Mount Hood in Oregon) to the Ts'elxwéyeqw Tribe of the Stó:lō. It's the formidable mountain that eastbound travellers on Trans-Canada Highway 1 in Chilliwack see towering over the Fraser Valley. The Skagit Range, to which it belongs, is a subrange of the Cascade Mountains.

From the logging road barricade, head north on the wide trail past the map board. In short order, American Border Peak, Canadian Border Peak, Tomyhoi Peak, and Mount Baker enter the view. The Mount Cheam Trail descends to the meadowy bowl below Cheam and Lady Peaks, crossing two creeks on wooden bridges and going by near-circular Spoon Lake.

After 20 minutes, follow the main path as it switchbacks up Lady Peak (Sqwema:y), then angles north and climbs steadily toward the Cheam-Lady

Cheam Peak (Lhílheqey) towers above the Fraser River (Stó:lō).

saddle. Blueberries and wildflowers—fireweed, green false hellebore, edible thistle, leafy aster, and red paintbrush—line the trail. Preserve the lush meadows: stay on the path and don't shortcut.

Begin switchbacking northwest on Cheam Peak itself, 1 hour in. Ponder the sheer north face of Lady Peak. Join Cascade golden-mantled ground squirrels and the selfie-obsessed #DoItForTheGram crowd on the southwest ridge, and embark on the final windy walk to your objective.

A well-worn track through the volcanic breccia leads to a wooden bench, then to the satisfying summit, 2 hours from the trailhead (49°11′11″ N, 121°40′56″ W). Clockwise from north, the breathtaking panorama includes the Fraser River (Stó:lō), Wahleach (Jones) Lake, Knight Peak and the rest of Cheam Ridge, Mount Shuksan, Mount Agassiz (Hike 60), Harrison Lake (Peqwpa:qotel), and Bear Mountain (Hike 61). Watch your step around the precipice. Reverse your ascent route on the descent.

The Mount Cheam Trail is managed by Recreation Sites and Trails B.C. and the Fraser Valley Regional District. Camping, fires, mountain biking, and motorized vehicles are prohibited, and dogs must be leashed. Visitors are asked not to build memorial monuments.

GETTING THERE

Vehicle: On Trans-Canada Highway 1 in Chilliwack, take Exit 119. Head south on Vedder Road for 5 km (3 mi). Just before the Vedder Bridge, go east on Chilliwack Lake Road. About 26 km (16 mi) later, turn left on Chilliwack Bench Forest Service Road (no shooting within 400 m/437 yd!). Bear left after the Foley Creek bridge. With high-clearance 4WD, turn right on Chipmunk Creek FSR and follow signs for the Mount Cheam Trail for 11.5 km (7.1 mi).

64
MOUNT THURSTON

Distance: 16 km (10 mi)
Time: 7 hours (round trip)
Elevation gain: 990 m (3,250 ft)
High point: 1,620 m (5,315 ft)

Quality: ★★★
Difficulty: ◆
Maps: NTS 92-H/4 Chilliwack; Trail Ventures BC Chilliwack East, Chilliwack West
Trailhead: 49°06'18" N, 121°49'14" W

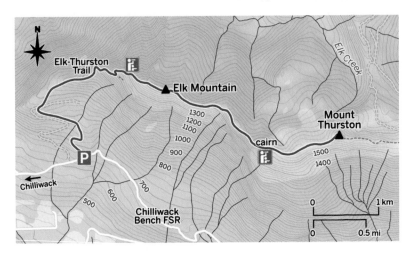

LOOKING FOR a day hike that will test your mettle and amply reward your efforts? The Chilliwack duo of Elk Mountain and Mount Thurston, in Stó:lō territory, is just the ticket with its gorgeous meadows and superlative views.

From Chilliwack Bench Forest Service Road, the popular Elk-Thurston Trail dives into the forest, crosses a logging road, and grinds steeply northward to Elk Mountain's west ridge. The path is badly braided due to shortcutting and is slippery when wet. A rocky lookout with a grand view of the Fraser Valley offers a taste of what's to come.

Head east through subalpine meadows with wildflowers and strawberries. Pass a windsock; paragliders launch here. At 4 km (2.5 mi), reach the gentle summit of Elk Mountain (1,432 m/4,700 ft; 49°06'47" N, 121°48'13" W), halfway to your objective. With the hardest part behind you, the best lies ahead.

Stroll along the ridge, savouring the high meadows and sweeping views of the Chilliwack River valley, far below to your right. Stay on the main path to preserve the vegetation. A cairn marks a false summit (1,542 m/5,060 ft) of Mount Thurston. For many hikers, this perch is a satisfying enough destination.

Looking back at Elk Mountain from Mount Thurston.

For the sake of completeness, press on to the true summit of Mount Thurston (49°06′25″ N, 121°46′05″ W), a couple of bumps east. The treed mountaintop is a bit of a letdown, but it does offer a vista of Cheam Peak (Lhílheqey to the Ts'elxwéyeqw Tribe; Hike 63) and Lady Peak (Sqwema:y).

Head back the way you came. Admire arctic lupine, red paintbrush, and spreading phlox in summer bloom and bask in the magnificence of the Cascade Mountains. Eye Mount McGuire (T'amiyehó:y to the Nooksack Tribe) due south, Lookout Ridge below to the west, and the mighty Fraser River (Stó:lō) on its way to the Salish Sea. Don't forget to bring plenty of water on this trip.

SHORTER OPTION

To do the Chilliwack Grind, top out at Elk Mountain and head back down for an 8 km (5 mi) round trip. This workout packs 800 m (2,625 ft) of elevation gain, just a tad less than the Grouse Grind.

GETTING THERE

Vehicle: On Trans-Canada Highway 1 in Chilliwack, take Exit 123. Head south on Prest Road and then east on Bailey Road. Keep right for Elk View Road, which becomes the gravel Chilliwack Bench Forest Service Road (2WD), and drive 10 km (6 mi) to find the trailhead on the left.

65
HOPE LOOKOUT TRAIL

Distance: 5 km (3.1 mi)
Time: 2.5 hours (round trip)
Elevation gain: 462 m (1,515 ft)
High point: 524 m (1,720 ft)

Quality: ★
Difficulty: ■
Maps: NTS 92-H/6 Hope
Trailhead: 49°22'21" N, 121°26'30" W

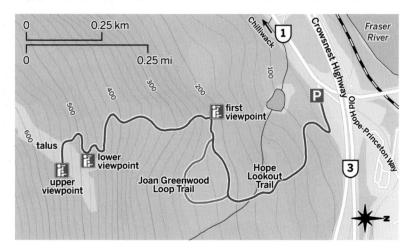

HOPE'S ANSWER to the vista-less Grouse Grind is home to a race called the Hope Hustle, but take some time to savour the scenery during this popular hike. Built in the 1990s, the Hope Lookout Trail lies at the foot of Hope Mountain (St'ám'ya to the Stó:lō people; Hike 66) and is earnestly maintained by the Hope Mountain Centre for Outdoor Learning.

From the trailhead kiosk next to the Highway 1–Highway 3 junction, walk past the gate and up the gravel road. Look left before the next gate to spot trail signs. Hikers are directed up the right-of-way for Kinder Morgan's Trans Mountain oil pipeline, while mountain bikers are to enter the woods. The easy-to-follow footpath soon heads right, into the trees, too—steadily gaining elevation, encountering benches and bike obstacles, and passing under a power line.

In 20 minutes, the Joan Greenwood Loop Trail strikes off to the left. The Hope Lookout Trail climbs a set of stairs to meet the other end of the loop. After a fixed chain comes the underwhelming first viewpoint (197 m/645 ft)— made possible by the power line—30 minutes in.

The partially shaded trail steepens, with switchbacks, stairs, and wooden handrails. Oregon grape, with its tart purple berries, is one of the shrubs

Fraser River (Stó:lō) and Hope from the upper viewpoint.

adorning the forest floor. Unfortunately, birdsong can't mask the noise pollution from the highway below. Over 1 hour from the start, a spur goes left to the lower viewpoint (49°21′55″ N, 121°26′21″ W), 472 m (1,550 ft) above sea level. It's merely a preview of what's to come.

Push on to the upper viewpoint (49°21′53″ N, 121°26′20″ W). Several benches sit on a talus slope with a commanding view of Hope (Ts'qó:ls), the Fraser River (Stó:lō) emerging from the Fraser Canyon, Kawkawa Lake (Q'áwq'ewem, drained by Sucker Creek), and Ogilvie Peak (Qemqemó). The Fraser is the longest river in B.C. and forms the boundary between the Coast Mountains and North Cascades.

A path continues up the talus but peters out quickly. Return the way you came. Camping and fires are not allowed on the Hope Lookout Trail.

LONGER OPTION

The Joan Greenwood Loop Trail takes only 10 minutes and will add a bit of uphill and a bunch of tall western red cedar and Douglas fir trees to your descent. Go left at the junction with the Ryan's Ravine bike trail to rejoin the Hope Lookout Trail.

GETTING THERE

Vehicle: Eastbound on Trans-Canada Highway 1 in Hope, take Exit 170. Go left at the Flood Hope Road intersection to stay on Highway 1. Turn right on Old Hope Princeton Way and immediately right again to take an access road back under the freeway overpass to the trailhead.

66
HOPE MOUNTAIN

Distance: 8.5 km (5.3 mi)
Time: 6 hours (round trip)
Elevation gain: 690 m (2,260 ft)
High point: 1,844 m (6,050 ft)

Quality: ★★★★
Difficulty: ■
Maps: NTS 92-H/6 Hope
Trailhead: 49°19'43" N, 121°22'57" W

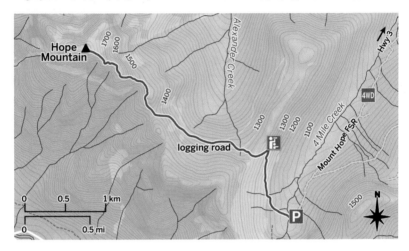

KNOWN AS St'ám'ya to the Stó:lō people, Hope Mountain overlooks its namesake municipality at the head of the Fraser Valley. This peak forms part of the Skagit Range and accords visitors fine views of its North Cascades relatives to the south.

From its cutblock trailhead (right of the start of the trail to nearby Wells Peak), the flagged route to Hope Mountain descends west to cross 4 Mile Creek. The trail then rises northward to the divide between 4 Mile and Alexander Creeks. Blueberries and saffron milk-cap mushrooms flourish along the path.

After pausing at the viewpoint on the divide, drop down the other side to pick up an old, easygoing logging road. Contour west across the head of a bowl scarred by clear-cuts, until the trail exits to the left, headed for Hope Mountain's southeast ridge. The path climbs steeply northwest—winding through heather, by ponds, and over rock—and crosses a ledge at one point.

Although three radio repeater cones litter the mountaintop (49°20'51" N, 121°25'04" W), the panorama more than compensates. Looking north from the summit cairn, you can see the Fraser River (Stó:lō) emerging from

Hiking down Hope Mountain (St'ám'ya).

the Fraser Canyon, Ogilvie Peak (Qemqemó) behind Hope (Ts'qó:ls) and Kawkawa Lake (Q'áwq'ewem), and the mountains around Coquihalla Pass.

An outcrop on the far side of a pond just below the summit offers a prime spot from which to admire the shapely valley of Silverhope Creek to the south. Wells Peak (1,863 m/6,110 ft) and the Silver Bluffs tower over Silver Lake. Mount Baker stands tall across the Canada–U.S. border. Retrace your steps to the trailhead.

GETTING THERE

Vehicle: From Trans-Canada Highway 1 in Hope, head east on Crowsnest Highway 3. Take Exit 177 at the Coquihalla Highway interchange. Shortly after, turn right on Mount Hope Forest Service Road. Stay on the rough mainline (keep left at forks). Cross 4 Mile Creek. At a signed fork, 8 km (5 mi) up, go straight to leave the main. Arrive at spur's end and the trailhead. High-clearance 4WD is required to make it all the way.

67
HOPE-NICOLA VALLEY TRAIL

Distance: 5.4 km (3.4 mi)
Time: 2 hours (loop)
Elevation gain: 205 m (670 ft)
High point: 347 m (1,140 ft)

Quality: ★
Difficulty: ●
Maps: NTS 92-H/6 Hope
Trailhead: 49°22'40" N, 121°22'11" W

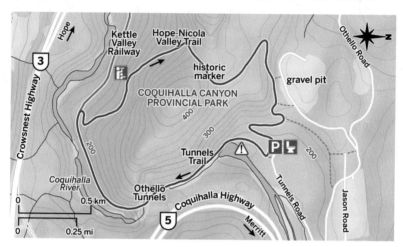

ONE HIKE, two historic routes. That's what awaits in Coquihalla Canyon Provincial Park on the outskirts of Hope (Ts'qó:ls), in Stó:lō territory. In the early 1900s, the Canadian Pacific Railway constructed the Kettle Valley Railway (KVR) to provide passenger and freight service between the Kootenays and the B.C. coast. The B.C. Department of Lands and Works built the Hope-Nicola Valley Trail, to move cattle and horses, over Coquihalla Pass in the late 1800s.

Our clockwise loop begins on the abandoned rail grade of the KVR. From the trailhead kiosk and outhouses, follow the tourists south on the wide gravel Tunnels Trail. To your left, the Coquihalla River rushes into its narrow granite gorge.

The impressive Othello Tunnels, built in 1914 and seen in the Hollywood films *First Blood* and *Shoot to Kill*, are reached in 10 minutes. Linked by wood-steel trestles, the five tunnels (closed in winter) offer a dark and cool respite from a hot day. Peer down at the rapids and up at the cliffs, and see how many selfies you can photo-bomb. From the gate at the end of the Quintette Tunnels, the KVR bed continues south into the woods on river right.

In 2.1 km (1.3 mi), turn right on the Hope-Nicola Valley Trail (49°21'59" N, 121°22'25" W). Leaving the throngs behind, head uphill under the cover of

ENGINEER'S MULE ROAD TO SIMILKAMEEN
BUILT FALL 1860 BY E. DEWDNEY FROM MILE 4 ON
THE HBC TRAIL, BETWEEN THE 2 CONICAL HILLS, TO
THE COQUIHALLA RIVER AND THEN UP THE NORTH
SIDE OF THE NICOLUM RIVER TO THE SKAGIT.

Coquihalla Canyon Provincial Park preserves part of the Hope–Nicola Valley Trail.

conifers. Benches offer vistas of Hope Mountain (St'ám'ya; Hike 66). At the apex, a metal plate notes that the Hope–Nicola Valley route was built by Edgar Dewdney, the engineer and B.C. lieutenant governor also behind the Dewdney Trail. Keep right on the descent, bypassing a gravel pit to the north, to reach your starting point.

Established in 1986, Coquihalla Canyon Recreation Area became a Class A park in 1997. Camping and angling are prohibited, swimming is discouraged (high drowning risk), and dogs must be on-leash.

LONGER OPTION

If you'd like to extend your outing, the Kettle Valley Railway Trail continues 2.7 km (1.7 mi) west from the Hope–Nicola Valley Trail junction to Kettle Valley Road.

GETTING THERE

Vehicle: From Trans-Canada Highway 1 in Hope, head east on Crowsnest Highway 3. Keep left for Yellowhead Highway 5 (Coquihalla Highway) northbound and take Exit 183. From the off-ramp, swing south, go under the highway, and make a left on the other side. After 3 km (1.9 mi) on Othello Road, turn left on Tunnels Road to find the big parking lot at Coquihalla Canyon Provincial Park.

68
TIKWALUS HERITAGE TRAIL

Distance: 12 km (7.5 mi)
Time: 7 hours (lollipop)
Elevation gain: 790 m (2,590 ft)
High point: 910 m (2,985 ft)

Quality: ★★★
Difficulty: ■
Maps: NTS 92-H/11 Spuzzum, 92-H/14
Boston Bar
Trailhead: 49°43'23" N, 121°25'18" W

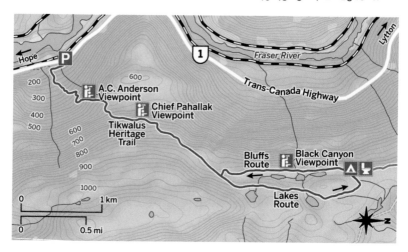

FOR MANY years, social studies teacher Charles Hou led Burnaby high-school students (including the author) up the First Brigade Trail in the Fraser Canyon in preparation for a weeklong backpacking trip on the Harrison-Lillooet Gold Rush Trail, north of Harrison Lake. In 2012, the former reopened as the Tikwalus Heritage Trail, complete with interpretative panels so all visitors may learn about its place in Indigenous, fur trade, gold rush, and railway history. The Hope Mountain Centre for Outdoor Learning, Spuzzum First Nation, and New Pathways to Gold Society deserve much credit for its restoration.

Originally an ancient Nlaka'pamux route bypassing the cliffs of Hells Gate and the Black Canyon (Ch.etwik in Nlaka'pamuchin) along the Fraser River (Quoo.ooy), the challenging trail over Lake Mountain was tapped for the fur trade by the Hudson's Bay Company in 1848 and 1849. In the first season, seventy horses died making the trip between Fort Kamloops and Fort Langley. Consequently, another route—the HBC (1849) Heritage Trail (Hikes 69, 70, and 73)—became the preferred way to cross the Cascade Mountains.

Black Canyon Viewpoint on Lake Mountain.

Start early and carry plenty of water to avoid heat exhaustion. Initially, the trail contours south before steeply switchbacking eastward up the forested mountainside. Within 2 hours, pass the A.C. Anderson Viewpoint and arrive at the Chief Pahallak Viewpoint, which has log benches and a geocache. Heading northeast, the trail passes spiny devil's club and drops a bit to visit some bark-stripped western red cedars (*quatqulhp*).

Three hours and 4.2 km (2.6 mi) from the highway, arrive at a key fork (49°44′25″ N, 121°24′08″ W). Go right to do a counterclockwise loop starting on the Lakes Route. After some more up, the trail breaks into the sunshine amid the scent of wildflowers before turning into a mellow ramble and passing through a patch of trees burned in a 2004 wildfire. From the high point at the 5 km (3.1 mi) mark, descend to the shady Lake House site. Yew Gardens is the next point of interest. At 6.5 km (4 mi) in, reach the campsite at trail's end. With a campfire ring, food cache, outhouse, butterflies, and views of Spuzzum Mountain and the Lillooet Ranges, it's a righteous lunch spot.

Returning via the undulating Bluffs Route, hike south with lakes on your left and cliffs on the right. The Black Canyon Viewpoint offers the most spectacular views of the Fraser Canyon downstream of Hells Gate. Back at the Lakes-Bluffs junction, go right and descend familiar terrain to the trailhead.

LONGER OPTION

For overnight hikers, the Bluffs Trail continues north from the Tikwalus Heritage Trail campsite to a junction with the 17 Mile Creek Mule Trail (left) and Gate Mountain Trail (right). The latter leads to summit views from The Notch and Gate Mountain.

GETTING THERE

Vehicle: From Hope, head north on Trans-Canada Highway 1. Find the trailhead at a pullout on the east shoulder, 22 km (13.7 mi) north of Yale (Xwoxwelá:lhp). Sadly, this parking lot is prone to break-ins.

69
MANSON'S RIDGE

Distance: 16.5 km (10.3 mi)
Time: 7 hours (round trip)
Elevation gain: 1,210 m (3,970 ft)
High point: 1,530 m (5,020 ft)

Quality: ★
Difficulty: ◆
Maps: NTS 92-H/6 Hope
Trailhead: 49°22'49" N, 121°18'14" W

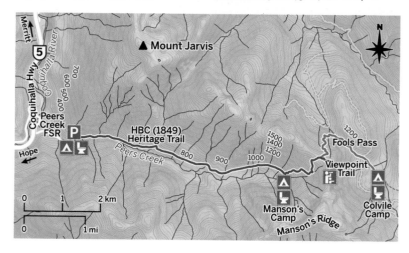

TRAVELLED BY First Nations, fur trade brigades, gold miners, and cattle ranchers, the Hudson's Bay Company (1849) Heritage Trail (Hikes 70 and 73) has a storied past. Crossing the Cascade Mountains, the HBC Trail extends 74 km (46 mi) between Hope and Tulameen, in the territories of the Nlaka'pamux, Stó:lō, and Upper Similkameen peoples. Officially reopened in 2016 by the Hope Mountain Centre for Outdoor Learning, the footpath and its ten campsites beckon backpackers seeking a 6-day hike into history.

The western section is the much more scenic half and lends itself to day hikes and overnighters. Be bear aware. To experience this initial leg of the journey from Fort Hope, head 6 km (3.7 mi) east from the trailhead up the deactivated Peers Creek logging road to Manson's Camp (950 m/ 3,120 ft; 49°22'23" N, 121°13'50" W). A pit latrine (bring your own toilet paper) and food cache are on site, but getting water requires a steep descent to the creek. This is the approximate location of the first slumber stop for the horse brigades, crewed largely by First Nations, Kanakas (Hawaiians), and French-Canadian voyageurs. For the next 2 km (1.2 mi), the stiff path switchbacks up Manson's Ridge under the cover of old-growth trees. In 1857, seventy horses perished on the ridge during a snowfall.

Tulameen Mountain, as seen from Manson's Ridge.

At a ridgetop clearing (1,450 m/4,760 ft; 49°22′31″ N, 121°12′57″ W), a signed Viewpoint Trail leaves to the right. Follow the rough, flagged route for 300 m (0.2 mi) to a little loop with vistas of the Hozameen Range in several directions. To the southeast, Mount Dewdney rises at the head of Sowaqua Creek (Skōkel, or "loon," in Halq'eméylem). Tulameen Mountain lies nearby to the east and the Coquihalla Pass summits farther away to the north. Retrace your steps down the Peers Creek valley to wrap up a strenuous day.

LONGER OPTION

To spend a night on the HBC (1849) Heritage Trail, continue east on the main path for 3 km (1.9 mi). Descend Manson's Ridge via suitably titled Fools Pass, home of the mountain beavers, to Colvile Camp (920 m/3,020 ft; 49°22′16″ N, 121°11′42″ W), a pleasant spot in the woods at Colvile Creek. It's named for Eden Colvile (1819–1893), a governor of Rupert's Land, the vast HBC-occupied territory in colonial British North America. Donald Manson (1798–1880) was a chief trader for the HBC.

GETTING THERE

Vehicle: From Trans-Canada Highway 1 in Hope, head east on Crowsnest Highway 3. Keep left for Yellowhead Highway 5 (Coquihalla Highway) northbound and take Exit 183 (Othello Road). From the off-ramp, swing south and immediately turn left onto a bridge over the Coquihalla River. Drive 1.5 km on Peers Creek Forest Service Road (2WD) to the trailhead and campsite.

70
PALMER'S POND

Distance: 11.5 km (7.1 mi)
Time: 7 hours (round trip)
Elevation gain: 950 m (3,120 ft)
High point: 1,855 m (6,085 ft)

Quality: ★★★★
Difficulty: ■
Maps: NTS 92-H/6 Hope, Clark Geomatics 104 Manning Park
Trailhead: 49°20'03" N, 121°07'41" W

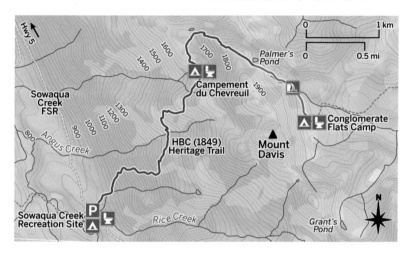

DESIGNATED AS a provincial recreation trail, most of the Hudson's Bay Company (1849) Heritage Trail (Hikes 69 and 73) is protected by a 200 m (220 yd) buffer under the Heritage Conservation Act. Motorized use is prohibited, as is the desecration or excavation of any objects of historical interest. It's gaining popularity with backpackers, naturalists, and trail runners (Mountain Madness ran an ultramarathon on this trail for the first time in 2017)—and with good reason.

The Mount Davis section of "Blackeye's Trail"—referring to the Upper Similkameen chief who showed the route to HBC trader A.C. Anderson in 1846—offers the most spectacular scenery. From the Sowaqua Creek (Skōkel in Halq'eméylem) logging road, head northeast on the steep trail, enduring switchbacks while feasting your eyes on arctic lupine, red paintbrush, Sitka columbine, and tiger lily. After 1.5 hours, cross Angus Creek and watch the forest give way to subalpine meadows.

Shortly after a wooden bench offers a rest with a view, a sign informs you of the campsite ahead. The path curves to the right (east), rewarding you with more stunning scenery. After the HBC Trail's 22 km (13.7 mi) marker, drop to

Palmer's Pond, east of Campement du Chevreuil on the HBC (1849) Heritage Trail.

a muddy section with avalanche lilies and cross a creek to the inviting kiosk, food cache, firepit, tent pads, and open-air toilet of Campement du Chevreuil (Deer Camp), 3.75 km (2.3 mi) from the logging road. Grand views of Mount Outram, Mount Hatfield, and Macleod Peak (Yusoló:luk) await just above the campsite (1,630 m/5,350 ft; 49°21'05" N, 121°06'31" W).

Your objective, Palmer's Pond, is 2 km (1.2 mi) and less than an hour away. The meadow path weaves through heather, blueberries (leave them for the bears), mud, and ponds with caddisflies. Enchanting vantages of Tulameen Mountain come with the steep ascent to the hike's high point—on the Cascade Divide, north of Mount Davis—before the emerald tarn enters the picture. The path dips to cross the streamlets feeding Palmer's Pond (49°21'03" N, 121°05'50" W). To protect the fragile environment, camping and fires are discouraged here.

The HBC Trail lies in the territories of the Nlaka'pamux, Stó:lō, and Upper Similkameen peoples. Credit for its restoration goes to the Hope Mountain Centre for Outdoor Learning, Back Country Horsemen Society of B.C., Okanagan Similkameen Parks Society, and New Pathways to Gold Society.

LONGER OPTION

Conglomerate Flats Camp (49°20'37" N, 121°05'12" W) lies 1 km (0.6 mi) east of Palmer's Pond on the HBC (1849) Heritage Trail at an elevation of 1,660 m (5,450 ft). It's a gorgeous stroll past a waterfall and more avalanche lilies to the muddy meadows below Mount Davis. Spend the night there, and hike a further 2 km (1.2 mi) to Grant's Pond or scramble up to the summit for spectacular views of the peaks in E.C. Manning Provincial Park. Black and grizzly bears are active in this area, and the weather can change in an instant: be prepared for both.

GETTING THERE

Vehicle: On Yellowhead Highway 5 (Coquihalla Highway), 20 km (12.4 mi) north of Hope, take Exit 192. Drive 20 km (12.4 mi) southeast on Sowaqua Creek Forest Service Road (2WD) to the Sowaqua Creek Recreation Site. Note: This road is actively used by logging trucks (be prepared to pull over), and the first pitch is steep, rocky, and rutted and can be difficult for 2WD vehicles when very dry or wet.

71
THE FLATIRON

Distance: 10 km (6.2 mi)
Time: 5 hours (round trip)
Elevation gain: 690 m (2,260 ft)
High point: 1,898 m (6,230 ft)

Quality: ★★★★
Difficulty: ■
Maps: NTS 92-H/11 Spuzzum, John Baldwin Coquihalla Summit
Trailhead: 49°35'43" N, 121°07'31" W

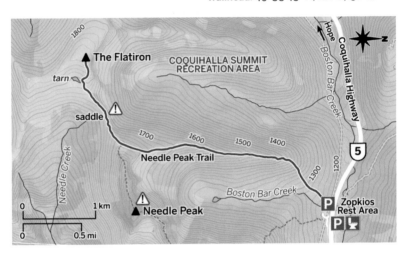

THE STRIKING peaks of the Cascade Mountains that tower over Coquihalla Pass are underlain by a body of rock that geologists call the Needle Peak Pluton. Their intrusive rock is the product of magma crystallizing within the Earth's crust during the Eocene epoch. Consequently, making an ascent of The Flatiron, south of the Coquihalla Highway, means treading on 39-million-year-old granite.

Find the trailhead just west of the parking area, across a creek and along a gas pipeline right-of-way. Make sure to carry plenty of water; sources are scarce by late summer. The Needle Peak Trail threads south into the woods, steepening as it weaves uphill amid Douglas fir and devil's club (*Oplopanax horridus*).

In 45 minutes, the forest opens up, inviting a look back at the exfoliating south face of Yak Peak on Zopkios Ridge. Following orange squares, gain the crest of a lovely spur ridge, extending north from Needle Peak's west shoulder, 15 minutes farther. The trail levels out before rising in a largely gentle fashion, encountering blueberries and Cascade golden-mantled ground squirrels and travelling over bare rock and through heather meadows.

Fall hike to The Flatiron, with Needle Peak looming large in the background.

Reach the signed "Needle Peak Saddle" (not a saddle) at the 3.3 km (2.1 mi) mark (1,800 m/5,905 ft; 49°34'12" N, 121°08'14" W). Watching for orange and pink flagging, drop southwest (right) to the actual Needle-Flatiron saddle (1,740 m/5,710 ft). The braided path skirts a cliff on your right, then climbs to a pretty tarn in the bowl on the east side of The Flatiron. Cross via an island and make a zigzagging ascent, following occasional cairns through rock and heather.

The broad summit plateau (49°33'56" N, 121°09'13" W) comes 1.5 km (0.9 mi) past the Needle Peak junction and 3 hours up. In addition to the two solar-powered radio repeater cones, you might spot a sooty grouse. Illal Mountain (Hike 72), Jim Kelly Peak, and Coquihalla Mountain lie across the Coquihalla River (and Coquihalla Fault) to the southeast. Nearby Portia Peak is due south. Needle Peak, a popular scramble via its southwest ridge, dominates to the northeast, with Markhor Peak behind it. Descend the way you came.

Established in 1986, Coquihalla Summit Recreation Area—which comprises the transition zone between the coast and southern Interior—lies in the territories of the Nlaka'pamux, Stó:lō, and Yale First Nations. The recreation area's 1990 master plan identifies designation as a Class A provincial park as an objective—which has not yet occurred. Campfires and tree cutting are banned. Dogs must be leashed but are discouraged in the backcountry. (Please pick up your dog's poop.)

GETTING THERE

Vehicle: On Yellowhead Highway 5 (Coquihalla Highway), 40 km (25 mi) north of Hope and past the Great Bear Snowshed, take poorly marked Exit 217. From the northbound off-ramp, immediately turn right onto a gravel road and right again into the Needle Peak trailhead parking area (below the highway maintenance sheds). Alternatively, go under the highway and park at the Zopkios Rest Area on the southbound side.

72
ILLAL MOUNTAIN

Distance: 13 km (8.1 mi)
Time: 7.5 hours (round trip)
Elevation gain: 745 m (2,445 ft)
High point: 2,020 m (6,630 ft)

Quality: ★★★★★
Difficulty: ◆◆
Maps: NTS 92-H/10, 92-H/11; John
Baldwin Coquihalla Summit
Trailhead: 49°32'04" N, 120°59'48" W

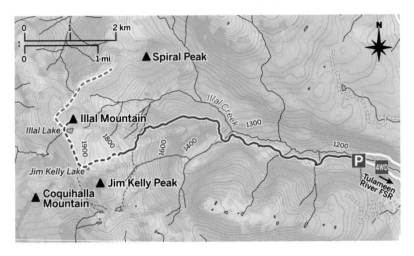

ILLAL MEADOWS is noted for high winds, scattered tarns, radiant wildflowers, and breathtaking sunsets. Less known is that the headwaters of Illal Creek are surrounded by volcanoes. A hike to this subalpine wonderland is also a tour of the Coquihalla Volcanic Complex, part of the Miocene-age Pemberton Volcanic Belt.

From the top of the Illal Creek road (1,275 m/4,180 ft), set off west on the unblazed but well-established trail. After a stream crossing, the path climbs in shady forest. About 1.5 hours in, tread across talus slopes, with rocks clinking like dinner plates, encountering blueberries and huckleberries. The trail rises higher, through meadows and stream beds, before levelling out in wide-open terrain and becoming less distinct. Please keep to established paths as much as possible in this fragile subalpine environment.

Occasional flagging and cairns mark the intermittent path up the south (left) side of Illal Meadows. Pass to the left of a pair of brook-fed ponds en route to crystal-clear Jim Kelly Lake (49°31'51" N, 121°02'40" W), just northwest of Jim Kelly Peak, an andesite dome. Ignore a track breaking off left near the Jim Kelly Peak–Coquihalla Mountain col. Continue west to the glorious

Illal Mountain and Illal Lake at sunrise.

crest of the windblown plateau and bear north (right) to close the distance with Illal Mountain. The hornblende andesite dome, with radiating columnar jointing and a talus apron, looms over striking Illal Lake (1,930 m/6,330 ft; 49°32′16″ N, 121°03′04″ W).

From the lake's west end, follow a path around the back of the mountain. Ascend its straightforward western slopes to the rocky summit (4 hours up; 49°32′23″ N, 121°02′51″W). Coquihalla Mountain, a stratovolcano, and Jim Kelly Peak loom behind Illal Meadows. The Flatiron (Hike 71), Needle Peak, and Yak Peak are northwest. Reverse your course for the descent.

Illal Meadows lies within the Similkameen Provincial Forest and the territories of the Nlaka'pamux, Stó:lō, and Yale First Nations. Illal Mountain belongs to the Bedded Range of the Cascade Mountains. In 2017, John Baldwin, author of *Exploring the Coast Mountains on Skis* (3rd edition, 2009), proposed the expansion of the Coquihalla Summit Recreation Area into the Bedded Range.

LONGER OPTION

Wander along the leisurely ridge extending northeast from Illal Mountain. The scenic bump before the col west of Spiral Peak (1,866 m/6,120 ft) is an agreeable destination before turning around. Dirt bikes ride the ridge. Scramblers may set their sights on the summit of Spiral, a dacite dome.

GETTING THERE

Vehicle: On Yellowhead Highway 5 (Coquihalla Highway), 55 km (34 mi) north of Hope, take Exit 228 (Coquihalla Lakes). Drive south on Tulameen River Forest Service Road for 19 km (12 mi). Cross the Illal Creek bridge and turn right on a gravel road. With high-clearance 4WD, continue 2.9 km (1.8 mi) to road's end. (2WD vehicles park near the bottom; add 40 minutes on foot each way.)

73
PODUNK CREEK

Distance: 23 km (14.3 mi)
Time: 8 hours (round trip)
Elevation gain: 215 m (705 ft)
High point: 1,470 m (4,820 ft)

Quality: ★★
Difficulty: ■
Maps: NTS 92-H/6 Hope, 92-H/7 Princeton
Trailhead: 49°21'11" N, 121°03'31" W

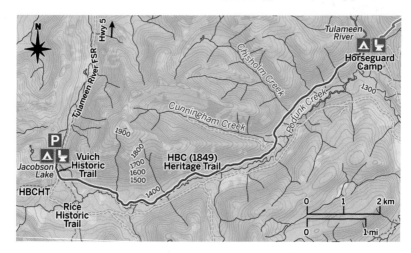

TRAVELLING EASTWARD, the Hudson's Bay Company (1849) Heritage Trail (Hikes 69 and 70) culminates with a ford of the Tulameen River, 3 km (1.9 mi) west of its namesake community. Backpackers must also make a wet crossing of the Tulameen upstream, just after the midpoint of the HBC Trail. It's optional on the pleasant day hike down Podunk Creek.

Starting at Jacobson Lake, go south on the Vuich Historic Trail for 410 m (0.25 mi). Turn east (left) on the HBC Trail (the Rice Historic Trail continues south) and follow the mellow path for 11.5 km (7.1 mi). Staying on river left, pass from the Engelmann spruce–subalpine fir to the montane spruce biogeoclimatic zone. Arctic lupine is plentiful.

Finally, the remote trail climbs some and drops more to Horseguard Camp (49°22'39" N, 120°56'33" W). The third campsite of the HBC fur trade brigades sits on the left bank of the Tulameen, just north of its confluence with Podunk Creek. Creature comforts include a campfire ring, open-air pit latrine, food cache, and tent sites above a cobble point bar. Bring a copy of B.C. poet Al Purdy's "Say the Names" to recite on the riverbank before retracing your steps—upstream—back to Jacobson Lake. "Tulameen Tulameen / till the heart stops beating…."

The HBC (1849) Heritage Trail's Horseguard Camp lies by the Tulameen River.

The Tulameen ("red earth" in the Nlaka'pamux language) was once known as the North Fork of the Similkameen River (nməlqaytkw to the Syilx people of the Okanagan Nation). The latter crosses the Canada–U.S. border and flows into the Okanogan River, a tributary of the mighty Columbia River.

LONGER OPTION

If the Tulameen River is low enough to safely ford, carefully cross to the right bank. You might spot a notice of a placer mineral claim in the silty woods. You can overnight at buggy Blackeye's Plateau Camp (1,860 m/6,100 ft) on the Tulameen Plateau, 6.5 km (4 mi) farther east. On the way, the HBC (1849) Heritage Trail passes Squakin Creek and navigates The Defiles, a lonely and beautiful stretch of steep-sided valley meadows.

GETTING THERE

Vehicle: On Yellowhead Highway 5 (Coquihalla Highway), 55 km (34 mi) north of Hope, take Exit 228 (Coquihalla Lakes). Drive 45 km (28 mi) south on Tulameen River Forest Service Road (2WD) to Jacobson Lake Recreation Site in the Okanagan-Similkameen regional district.

74
SKAGIT RIVER TRAIL

Distance: 18 km (11.2 mi)
Time: 6.5 hours (round trip)
Elevation gain: 60 m (200 ft)
High point: 625 m (2,050 ft)

Quality: ★★★
Difficulty: ■
Maps: NTS 92-H/3 Skagit River, Clark
Geomatics 104 Manning Park
Trailhead: 49°12'34" N, 121°04'47" W

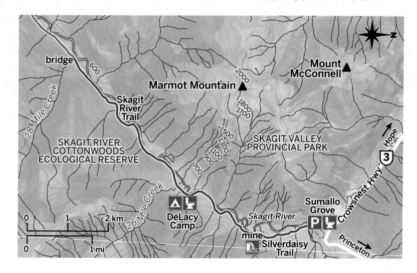

IN 1858, the Whatcom Trail was built as a way for American prospectors headed for the Fraser Canyon gold rush to bypass Victoria. The short-lived pack trail, also used by First Nations as a trade route, connected the Bellingham area with the Hudson's Bay Company (1849) Heritage Trail (Hikes 69, 70, and 73). Today, the Skagit River Trail follows a section of the historic Whatcom Trail.

Hiking south from Sumallo Grove in the "panhandle" of E.C. Manning Provincial Park, enter Skagit Valley Provincial Park and cross a bridge over the Skagit River, below its confluence with the Sumallo River. At 1.5 km (0.9 mi) downstream, the Silverdaisy Trail leaves to the left. Due to mining interests, Silverdaisy Mountain lies in an unprotected "donut hole" surrounded by Manning and Skagit Valley parks. (An old mining tramway cut is visible from the Skagit River bridge.) Shortly after the Silverdaisy turnoff, an abandoned truck, cabin, and mine entrance are found just left of the trail by a waterfall.

Reach DeLacy Camp further downstream at the 4 km (2.5 mi) mark. See if you can spot harlequin ducks in the swift water. The Skagit River, which

Harlequin duck in the Skagit River.

divides the Skagit and Hozameen Ranges of the Cascade Mountains, provides breeding habitat for these diving birds. Continue south to cross 26 Mile Creek.

At 6 km (3.7 mi), enter Skagit River Cottonwoods Ecological Reserve, home to old-growth groves of Douglas fir and western red cedar and the most beautiful section of the trail. Covering 69 ha (170 acres), this protected area was established in 1978 to preserve alluvial stands of black cottonwood trees. Red-osier dogwood, beaked hazelnut, salmonberry, and thimbleberry shrubs populate the floodplain understory.

The bridge over 28 Mile Creek comes soon after you exit the ecological reserve. After 3 hours of downstream hiking, it's a good place to turn around. Your return is all uphill from here.

Skagit Valley Provincial Park protects endangered spotted owl habitat and lies in the territories of the Nlaka'pamux and Stó:lō peoples. Fires and bikes are prohibited, and dogs must be leashed in the park. Camping, hunting, and fishing are banned in the ecological reserve.

SHORTER OPTION

With two cars, a one-way trip down the whole Skagit River Trail (15 km/9.3 mi with 90 m/295 ft of elevation loss) is an attractive and surprisingly shorter proposition. Continue south to Harlequin Flats Camp at 11 km (6.8 mi) and a patch of red rhododendrons that bloom in late spring. Go right at the Centennial Trail junction after 13 km (8.1 mi) to reach the 26 Mile Bridge parking lot (49°07'11" N, 121°09'57" W) on Silver-Skagit Road, south of Hope.

GETTING THERE

Vehicle: On Crowsnest Highway 3, 26 km (16 mi) east of Hope, turn south into Manning Provincial Park's Sumallo Grove day-use area.

75
WINDY JOE MOUNTAIN

Distance: 15 km (9.3 mi)
Time: 5.5 hours (round trip)
Elevation gain: 677 m (2,221 ft)
High point: 1,825 m (5,989 ft)

Quality: ★★
Difficulty: ■
Maps: NTS 92-H/2 Manning Park, Clark
Geomatics 104 Manning Park
Trailhead: 49°03'50" N, 120°47'53" W

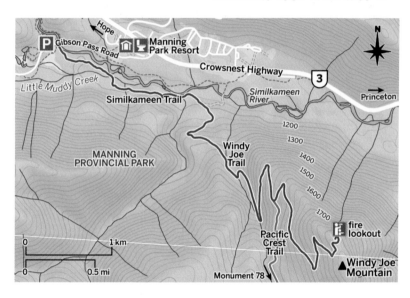

FOR THOSE of us harbouring long-distance hiking dreams, a visit to Windy
Joe Mountain is a must. On a mere day hike, you can experience the home
stretch of the epic Pacific Crest Trail, which runs 4,260 km (2,650 mi) from
Mexico to Canada. If you're lucky enough to encounter a thru-hiker, they will
have just spent around five months backpacking the PCT.

But there are lots of other reasons to hike Windy Joe. First of all, it's in
British Columbia's beloved E.C. Manning Provincial Park and, therefore,
lies among the northernmost peaks of the Cascade Range (officially the Cascade Mountains in Canada). Secondly, it's topped by an intact fire lookout,
complete with an old-school fire finder and boasting views in every direction.
Thirdly, the old road to the top welcomes use in all seasons (with snowshoes
in winter).

From the trailhead, head southeast on the more or less level Similkameen
Trail. After 2 km (1.2 mi), go right on the Windy Joe Trail and start gaining

altitude. At 5.5 km (3.4 mi), the trail forks and you head left for the top. (Right leads to the PCT and Frosty Mountain [Hike 76].)

An 8 km (5 mi) marker is nailed to the Windy Joe Fire Tower, a two-storey hut dating back to 1950. On the second floor, signs help hikers identify The Parks, jagged Castle Peak,

Winter snow at the old fire lookout on Windy Joe Mountain.

Frosty, and other prominences. Don't leave without trying out the fire finder. Retrace your steps to the trailhead.

For decades, fire lookouts like this one were staffed and played a lead role in wildfire detection in B.C. The province is home to more than 300 fire-lookout sites, but only around 25 are considered active. Since fire lookouts needed to command an excellent view of the surrounding landscape, today they tend to make attractive hiking destinations.

For peak baggers, Windy Joe's true summit (49°02′24″ N, 120°45′12″ W) lies off-trail to the south at an elevation of 1,843 m (6,047 ft). Horseback riders, mountain bikers, trail runners, and ski tourers also use the Windy Joe Trail, which is in the vicinity of the Coldspring and Lightning Lake campgrounds. Dogs must be on-leash at all times.

Established in 1941, Manning Provincial Park is located east of Skagit Valley Provincial Park (you know, beyond Hope) in the territories of the Nlaka'pamux, Syilx (Okanagan), and Stó:lō peoples. Sunshine Valley, just outside the west entrance, is a former World War II–era Japanese Canadian internment camp.

LONGER OPTION

Choose right instead of left at the 5.5 km (3.4 mi) junction and then left 1.6 km (1 mi) later if you wish to hike the entire Canadian extension of the Pacific Crest Trail. Continue south to Monument 78, one of many markers of the Canada–U.S. border on the 49th parallel. It's a 26 km (16 mi) round trip from the trailhead.

GETTING THERE

Vehicle: On Crowsnest Highway 3, 60 km (37 mi) east of Hope (just past the Manning Park Resort), turn south on Gibson Pass Road. Drive 1 km (0.6 mi) and cross the Similkameen River (nməlqaytkw to the Syilx) to find the trailhead parking area on the left.

76
FROSTY MOUNTAIN

Distance: 22 km (14 mi)
Time: 7.5 hours (round trip)
Elevation gain: 1,160 m (3,805 ft)
High point: 2,409 m (7,900 ft)

Quality: ★★★★★
Difficulty: ■
Maps: NTS 92-H/2 Manning Park, Clark Geomatics 104 Manning Park
Trailhead: 49°03'39" N, 120°49'27" W

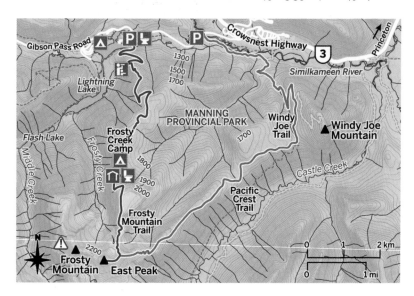

FROSTY MOUNTAIN (2,426 m/7,960 ft) has the distinction of being the highest summit in E.C. Manning Provincial Park. However, the destination for hikers is the lower east peak. You'll see why at the top.

From the Lightning Lake day-use area, head south across the dam at the east end of the lake to find the trailhead in short order. Leaving the Lightning Lake Trail, the well-graded Frosty Mountain Trail zigzags upward in the Engelmann spruce–subalpine fir biogeoclimatic zone. Soon there are picturesque down-valley views of Lightning Lake, Flash Lake (Hike 77), and Lone Mountain. Butterflies aplenty flutter over colourful meadows of arctic lupine and Sitka valerian on the steep slopes.

In 7 km (4.3 mi), reach Frosty Creek Camp (1,850 m/6,070 ft; 49°01'51" N, 120°49'49" W), with its rustic shelter (backcountry camping fee required). Beyond lies a subalpine larch forest. When the larch's deciduous needles change from pale blue-green to golden yellow in autumn, it's an incredible

Looking up at Frosty Mountain from Lightning Lake.

sight. Past the larches, the east and west peaks of Frosty Mountain reveal themselves.

After enjoying a largely pleasant grade, switchback sharply up the harsh talus—home to moss campion and American (well, Canadian in this case) pikas—to the rocky crest, merging with the alternate approach from the Windy Joe Trail (Hike 75). Turn west (right) for a magnificent ridge walk to the summit post and elating panorama of the east peak (4 hours up; 49°00′39″ N, 120°50′15″ W). From this perch 1.2 km (0.7 mi) from the Canada–U.S. border, survey Mount Winthrop and Castle Peak in North Cascades National Park to the south, Mount Outram and Three Brothers Mountain (Hike 79) to the north, and Chuwanten Mountain to the east. Return the way you came.

Established in 1941, Manning Provincial Park lies within the territories of the Nlaka'pamux, Syilx (Okanagan), and Stó:lō peoples. The Frosty Mountain larches are designated a special feature zone. Dogs must be on-leash in provincial parks but are discouraged in the backcountry.

LONGER OPTION

If you're a glutton for punishment, ascend Frosty Mountain's east peak via the Windy Joe Trail, as runners in Trail Whisperer's annual Frosty Mountain Ultra race do. From the Windy Joe trailhead, it's an out-and-back hike of 29 km (18 km).

GETTING THERE

Vehicle: From Crowsnest Highway 3, 60 km (37 mi) east of Hope (just past the Manning Park Resort), head south on Gibson Pass Road. Turn left into the Lightning Lake day-use area.

77
LIGHTNING LAKES

Distance: 20 km (12.4 mi)
Time: 7 hours (reverse lollipop)
Elevation gain: 50 m (160 ft)
High point: 1,250 m (4,100 ft)

Quality: ★★★
Difficulty: ■
Maps: NTS 92-H/2 Manning Park, Clark
Geomatics 104 Manning Park
Trailhead: 49°03'31" N, 120°50'26" W

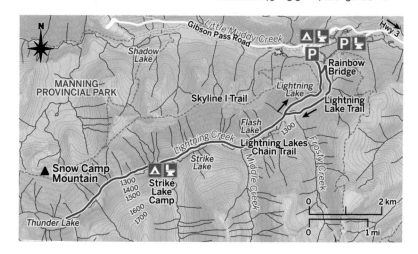

E.C. MANNING Provincial Park's Lightning Lake has a lot to offer—car camping, canoeing, hiking, fishing, kayaking, and swimming—so it's not lacking for summer visitors. Leave the masses behind with a hike to the quieter of the Lightning Lakes: Flash, Strike, and Thunder.

Head south from the Spruce Bay parking lot, quickly turning left on the Lightning Lake Trail to visit picturesque Rainbow Bridge. Frosty Mountain (Hike 76) rises due south. Cross the narrows of Lightning Lake, turn right, and continue south through lovely Engelmann spruce, subalpine fir, and lodgepole pine. At the lake's southwest end, cross Lightning Creek and go left for the Lightning Lakes Chain Trail.

Follow the old trappers' path, which negotiates several rockslides, down the valley to marshy Flash Lake and Strike Lake. (An optional loop accesses the south side of the former.) Watch for rainbow trout jumping. Other potential wildlife sightings include black bears (got bear spray?), mule deer, beavers, Townsend's chipmunks, merganser ducks, western terrestrial garter snakes, and damselflies.

Rainbow Bridge reflected in Lightning Lake.

The wooded Strike Lake Camp comes 4 km (2.5 mi) past the end of Lightning Lake. There are eight tent sites (backcountry camping fee required), outhouses, and a bear cache. You're now 3.5 km (2.2 mi) from trail's end.

Pushing on, your path crosses scree slopes and enters a drier environment. Above remote Thunder Lake, which lies between Snow Camp Mountain (Hike 78) and Lone Mountain, there are terraces of glacial deposits. Heading upstream on the way back, stay left at all junctions, except the one for the Skyline I Trail, to return to the parking lot.

During the Wisconsin Glaciation, erosion by ice and meltwater deepened and widened the Lightning Creek valley. Although the chain, formerly known as the Quartet Lakes, may have drained eastward in the past, its waters now flow west. The exception is Lightning Lake, which drains in both directions due to a dam built at its northeast end in 1968.

Established in 1941, Manning Provincial Park lies within the territories of the Nlaka'pamux, Syilx (Okanagan), and Stó:lō peoples. Dogs must be leashed. Avalanches make the Lightning Lakes Chain Trail dangerous to travel in winter and spring.

GETTING THERE

Vehicle: On Crowsnest Highway 3, 60 km (37 mi) east of Hope (just past the Manning Park Resort), turn south on Gibson Pass Road. Drive 5 km (3 mi), go left at the Lightning Lake campground turnoff, and keep right to find the Spruce Bay parking lot.

78
SNOW CAMP MOUNTAIN

Distance: 17 km (10.6 mi)
Time: 6 hours (round trip)
Elevation gain: 600 m (1,970 ft)
High point: 1,980 m (6,497 ft)

Quality: ★★★★
Difficulty: ■
Maps: NTS 92-H/2 Manning Park, Clark
Geomatics 104 Manning Park
Trailhead: 49°03'59" N, 120°53'02" W

WITH ITS sharp greenstone towers, Hozomeen Mountain (2,447 m/8,028 ft) in Washington's North Cascades is an unmistakable landmark for hikers across the border in E.C. Manning Provincial Park. Venturing onto the Skyline Trail, which links Manning with Skagit Valley Provincial Park, means getting an eyeful of the double peak that Jack Kerouac described as the "most mournful mountain I ever seen" in his 1958 novel *The Dharma Bums*.

Indigenous peoples blazed the Skyline Trail, which would later be travelled by fur traders and gold prospectors, known as the Roach River Trail for a time, and incorporated into the fading Centennial Trail of the 1960s. Today, Snow Camp Mountain makes a fine destination for day trippers.

Head west from the Strawberry Flats trailhead and go left at the Three Falls Trail junction. The Skyline I Trail climbs steadily southwest—first in forest, then through subalpine meadows and across steep rocky slopes. At the 5.9 km (3.7 mi) mark (49°02'20" N, 120°55'11" W), Skyline I goes left to its eventual terminus at Lightning Lake. But you turn right on the Skyline II Trail, part of the National Hiking Trail.

Drop west to aptly named Despair Pass, then rise up to the colourful wildflowers of Snow Camp Mountain. A path to the grassy summit (49°02'00" N,

Red paintbrush in bloom along the Skyline II Trail.

120°56′34″ W) strikes off to the right. From your perch above Thunder Lake (Hike 77), Hozomeen Mountain dominates the southern landscape, while Lone Goat Mountain and Red Mountain lie nearby to the west. Three Brothers Mountain (Hike 79) is visible on the northeast horizon. Steel yourself for the return via Despair Pass.

Manning Provincial Park lies within the territories of the Nlaka'pamux, Syilx (Okanagan), and Stó:lō peoples.

LONGER OPTION
Day hikers can keep going west on the Lightning Creek–Nepopekum Creek divide to Lone Goat Mountain (2,004 m/6,575 ft; 49°02′04″ N, 120°58′03″ W). Backpackers push on to Mowich Camp for the night (12.5 km/7.8 mi from Strawberry Flats, backcountry camping fee required), perhaps en route to completing the Skyline II Trail crossover to Silver-Skagit Road (13 km/8.1 mi farther), south of Hope.

GETTING THERE
Vehicle: On Crowsnest Highway 3, 60 km (37 mi) east of Hope (just past the Manning Park Resort), turn south on Gibson Pass Road. Drive 8 km (5 mi) to the Strawberry Flats parking lot.

79
THREE BROTHERS MOUNTAIN

Distance: 21.5 km (13.4 mi)
Time: 6.5 hours (round trip)
Elevation gain: 480 m (1,575 ft)
High point: 2,272 m (7,453 ft)

Quality: ★★★★★
Difficulty: ■
Maps: NTS 92-H/2 Manning Park, Clark Geomatics 104 Manning Park
Trailhead: 49°05'56" N, 120°45'54" W

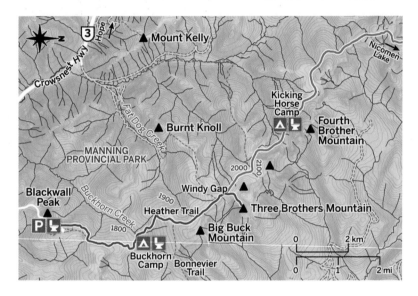

READY FOR one of the best wildflower hikes in southwestern B.C.? It's no secret why hikers flock to the Heather Trail every July and August. At peak bloom, the subalpine meadows burst into a sea of red (Sitka columbine), orange (slender agoseris), yellow (mountain arnica), blue (arctic lupine), purple (silky phacelia), pink (spreading phlox), and white (Douglas's catchfly).

From the trailhead (1,980 m/6,500 ft) below Blackwall Peak, head north on the Heather Trail, contouring along the western slopes of Lone Man Ridge and merging with a trail from the upper parking lot. Lose a bunch of elevation—which you can look forward to regaining on the return—on the way to the backcountry campsite (no fires, camping permit required) and low point at Buckhorn Creek, 5 km (3.1 mi) in.

Switchbacks lead up and out of the valley. Stay left at the Bonnevier Trail junction at the 7 km (4.3 mi) mark. Stroll northwest through the floral rainbow, taking care to stay on the path to avoid trampling the fragile meadows, which climate change could diminish in extent. Traversing the west side of

Subalpine meadows along the Heather Trail on Big Buck Mountain.

Big Buck Mountain, there's ample opportunity to survey Frosty Mountain (Hike 76), the fearsome towers of Hozomeen Mountain, and the rest of the North Cascades to the south. Vidler's alpines and other butterflies flutter above lingering snow.

At Windy Gap, part ways with the Heather Trail, 10 km (6.2 mi) from the start. Go right to ascend the rocky path to the saddle east of Second Brother Mountain. Once on the crest, face northeast and relish the elating ridge walk to sometimes-buggy First Brother Mountain (49°09'58" N, 120°46'06" W), the highest summit of Three Brothers Mountain. This mountaintop pierces the alpine tundra biogeoclimatic zone; look for krummholz, stunted trees deformed by freezing winds. For peak baggers, the second and third siblings are within scrambling range. Fourth Brother Mountain stands estranged, farther northwest.

Returning via the Heather Trail, you'll see more than one species of its namesake evergreen shrub. Four-angled, pink, and yellow mountain-heather grow in the subalpine here. E.C. Manning Provincial Park lies within the territories of the Nlaka'pamux, Syilx (Okanagan), and Stó:lō peoples.

LONGER OPTION

For the multi-day Heather Trail experience, backpack all the way to the Kicking Horse (no fires) and Nicomen Lake campsites. It's 23 km (14 mi) one way, without counting summit side trips. From trail's end, either hike back to the Blackwall Peak trailhead or cross over via the Grainger Creek Trail and Hope Pass Trail to the Cayuse Flats parking lot. Backcountry permits are required for overnight stays at all the campsites on this trail; buy them online or at the park's visitor centre before you set out.

GETTING THERE

Vehicle: On Crowsnest Highway 3, 60 km (37 mi) east of Hope (just past the Manning Park Resort), turn north and immediately left on Blackwall Road. Drive 14 km (6.7 mi), passing Cascade Lookout, to the lower Blackwall Peak parking area.

80
MOUNT GARDNER

Distance: 17 km (10.6 mi)
Time: 7 hours (lollipop)
Elevation gain: 720 m (2,360 ft)
High point: 727 m (2,385 ft)

Quality: ★★★
Difficulty: ■
Maps: NTS 92-G/6 North Vancouver
Trailhead: 49°22'48" N, 123°20'08" W

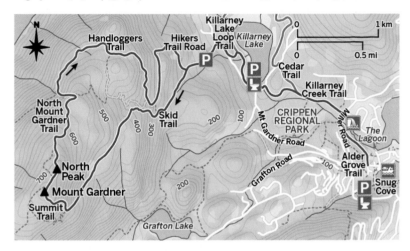

AN ISLAND day hike can feel as invigorating as a week away. The ferry from Horseshoe Bay (Ch'axáy) to Bowen Island (Nex̱wlélex̱wem), in Squamish Nation territory, takes just 20 minutes. Foot passengers can scale the island's tallest peak and be back in Vancouver for dinner.

From the Snug Cove ferry dock, walk up Bowen Island Trunk Road for a few minutes to find a trailhead on the right. Head north into Crippen Regional Park (dogs must be leashed). Quickly turn left on the Alder Grove Trail. Detour right to see Bridal Veil Falls. Go right on Miller Road, then left on the Killarney Creek Trail. At the fork with the Cedar Trail, stay left to reach the Killarney Lake dam and picnic area.

Continue north on the Killarney Lake Loop Trail. Forty minutes from Snug Cove, a signpost points left for Mount Gardner Road. Follow the trail to the road and go right. Take a left on Hikers Trail Road for the Mount Gardner trailhead (49°23'33" N, 123°21'42" W). Plod up the road for several minutes, passing parking spots and coming to a gate next to the David Otter Nature Reserve.

At Junction 1, go left on the Skid Trail, which crosses a bridge and steadily rises in the dappled light of the cool forest. Stay left at Junction 2 to stick with

Helipad on Mount Gardner's north peak.

the Skid Trail and surmount stiff switchbacks. A Douglas squirrel may scold you for invading its territory. Follow orange-painted can lids to stay on the correct path.

Junction 3 (49°22′28″ N, 123°23′14″ W) comes 3.5 km (2.2 mi) from Mount Gardner's base. Ignoring the "No view at south summit" warning, turn right on the steep and overgrown Summit Trail. Small outcrops might require your hands to clamber over. In 20 minutes, earn vistas of Whytecliff Park (St'éxw't̲e̲kw's), Burnaby Mountain, and Point Grey through shore pine. A cairn marks the south peak (49°22′34″ N, 123°23′25″ W), the true summit with no view.

Look for pink tapes and continue north. Keep right to gain the north peak (719 m/2,360 ft; 49°22′46″ N, 123°23′19″ W), a suitable lunch spot in spite of its jumble of telecommunications towers. Wooden helipads offer vantages east (Burrard Inlet) and west (Mount Elphinstone and Keats Island [Hike 81]).

From the west-facing pad, follow markers down an abrupt gully, aided by a fixed cord. Go right at the next junction and pass a bluff viewpoint on the North Mount Gardner Trail. Take the scenic route down: 45 minutes from the north peak, turn left to drop to the Handloggers Trail and go right. The mellow path leads to Hikers Trail Road. Bear left to descend to the Mount Gardner trailhead, and return to Snug Cove.

SHORTER OPTION
Complete the easy Killarney Lake loop. Return via the Cedar Trail for an 8.5 km (5.3 mi) round trip from the ferry dock.

GETTING THERE
Transit: TransLink Bus 250, 257, or 259, or Community Shuttle C12 to Horseshoe Bay.
Vehicle: From Vancouver, head east on Trans-Canada Highway 1 to the B.C. Ferries terminal at Horseshoe Bay. Park in the long-term parking lot.

81
LOOKOUT PEAK

Distance: 9 km (5.6 mi)
Time: 4 hours (one way)
Elevation gain: 189 m (620 ft)
High point: 189 m (620 ft)

Quality: ★★★
Difficulty: ●
Maps: NTS 92-G/6 North Vancouver
Trailhead: 49°23'38" N, 123°29'01" W

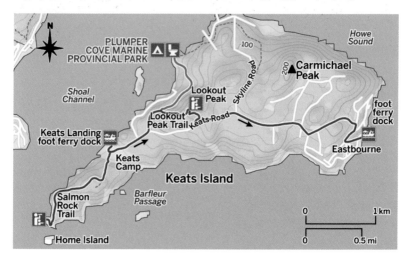

STANDING ATOP Lookout Peak, it may seem fitting to recite the untitled John Keats poem that begins "I stood tip-toe upon a little hill." However, Keats Island in Howe Sound, where said knoll stands, is named for Sir Richard Goodwin Keats (1757–1834), a British naval admiral and colonial governor of Newfoundland—not the English poet of the Romantic era.

Covering 600 ha (1,500 acres), Keats Island lies between Gibsons (Ch'ḵw'elhp), Gambier Island (Chá7elkwnech), and Bowen Island (Nex̱wlélex̱-wem; Hike 80) in Squamish Nation territory. A visit from Vancouver entails a trip on B.C. Ferries' Horseshoe Bay–Langdale route followed by a passenger ferry to Keats Landing or Eastbourne. Paddling the Sea to Sky Marine Trail (áyelhḵw shewálh) is another option.

Our hike begins at Keats Landing. From the wharf, walk up the gravel road through the Bible camp and swing right at the big field to pick up the Salmon Rock Trail. Keep right at a fork, ignoring the Katimavik Trail. Follow the forest path and its signs retelling Christian mythology to the gorgeous southwest toe of the sleepy island, where Salmon Rock, also known as Home Island, lies offshore.

Tombolo (sandy isthmus) at the south end of the Salmon Rock Trail.

Retrace your steps to the fork below the Bible camp field. This time, go east on Keats Road, the island's main drag. Hang a left on the signed Marine Park Trail. Next, take the right fork for the Lookout Peak Trail. The path climbs steeply through the woods to the island's rocky central hilltop, rewarding you with vistas of Gibsons and Barfleur Passage. Lookout Peak (49°23′57″ N, 23°27′56″ W), officially named Stony Hill, is a tad lower than Carmichael Peak to the east.

The Lookout Peak Trail descends east then south to Keats Road. Turn left and follow the thoroughfare east to the ferry dock at Eastbourne (49°23′42″ N, 123°26′07″ W). Make sure to arrange your departure with the ferry operator in advance.

Keats Island is part of the Gambier Island Local Trust Area and the Sunshine Coast Regional District's West Howe Sound electoral area. Remember to carry sufficient food and water, as there are no stores or public services.

LONGER OPTION

To lengthen your outing, continue north on the Marine Park Trail to visit Plumper Cove Marine Provincial Park prior to ascending Lookout Peak. A stop for kayakers and canoeists on the Sea to Sky Marine Trail, Plumper Cove (Ch'á७elsem) has twenty walk-in campsites and a pebble beach. Note: No water is available from mid-September to mid-May, and a boil-water advisory is in effect the rest of the year.

GETTING THERE

Transit: TransLink Bus 250, 257, or 259, or Community Shuttle C12 to Horseshoe Bay. Or, Sunshine Coast Regional Transit Bus 1 or 90 to Langdale ferry terminal.

Vehicle: From Vancouver, head east on Trans-Canada Highway 1 to the B.C. Ferries terminal at Horseshoe Bay. Park in the long-term parking lot.

82
CHAPMAN LAKE

Distance: 20 km (12.4 mi)
Time: 8 hours (round trip)
Elevation gain: 310 m (1,020 ft)
High point: 1,130 m (3,710 ft)

Quality: ★★★
Difficulty: ◆
Maps: NTS 92-G/12 Sechelt Inlet
Trailhead: 49°36'08" N, 123°41'07" W

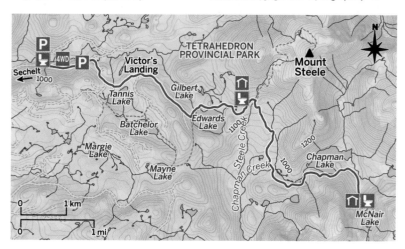

SEARCHING FOR solitude? In Tetrahedron Provincial Park, you have a better chance of finding it down by Chapman Lake than up on Mount Steele (Hike 83). This hike ventures off the beaten path and explores the bottom of a wild, remote valley. The price of admission: nearly as much outbound elevation gain as there is inbound. Route-finding skills are essential, as the path can be indistinct here and there. Be bear aware!

Head east from Branch 500, passing first the right-hand turnoff for Batchelor Lake and then Victor's Landing. At Edwards Lake, the trail swings left to rise above its north shore. At 4.9 km (3 mi) in, arrive at Edwards Lake Cabin (1,130 m/3,710 ft; 49°35'40" N, 123°37'25" W). If you spend the night, please clean up after yourself and pay the posted hut fee to the Tetrahedron Outdoor Club for maintenance.

Steele Creek is crossed in another 500 m (0.3 mi). Turn right at the Mount Steele junction; it's 5.2 km (3.2 mi) via Chapman Lake to trail's end. The southward path loses plenty of elevation en route to a mangled bridge over Chapman Creek. This watershed is the primary drinking-water source for the Sunshine Coast Regional District. Accordingly, dogs, swimming, mountain biking, snowmobiling, and open fires are prohibited in the park, which lies within the territories of the shíshálh (Sechelt) and Squamish First Nations.

Mount Steele stands behind Chapman Lake.

After passing several ponds, the muddy path reaches the south shore of Chapman Lake (974 m/3,195 ft), whose outflow is controlled by a concrete dam. The Sunshine Coast Conservation Association has opposed the expansion of water-supply infrastructure here. The lake supports Dolly Varden char and aquatic flora such as western quillwort and narrow-leaved bur-reed. Mountain hemlock, amabilis fir, and yellow cedar trees, as well as Alaskan and oval-leaved blueberry shrubs, surround it.

Next, the route takes aim at Panther Peak before curving south and ascending to far-flung McNair Lake Cabin (49°34'41" N, 123°35'20" W), often buried by snow in winter. The lake itself lies beyond the cabin, over the Howe Sound divide. Head back the way you came.

GETTING THERE

Vehicle: From Highway 101 (Sunshine Coast Highway) in Sechelt, head north on Wharf Avenue. Go right on Porpoise Bay Road, which becomes Sechelt Inlet Road. In 8 km (5 mi), shortly after crossing Gray Creek, turn right on the gravel Gray Creek Road (Sechelt Dakota Forest Service Road). Just 1 km (0.6 mi) later, take the left fork for Sechelt Gray FSR (rough 2WD). Keep right at the next fork to recross Gray Creek. The main parking lot is 11 km (6.8 mi) from the pavement. (In summer, 4WD vehicles can go 1 km [0.6 mi] farther on Branch 500 to the upper parking area.)

83
MOUNT STEELE

Distance: 18 km (11 mi)
Time: 8 hours (round trip)
Elevation gain: 840 m (2,755 ft)
High point: 1,659 m (5,440 ft)

Quality: ★★★★
Difficulty: ◆
Maps: NTS 92-G/12 Sechelt Inlet
Trailhead: 49°36'08" N, 123°41'07" W

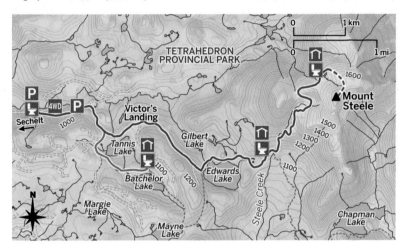

CREATED IN 1995 as part of the Lower Mainland Nature Legacy Program, Tetrahedron Provincial Park lies within the territories of the shíshálh (Sechelt) and Squamish First Nations. Mount Steele is the main draw for hikers, snowshoers, and ski tourers. The sensational summit panorama stars Tetrahedron Peak and Panther Peak, also in the park, alongside Salmon Inlet (skúpa in sháshishálem), the Earle Range, Phantom Mountain, Tantalus Range (Tsewílx in Skwxwú7mesh), and the Gulf Islands.

From Branch 500, hike east on a degrading logging road, passing first the right-hand turnoff for Batchelor Lake and then Victor's Landing, 1.5 km (0.9 mi) in. Clear-cuts give the trail a disheartening kickoff, but the scenery changes for the better as you approach Edwards Lake. The trail swings left to rise above its north shore en route to Edwards Lake Cabin (1,130 m/3,710 ft; 49°35'40" N, 123°37'25" W), erected by the Tetrahedron Outdoor Club (formerly the Tetrahedron Ski Club) in 1987, 4.9 km (3 mi) from your start. If you stay overnight, be sure to pay the posted hut fee to the club for maintenance.

Steele Creek is crossed 500 m (0.3 mi) past the cabin. Turn left (right goes to Chapman Lake [Hike 82]) to climb steeply over the next 2.9 km (1.8 mi) to Mount Steele Cabin (49°36'32" N, 123°36'32" W), 150 m (490 ft)

Sunset view of the Salish Sea from Mount Steele.

below the peak. The path switchbacks northeast, then curves 180 degrees in a scenic subalpine bowl before turning back eastward in the saddle between Lesser Mount Steele and your objective. A glorious ramble up the northeast ridge is all that separates the cabin and summit. Return the way you came.

Tetrahedron has a "limited recreational carrying capacity" of around 4,000 visitors per year, according to its 1997 management plan. The park's boundaries contain the headwaters of Chapman and Gray Creeks, which supply the drinking water for residents of the Sunshine Coast Regional District and support salmon populations. Understandably, dogs, swimming, mountain biking, snowmobiling, and open fires are prohibited.

SHORTER OPTION
Batchelor Lake (49°35′33″ N, 123°39′16″ W), a kettle lake north of Mount Crucil, is a 2.5 km (1.6 mi) walk from the parking lot (one way).

GETTING THERE
Vehicle: From Highway 101 (Sunshine Coast Highway) in Sechelt, head north on Wharf Avenue. Go right on Porpoise Bay Road, which becomes Sechelt Inlet Road. In 8 km (5 mi), shortly after crossing Gray Creek, turn right on the gravel Gray Creek Road (Sechelt Dakota Forest Service Road). Just 1 km (0.6 mi) later, take the left fork for Sechelt Gray FSR (rough 2WD). Keep right at the next fork to recross Gray Creek. The main parking lot is 11 km (6.8 mi) from the pavement. (In summer, 4WD vehicles can go 1 km [0.6 mi] farther on Branch 500 to the upper parking area.)

84
TRIANGLE LAKE

Distance: 8 km (5 mi)
Time: 3 hours (lollipop)
Elevation gain: 185 m (610 ft)
High point: 210 m (690 ft)

Quality: ★★
Difficulty: ●
Maps: NTS 92-G/5 Sechelt
Trailhead: 49°28'43" N, 123°52'01" W

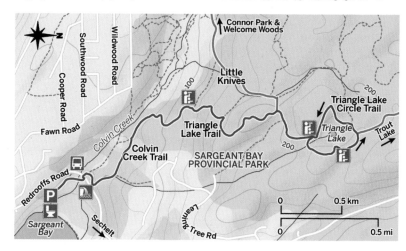

A **BARRIER** beach, tidal marsh, salmon-bearing stream, rain-fed bog, deer trails, and eelgrass beds—all of these natural features are preserved by Sargeant Bay Provincial Park on the Sechelt Peninsula. The Class A park was established in 1990, thanks to the efforts of the Sargeant Bay Society. Volunteers from the society also blazed this trail to Triangle Lake in 1995, and this area was added to the park the following year.

From Redrooffs Road, go right on the hiking-only Colvin Creek Trail (part of the National Hiking Trail), following signs for Triangle Lake. Cross a bridge by a waterfall and head north into a mossy second-growth forest of Douglas fir, western red cedar, and western hemlock. Tree roots spread like tentacles over rocks and stumps. Columbian black-tailed deer are a common sight. Stay right at a junction in 0.8 km (0.5 mi) to diverge from the riparian zone and strike off on the Triangle Lake Trail.

A signpost at 1.7 km (1.1 mi) indicates a viewpoint to the left; continue right. Stay right at the next signed junction. Reached in another 1.6 km (1 mi), Triangle Lake is a sphagnum bog that's known as s-ch'ewk' (a reference to frybread) to the shíshálh (Sechelt) Nation. A viewpoint with a bench overlooks the serene bog.

Black-tailed deer, spotted from the Colvin Creek Trail.

Head counterclockwise on the Triangle Lake Circle Trail (1.7 km/1.1 mi) to find a clifftop bench viewpoint on the bog's east margin. The wetland flora include bog cranberry, Labrador tea, and shore pine. Listen for songbirds such as the common yellowthroat ("witchety-witchety-witchety") and olive-sided flycatcher ("quick-three-beers"). Slow down—this is a hike for relaxed strolling and pleasant conversation. When the circumnavigation is complete, retrace your steps to the trailhead.

LONGER OPTION

Extend your woodland wander. A variety of biking-hiking trails in the Sechelt Provincial Forest link the Triangle Lake area with Welcome Woods Wilderness Park and Connor Park to the west and Trout Lake Park to the north. Or, visit the beavers at Colvin Lake behind the beach berm on Sargeant Bay (k'wéxwmínem).

GETTING THERE

Transit: Sunshine Coast Regional Transit Bus 4 (Halfmoon Bay) to 7600 block of Redrooffs Road.

Vehicle: From Highway 101 (Sunshine Coast Highway) at the western edge of Sechelt, go west on Redrooffs Road. In 1.7 km (1.1 mi), turn left into the parking lot at Sargeant Bay Provincial Park. Walk back to Redrooffs Road to find the trailhead on the north shoulder.

85
MOUNT DANIEL

Distance: 4.5 km (2.8 mi)
Time: 2 hours (round trip)
Elevation gain: 365 m (1,200 ft)
High point: 440 m (1,440 ft)

Quality: ★★★★
Difficulty: ■
Maps: NTS 92-F/9 Texada Island
Trailhead: 49°38'48" N, 124°00'22" W

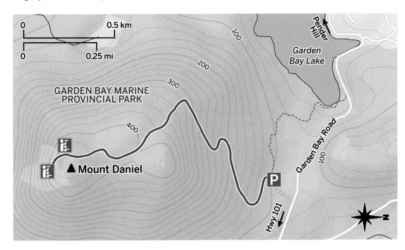

OVERLOOKING PENDER Harbour, Mount Daniel rises in the heart of shíshálh (Sechelt) Nation territory. Known as shélkém in the language of sháshishálem, this roche moutonnée, shaped by glaciers, has served as an important cultural, spiritual, and defence site for the shíshálh people. Today, Mount Daniel is protected by B.C.'s Garden Bay Marine Provincial Park and the First Nation's kálpilín–stséxwena kw'enit sim alap (Pender Harbour–Sakinaw Cultural Emphasis Area).

From the access road, the four-season trail zigzags south, making a steady ascent in a mixed forest with arbutus trees and a ferny understory. Dogs must be leashed in the park. Watch out for slugs and snails underfoot. A clearing on the right calls for a break, 45 minutes up. The trail jogs left and drops briefly before rising to bluff-top viewpoints near the summit (49°38'12" N, 124°00'25" W) 15 minutes later.

Feast on the delicious Salish Sea views. Garden Bay (séxw?ámin), Gerrans Bay, Lily Lake, Francis Peninsula, Bargain Bay, the Malaspina Strait and Strait of Georgia (sinkwu), and Texada Island (spílksen) lie below you to the southwest. Cecil Hill (wah-wey-we'-lath) looms across Gunboat Bay.

Cairn on Mount Daniel (shélkém).

SHORTER OPTION
Pender Hill (231 m/760 ft; 49°38′24″ N, 124°03′19″ W) overlooks the entrance to Pender Harbour. Short and steep, it's a 1-hour round trip (3 km/ 1.9 mi) to the top. Dogs must be on-leash. Find Pender Hill Park at 4331 Coastview Drive, west of the Mount Daniel trailhead, via Garden Bay Road, Irvines Landing Road, and Lee Road.

Both Mount Daniel and Pender Hill make ideal outings for cycle campers staying at Porpoise Bay Provincial Park on Sechelt Inlet. Bike the Suncoaster Trail to bypass a chunk of Highway 101.

GETTING THERE
Vehicle: From Highway 101 (Sunshine Coast Highway) in Kleindale, 35 km (21 mi) north of Sechelt, head west on Garden Bay Road. Three km (1.9 mi) later, after passing Oyster Bay Road, turn left onto a dirt road. Park near the entrance, or just up the road where a Mount Daniel sign points to the left fork.

86
FAIRVIEW BAY

Distance: 13.5 km (8.4 mi)
Time: 4 hours (round trip)
Elevation gain: 95 m (310 ft)
High point: 100 m (330 ft)

Quality: ★★★
Difficulty: ●
Maps: NTS 92-F/16 Haslam Lake, Tourism
Powell River Recreation Map
Trailhead: 49°47'03" N, 124°10'30" W

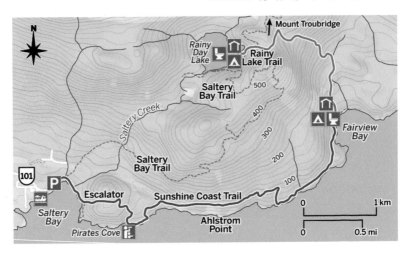

JOLTED INTO action by the disappearing old-growth forests of the Upper Sunshine Coast, Eagle Walz and his merry band of outdoor enthusiasts began building the Sunshine Coast Trail (Hikes 87, 88, and 89) in 1992 and formed the Powell River Parks and Wilderness Society in 1993. Completed circa 2000, the SCT extends from Sarah Point (saysimaʔaq) on Desolation Sound to Saltery Bay on Jervis Inlet, within the Powell River Regional District and Tla'amin Nation territory. An end-to-end journey of 10-plus days, the epic footpath covers 178 km (111 mi), boasts thirteen huts, and forms part of the National Hiking Trail.

To day-hike the final leg of the SCT, set out from the Saltery Bay trailhead on the scenic Fairview Bay Trail. Follow the SCT distance markers and signs east for 6.8 km (4.2 mi). Cross Saltery Creek, keep left at the next junction, ascend the Escalator switchbacks, and arrive at the Pirates Cove picnic site.

The SCT heads up to a power line road and east to the big hydro pylons at Ahlstrom Point, near a noisy fish farm, before getting lower and closer to the water. Feel the peeling reddish-brown bark and greenish under-bark of an arbutus. Also known as Pacific madrone, this iconic broadleaf evergreen tree is found within 8 km (5 mi) of the ocean on the South Coast.

Purple sea star in the intertidal zone at Fairview Bay.

Lovely Fairview Bay Hut (49°47'23" N, 124°07'19" W) is the southern-most and only seaside overnight shelter on the SCT. Peruse the logbook for the reflections of thru-hikers. The rocky beach outside is littered with oyster shells, purple sea stars, and rusty chains. Once you've drunk in the views, return the way you came.

Thinking about thru-hiking or section-hiking the SCT? Walz's *The Sunshine Coast Trail* (4th edition, End of the Road Press, 2013) is the essential guide.

LONGER OPTION

Experience more of the Sunshine Coast Trail by continuing 2.7 km (1.7 mi) north to the Rainy Day Lake Trail junction (450 m/1,480 ft; 49°48'01" N, 124°08'13" W). Hang a left to reach Rainy Day Lake Hut, an open shelter with a sleeping loft, on Hailstone Bluff in 500 m (0.3 mi). Take a dip in the lake!

Spend a night or two at the hut and ascend Mount Troubridge (1,305 m/ 4,280 ft; 49°48'44" N, 124°10'07" W). The highest summit on the SCT is 9.7 km (6 mi) north of Rainy Day Lake via the East Mount Troubridge Trail. From the lake, the Saltery Bay Trail provides an alternative but less scenic way back to the trailhead.

GETTING THERE

Transit: Powell River Regional Transit Bus 12 (Stillwater) offers limited request-stop service to Saltery Bay (call 604-483-2008 to book).
Vehicle: At the entrance to the B.C. Ferries terminal at Saltery Bay, southeast of Powell River, turn east from Highway 101 (Sunshine Coast Highway) onto Saltery Bay Forest Service Road. Go 200 m (0.1 mi) to the SCT trailhead kiosk and parking lot.

87
WALT HILL

Distance: 22.5 km (14 mi)
Time: 8 hours (round trip)
Elevation gain: 890 m (2,920 ft)
High point: 1,050 m (3,440 ft)

Quality: ★★★
Difficulty: ■
Maps: NTS 92-F/16 Haslam Lake, Tourism Powell River Recreation Map
Trailhead: 49°47'46" N, 124°19'43" W

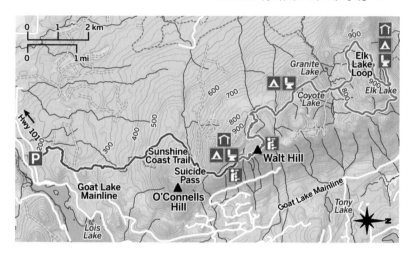

TO BACKPACK the entire Sunshine Coast Trail (Hikes 86, 88, and 89) is to take a long walk in the woods. Indeed, staring up at "grandpa trees" is a big highlight of the journey through Tla'amin Nation territory. However, clearcuts are also a major part of the SCT experience. Indeed, a newfound interest in or renewed concern about silvicultural practices in B.C. is one potential side effect of the trek.

On the hike to Walt Hill (officially named Walts Hill) in the Smith Range, you'll make use of an old logging rail grade, tour cutblocks and riparian management zones, and spend quality time in lush forest. Keep an eye out for reroutes due to logging. From Dixon Road, go northbound on the Eagle River Trail section of the SCT, following the trademark orange markers as they count down from kilometre 134 to kilometre 123 (in relation to the northernmost trailhead at Sarah Point, also known as saysimaʔaq). Deer and sword ferns and salal line the path. Bears also frequent this area.

In short order, cross Goat Lake Mainline (49°48'27" N, 124°19'24" W) and ascend Smokey's Blue Ridge Trail (4.2 km/2.6 mi) on the lower slopes of O'Connells Hill. Clusters of Pacific golden chanterelle cover the mossy forest

Looking north to Dodd Lake from Walt Hill on the Sunshine Coast Trail.

floor. On the far side of another logging road, the Suicide Pass Trail (2 km/ 1.2 mi) follows a rail grade and creek up to the Walt Hill Trail for the final push. Cross Walt Creek and climb steeply among old-growth, pausing to savour the occasional vista.

Walt Hill Hut, a cozy winterized cabin, awaits atop Penstemon Bluff (49°51′21″ N, 124°19′39″ W). A water source is accessed via a dark spur just up the trail. At sunset, the scenery from the bluff is sublime. The eastern lakes of the Powell Forest Canoe Route—Dodd, Horseshoe, and Lois—lie in the Horseshoe Valley below. Beyond looms Mount Troubridge—the highest summit on the SCT—and The Knuckles. Return the way you came.

LONGER OPTION

Explore more of the Sunshine Coast Trail and Smith Range by staying a night or two and continuing on to Elk Lake (49°53′55″ N, 124°22′21″ W). The pretty lake, with its open shelter and swimming dock, is found 14 km (8.7 mi) to the north via either side of the Elk Lake Loop.

GETTING THERE

Transit: Powell River Regional Transit Bus 12 (Stillwater) offers service to Lang Bay three times a day, four days a week (call 604-483-2008 to book). From the bus stop, walk north on Dixon Road.

Vehicle: On Highway 101 (Sunshine Coast Highway) at Lang Bay, 12 km (7.5 mi) west of the B.C. Ferries terminal at Saltery Bay, turn north on Dixon Road, which turns to gravel. About 2 km (1.2 mi) from the highway, look for the Sunshine Coast Trail crossing the road.

88
CONFEDERATION LAKE

Distance: 20 km (12.4 mi)
Time: 7 hours (round trip)
Elevation gain: 530 m (1,740 ft)
High point: 630 m (2,070 ft)

Quality: ★★★
Difficulty: ■
Maps: NTS 92-F/16 Haslam Lake, Tourism Powell River Recreation Map
Trailhead: 49°55'01" N, 124°28'57" W

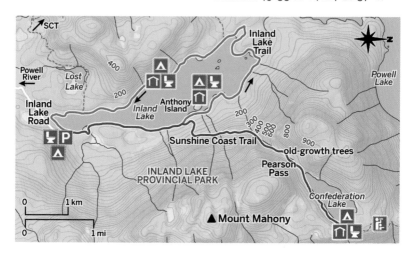

OLD-GROWTH WESTERN red cedar and Douglas fir trees are the giants of British Columbia's coastal western hemlock biogeoclimatic zone. By definition, "old-growth" refers to trees on the B.C. coast more than 250 years old and in the Interior over 120 or 140 years old, depending on forest type. Ancient groves of *Thuja plicata* and *Pseudotsuga menziesii* are the raison d'être of the 178 km (111 mi) Sunshine Coast Trail (Hikes 86, 87, and 89). You'll understand why on the hike to secluded Confederation Lake in Tla'amin Nation territory.

From the B.C. Parks campground, head counterclockwise on the scenic and wheelchair-accessible Inland Lake Trail. Dogs must be on-leash, and open fires are prohibited. Inland Lake (Thah yelh to the Tla'amin) is an optional side trip on the Powell Forest Canoe Route, an epic paddle entailing eight lakes and five portages over 57 km (35 mi).

After 2.8 km (1.7 mi), turn right and away from the lake on the strenuous Confederation Lake Trail (49°56'29" N, 124°29'06" W). Follow SCT signs for another 7.3 km (4.5 mi) as you gain height on the lush western slopes of Mount Mahony. A set of stairs and switchbacks help negotiate the stubbornly

The Confederation Lake Trail tackles steep woods.

steep climb. There are plenty of majestic trees to hug and intriguing mushrooms to see.

The grade relents as you crest Pearson Pass and continue around the east shore of Confederation Lake (named by the Powell River Wilderness Access Group in the 1970s) in its lofty bowl. In 2016, the Powell River Parks and Wilderness Society constructed a new Confederation Lake Hut (49°58'33" N, 124°27'20" W) next to the original, deteriorating log cabin near the 74 km (46 mi) mark of the SCT. Use the composting toilet and contemplate the peaceful surroundings. A sign just past the cabin may entice you farther: Vomit Vista lies 800 m (0.5 mi) north. Retrace your steps to Inland Lake on the return.

SHORTER OPTION
Leave Confederation Lake for another day and circumnavigate Inland Lake, also known as Loon Lake. The easy 13 km (8.1 mi) loop takes 3 hours. Along the way, stop for a swim at Anthony Island and enjoy numerous boardwalks, campsites (fee required), picnic spots, and fishing wharves. There are wheelchair-accessible huts on Anthony Island and on the west side of Inland Lake.

GETTING THERE
Vehicle: From the B.C. Ferries terminal at Saltery Bay, drive northwest on Highway 101 (Sunshine Coast Highway) for 25 km (16 mi), continuing onto Thunder Bay Street in Powell River. Turn right on Joyce Avenue and, when it ends, left on Manson Street. Go right on Cassiar Street, left on Yukon Avenue, and right on Haslam Street. Turn left on the gravel Inland Lake Road, right at the Haywire Bay Road intersection, and left in Inland Lake Provincial Park to reach the parking lot.

89
MANZANITA BLUFF

Distance: 10.5 km (6.5 mi)
Time: 4.5 hours (round trip)
Elevation gain: 165 m (540 ft)
High point: 340 m (1,115 ft)

Quality: ★★
Difficulty: ■
Maps: NTS 92-F/15, 92-K/2; Tourism
Powell River Recreation Map
Trailhead: 49°58'24" N, 124°42'35" W

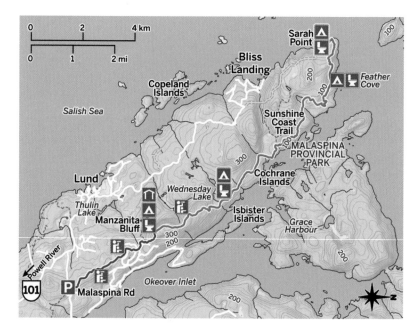

ON ITS 178 km (111 mi) journey from Sarah Point to Saltery Bay, the Sunshine Coast Trail (Hikes 86, 87, and 88) traverses lands subject to the laws of the Tla'amin Nation. In 2016, a treaty between the Tla'amin, Canada, and British Columbia took effect. The SCT has its own appendix in the final agreement, addressing such issues as trail maintenance and public access. The Malaspina Peninsula section of the SCT, north of Powell River (Tees kwat to the Tla'amin), is a popular destination for day and overnight hikes. Manzanita Bluff is its scenic zenith.

From Malaspina Road, go north on the Gwendoline Hills Trail, quickly encountering old-growth Douglas fir giants. Reforested clear-cuts follow, before Three K Bluff, 2.8 km (1.7 mi) in, grants a vista of Okeover Inlet. Heed the SCT signs and ignore westward turnoffs. Don't forget to fill your water

Manzanita Hut is a BYOW (bring your own water) overnight shelter.

bottles at Thulin Springs, 1 km (0.6 mi) later. The trail is dry from here to Wednesday Creek, on the far side of lovely Manzanita Hut (50°00'09" N, 124°44'23" W), which you reach after 5.3 km (3.3 mi) of hiking.

Erected in 2011, the partially enclosed shelter contains a sleeping loft with space for eight. A perfectly placed wooden bench overlooks crescent-shaped Savary Island (Kayikwen) and the Salish Sea. If you overnight in an SCT hut, consider making a donation to the Powell River Parks and Wilderness Society, whose tireless volunteers build and maintain the trail and its facilities.

Hairy manzanita is a shrub with peeling red bark that bears some resemblance to the beloved arbutus tree. Growing up to a few metres tall, these plants bloom with white flowers in early spring and are at home on rock outcrops. Look for them around the bluff and on the way back to Malaspina Road.

LONGER OPTION

Keep going to kilometre 0 of the Sunshine Coast Trail. Where the Gwendoline Hills Trail ends, the Land's End Trail begins. Over 16 km (9.9 mi), the path north of Manzanita Bluff enters Malaspina and Desolation Sound Marine Provincial Parks (which also lie in Klahoose First Nation territory), visits Wednesday Lake and Hinder Lake, and passes Feather Cove (sawʊsʔamɛn). Stock up on fresh water at the lakes; there's no source at the Sarah Point (saysimaʔaq) campsite (50°03'41" N, 124°50'31" W; backcountry camping permit required).

GETTING THERE

Transit: Powell River Regional Transit Bus 14 (Lund) offers by-request service to Highway 101 at Malaspina Road. Walk 1.4 km (0.9 mi) east on Malaspina Road.

Vehicle: From Powell River, drive north on Highway 101 (Sunshine Coast Highway) toward Lund. At 18 km (11 mi) past the Powell River bridge, turn east on Malaspina Road. In 1.4 km (0.9 mi), the trailhead is on the left.

90
MOUNT ERSKINE

Distance: 5.5 km (3.4 mi)
Time: 2.5 hours (lollipop)
Elevation gain: 380 m (1,245 ft)
High point: 448 m (1,470 ft)

Quality: ★★★★★
Difficulty: ■
Maps: NTS 92-B/13 Duncan, Wild Coast Gulf Islands
Trailhead: 48°51'23" N, 123°33'33" W

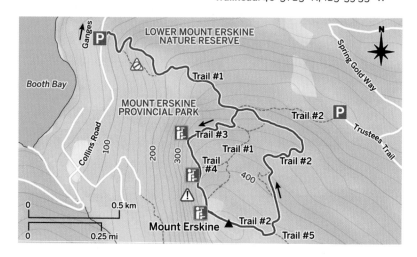

SURE, MOUNT Erskine isn't the loftiest peak on Saltspring Island, in the territories of the Hul'qumi'num Treaty Group and Hwlitsum, Tsawwassen, and W̱SÁNEĆ First Nations. Those bragging rights belong to Bruce Peak. No matter—Erskine is undoubtedly the most magical of Saltspring's prominences.

From Collins Road, enter the Islands Trust Fund's Lower Mount Erskine Nature Reserve, home to arbutus and hairy manzanita groves. Keep left at the first fork. At the Mount Erskine Provincial Park boundary, the Jack Fisher Trail becomes the Mount Erskine Trail (Trail #1). Map boards assist with navigation. A half-hour in, follow Trail #1 right at a four-way junction to start a counterclockwise loop.

Go right at the next fork for Trail #3 to discover charming little fairy doors and two enchanting viewpoints popular with dragonflies. To the northwest, the Shoal Islands and Penelakut Island line Stuart Channel. (Penelakut was the site of the Catholic-run Kuper Island residential school, where Coast Salish children were subjected to cruel experiments, sexual abuse, and other atrocities. Opened in 1890, the school finally closed circa 1975.)

Trail #4 enters from the left before the upper viewpoint, after which Trail

There be fairy doors on Trail #3.

#3 swings sharply left at a log with an orange marker. A fairy door lies on the other side. (A sketchy path continues south, passing a cave before petering out on a ledge. An exposed scramble and more ledges ensue. Not for kids or acrophobes.)

Trail #3 merges with Trail #1 en route to the avuncular summit (48°50′ 50″ N, 123°32′59″ W) with its expansive views. A concrete water bowl is dedicated to Rosie the dog (1990–2001), a wooden memorial bench offers a breather, and a capsule houses a logbook that awaits your insight du jour.

Continue southeast to pick up mellow Trail #2. Turn left at the junction with Trail #5. Descend in shady forest to the four-way junction, where you go straight to follow Trail #1 back to the trailhead.

Dogs must be leashed in Mount Erskine Provincial Park, established in 2006 after a Salt Spring Island Conservancy–led campaign. The largest of the Gulf Islands is known as Klaathem to the Cowichan Tribes and ĆUÁN to the W̱SÁNEĆ.

GETTING THERE

Vehicle: B.C. Ferries offers daily sailings to Saltspring Island via three routes: Tsawwassen–Long Harbour, Swartz Bay–Fulford Harbour, and Crofton–Vesuvius Bay. From the Long Harbour terminal, head west on Long Harbour Road. Turn left on Upper Ganges Road and right on Lower Ganges Road. Go left on Booth Canal Road, which merges with Rainbow Road. (From Fulford Harbour, take Fulford-Ganges Road north to Lower Ganges Road, where you go left. Turn left on Rainbow Road.) Take a left on Collins Road. In 750 m (0.5 mi), the trailhead is on the left.

91
MOUNT MAXWELL

Distance: 6.5 km (4 mi)
Time: 2.5 hours (lollipop)
Elevation gain: 280 m (920 ft)
High point: 593 m (1,945 ft)

Quality: ★★★
Difficulty: ◼
Maps: NTS 92-B/13 Duncan, 92-B/14 Mayne Island; Wild Coast Gulf Islands
Trailhead: 48°48'19" N, 123°29'42" W

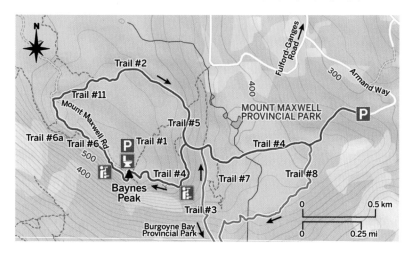

KNOWN AS Hwmet'utsum to the Hul'qumi'num people, Mount Maxwell on Saltspring Island is designated as a Hul'qumi'num Mustimuhw intensive traditional-use area for its importance as a cultural and resource-harvesting site. From the top, scan the vicinity for bald eagles, red-tailed hawks, and turkey vultures.

Strike off west on the Salt Spring Parks and Recreation Commission's Armand Way Trail (Trail #4). (No smoking, fires, or camping. Dogs must be leashed.) Breach the B.C. Parks boundary, stay right at junctions with Trails #8 and #7, cross Trail #3, and sweat your way up the steep path. Keep left to stick with Trail #4, and begin a clockwise loop. Soon, encounter foxgloves, grasses, and wow views of Fulford Harbour (Hwnen'uts), Portland Island, the San Juan Islands, and Mount Baker. Trail #4 swings right to meet Trail #1 near the mountaintop toilets and parking lot.

Find the conglomerate summit of Baynes Peak (1 hour up; 48°48'05" N, 123°31'02" W) above fenced-off cliffs flocked to by picture-taking sightseers who drove all the way up. Look out at Burgoyne Bay (Xwaaqw'um) and Maple Bay (Hwtl'upnets) in Sansum Narrows. Peregrine falcons, a species of special

Mount Maxwell (Hwmet'utsum) overlooks Burgoyne Bay (Xwaaqw'um).

concern in Canada, nest on the escarpment. Bold Bluff Point, to the southwest, is a fabled home of the Thunderbird (*S'hwa'hwa'us*).

Follow the fence west to pick up the Rim Trail (#6). Keep right to take the Brian Trail (#11) across Mount Maxwell Road and the Gary Trail (#2) east to the Link Trail (#5), ignoring Trail #1 on the left and then the right. Upon reaching Trail #4, turn left to return to Armand Way.

Created in 1938, Mount Maxwell Provincial Park protects Garry oak ecosystems and old-growth Douglas firs, and it neighbours Mount Maxwell Ecological Reserve and Burgoyne Bay Provincial Park. Stay on trails and abide by "Pack it in, pack it out" ethics. Saltspring Island lies in the territories of the Hul'qumi'num Treaty Group and Hwlitsum, Tsawwassen, and W̱SÁNEĆ First Nations. It's known as Klaathem to the Cowichan Tribes and ĆUÁN to the W̱SÁNEĆ.

LONGER OPTION
Expand your outing to include Daffodil Point. Drop down the Sunshine Trail (#8) and Girlfriend Trail (#3) to access the Boulders Trail (#10) and Daffodil Trail (#9) in Burgoyne Bay Provincial Park.

GETTING THERE
Vehicle: B.C. Ferries offers daily sailings to Saltspring Island via three routes: Tsawwassen–Long Harbour, Swartz Bay–Fulford Harbour, and Crofton–Vesuvius Bay. From the Long Harbour terminal, head west on Long Harbour Road. Turn left on Upper Ganges Road and right on Lower Ganges Road. Take a right on Fulford-Ganges Road. (From Fulford Harbour, take Fulford-Ganges Road north.) Turn west on Dukes Road. Go left on Seymour Heights (gravel) and left on Armand Way to the cul-de-sac.

92
MOUNT WORK

Distance: 6 km (3.7 mi)
Time: 2.5 hours (round trip)
Elevation gain: 300 m (985 ft)
High point: 449 m (1,475 ft)

Quality: ★★
Difficulty: ●
Maps: NTS 92-B/11 Sidney, TRIM 092B053
Trailhead: 48°33'00" N, 123°29'24" W

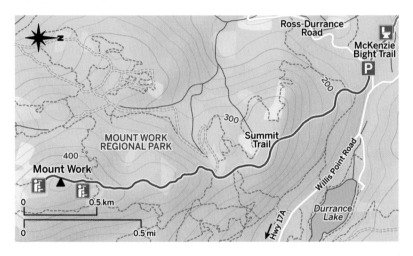

MOUNT WORK is gneiss—its exposed bedrock is, at least—and popular with trail runners. The highest peak on the Saanich Peninsula is a monadnock that survived the erosion of the Fraser Glaciation, 15,000 years ago. It's in the Gowlland Range, part of the Insular Mountains, which run from Vancouver Island to Haida Gwaii.

From the map board at Mount Work Regional Park's large gravel parking lot (open sunrise to sunset), start up the wide path. In 180 m (0.1 mi), fork right for the Summit Trail. The understory includes bracket fungi, Oregon grape, and sword fern. As you ascend southward, the mixed forest thins out and arbutus trees, with peeling cinnamon bark, increase in numbers. Look for yellow plates to stay on the rocky and rooty trail, and ignore numerous side paths.

In 1 hour, reach a broad viewpoint overlooking Jocelyn Hill (Hike 93), Pease Lake, and Saanich Inlet, a glacially carved fjord, to the northwest. Kinnikinnick and hairy manzanita line the path. A metal sign marks the view-challenged summit (48°31'51" N, 123°28'49" W), 2.9 km (1.8 mi) up.

Don't stop here; continue several minutes south for mossy ground, open rock, and expansive views. Watch the ravens and bald eagles, and survey the

Mount Work is the top of the Saanich Peninsula.

subdivisions on Skirt Mountain (SPAET to the W̱SÁNEĆ people), Mount Finlayson (W̱QENNELEL; Hike 94), the anchorage of Royal Roads, the Salish Sea, and Washington's snowy Olympic Mountains to the south. Return the way you came.

Mount Work Regional Park sits on land subject to the 1852 Douglas Treaty covering North Saanich and lies within the territories of the Malahat and W̱SÁNEĆ First Nations. The mountain is named for John Wark (c. 1792–1861), a chief factor of the Hudson's Bay Company and legislative councillor for the British crown colony of the Island of Vancouver and its Dependencies. No smoking, fires, camping, or flower-picking.

LONGER OPTION
Legs aren't sufficiently worked? After summiting Mount Work, cross Ross-Durrance Road to enter Gowlland Tod Provincial Park. Follow the McKenzie Bight Trail to the shore of Saanich Inlet and back.

GETTING THERE
Vehicle: On Highway 17A (West Saanich Road) in Saanich, north of Victoria, turn west on Wallace Drive. Go left on Willis Point Road. Take a left on Ross-Durrance Road to enter Highlands and find Mount Work Regional Park's main entrance on the left.

93
JOCELYN HILL

Distance: 9 km (5.6 mi)
Time: 4 hours (circuit)
Elevation gain: 210 m (690 ft)
High point: 434 m (1,425 ft)

Quality: ★★★★
Difficulty: ●
Maps: NTS 92-B/12 Shawnigan Lake,
TRIM 092B053
Trailhead: 48°30'32" N, 123°31'57" W

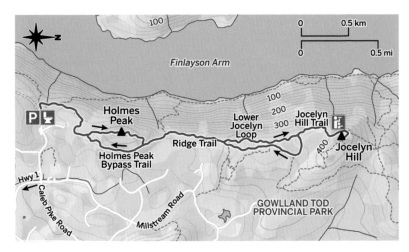

RISING IN the Gowlland Range of the Saanich Peninsula, Jocelyn Hill over-looks deep and steep-sided Finlayson Arm. Orcas, grey and pilot whales, and harbour seals frequent this unique fjord, which sees its anoxic water refreshed only once a year. Jocelyn Hill is the centrepiece of Gowlland Tod Provincial Park, created in 1995 as part of the Commonwealth Nature Legacy Program, in the territories of the Malahat and W̱SÁNEĆ First Nations.

Set off north on the undulating Ridge Trail, quickly turning right at a fork but thereafter keeping left all the way. Follow orange markers on rocks and trees under two sets of transmission lines with Scotch broom–infested corridors and up the wooded ridge. Spurning a bypass trail, surmount Holmes Peak (327 m/1,070 ft; 48°30'59" N, 123°31'47" W) in 1.3 km (0.8 mi). Pause and take a gander at the Warwick Range across Finlayson Arm, accompanied by the noise pollution of Malahat Drive.

Continue north along the lovely, lovely ridge (good for trail running and rainy days). Watch your step on the bluffs. Stay on designated trails to preserve the sensitive habitat of the rare, rain-shadowed coastal Douglas fir biogeoclimatic zone. Logged in the 1940s and '50s, the uplands are speckled

Finlayson Arm, viewed from Holmes Peak, is a fjord.

with very gneiss outcrops adorned with arbutus (B.C.'s only evergreen broad-leaf tree), hairy manzanita (a shrub related to arbutus), shore pine, and Garry oak.

En route to the Lower Jocelyn Loop fork, you're treated to more sweet views of Finlayson Arm. Stay left for the Jocelyn Hill Trail. The best vantages come before the summit, when you break out of the trees and onto stunning mossy bluffs. The trail U-turns before arriving at the Jocelyn Hill viewpoint (48°32'16" N, 123°31'47" W), off to the left at the 4.4 km (2.7 mi) mark.

Jocelyn Hill was officially named on a British admiralty chart in 1911, two decades before the Dominion of Canada gained independence with the passage of the Statute of Westminster. From the grassy, arbutus-fringed outcrop, gaze north up Squally Reach to the mouth of Saanich Inlet and Saltspring Island (ĆUÁN in the SENĆOŦEN language of the W̱SÁNEĆ) beyond. Malahat Ridge rises across the fjord.

Retrace your steps to the Caleb Pike entrance. Vary portions of your return by taking the eastern branch of the Lower Jocelyn Loop and the Holmes Peak Bypass Trail. Fires are prohibited in Gowlland Tod, and dogs must be on-leash in provincial parks.

GETTING THERE

Vehicle: On Trans-Canada Highway 1 in Langford, west of Victoria, take Exit 14. Proceed north on Millstream Road to Highlands. In 6.5 km (4 mi), turn left on Caleb Pike Road and pull into Gowlland Tod Provincial Park's south entrance.

94
MOUNT FINLAYSON

Distance: 7 km (4.3 mi)
Time: 2.5 hours (loop)
Elevation gain: 415 m (1,360 ft)
High point: 419 m (1,375 ft)

Quality: ★★★
Difficulty: ◆
Maps: NTS 92-B/5 Sooke, TRIM
092B043
Trailhead: 48°28'44" N, 123°32'45" W

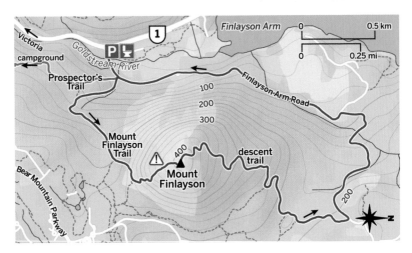

MOUNT FINLAYSON is known as WQENNELEL ("looking up") in the SENĆOŦEN language of the W̱SÁNEĆ Nation. In geomorphological terms, this rounded peak in the Gowlland Range is a roche moutonnée eroded by a passing glacier. For hikers, it's the big draw in Goldstream Provincial Park, even though it was only added to the park in 1994.

From the day-use area, walk east on Finlayson Arm Road over the salmon-bearing Goldstream River. Find the start of the steep Mount Finlayson Trail (and the end of the Prospector's Trail) on the right. (No camping or fires. Dogs must be leashed. Not recommended for young kids or rainy days.) Keeping left, ascend Finlayson's lower slopes, heading southeast and then northeast under cover of western red cedar, Douglas fir, and bigleaf maple. After dropping to cross a creek, the wide, rooty, and rocky path rockets up through the arbutus trees following orange bars.

In a half-hour, reach the bluffs. Get ready for some scrambly fun. Heeding arrows, head up the rock and traverse to the right. (Dangerous when wet!) Follow a crack up to a ramp that rises to the right, but cut back left before it tops out. Notice the profusion of yellow flowers belonging to Scotch broom,

Mount Finlayson (WQENNELEL) is an example of a roche moutonnée.

an invasive ornamental shrub. Also take note of the urban sprawl encroaching on the woody blanket of Skirt Mountain (SPAET) to the south.

Ascend more ramps to the right, and switchback up ledges and rocky slopes to the open summit (48°28'58" N, 123°32'18" W), with its commemorative plaques, after 1.7 km (1.1 mi) and 1 hour of hiking. Spot the turkey vultures. Gaze south at the snow-capped Olympic Mountains across the Juan de Fuca Strait, and see Mount Wells, another roche moutonnée.

Arrows point the way to the mellow second half of today's counterclockwise loop. Keep left on the descent trail as it zigzags 2.2 km (1.4 mi) north to Finlayson Arm Road. Hang a left and follow the quiet byroad for 3.1 km (1.9 mi) to the day-use area. Established in 1958, Goldstream Provincial Park lies within the territories of the Malahat and W̱SÁNEĆ First Nations and was the site of a gold rush in the mid-1800s.

LONGER OPTION

For an extended hike to Mount Finlayson, start at the Goldstream campground instead of the day-use area. Set off northwest on the Prospector's Trail (1.5 km/0.9 mi), which joins the Mount Finlayson Trail to the summit.

GETTING THERE

Vehicle: On Trans-Canada Highway 1 in Langford, 16 km (10 mi) northwest of Victoria, turn east on Finlayson Arm Road to enter the Goldstream Provincial Park day-use area. (South of the day-use area, go west on West Shore Parkway from Highway 1 to reach the campground via Amy Road, Sooke Lake Road, and Golden Gate Road.)

95
FRAGRANCE LAKE

Distance: 13 km (8 mi)
Time: 5 hours (circuit)
Elevation gain: 541 m (1,775 ft)
High point: 559 m (1,835 ft)

Quality: ★
Difficulty: ■
Maps: USGS Bellingham South, Square One Chuckanut Recreation Area
Trailhead: 48°39'12" N, 122°29'24" W

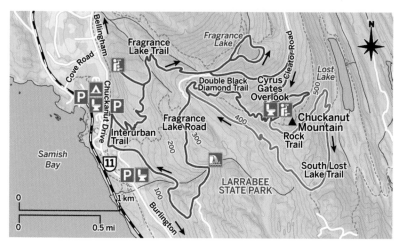

DESIGNATED AS a Washington State scenic byway, Chuckanut Drive attracts many drivers and cyclists to its winding roadbed between Bellingham and Burlington. There are plenty of reasons for hikers, mountain bikers, and horse riders to visit too, with more than a dozen trails penetrating the Chuckanut Mountains, which overlook the Salish Sea's Puget Sound. Fragrance Lake is one of the most popular destinations.

From Chuckanut Drive, the Fragrance Lake Trail leads uphill into the woods, across the Interurban Trail, and to a junction. Go left to see Samish Bay from a viewpoint. Push on to reach the lake (no camping—but the swimming is excellent), 3 km (1.9 mi) from the trailhead, after 1.5 hours of hiking. The scenic lake loop covers 1 km (0.6 mi), passes sandstone outcrops, and provides ample reward for your modest efforts thus far.

Done with the loop, double back on the Fragrance Lake Trail to its junction with Fragrance Lake Road, where you go left and head east to Cleator Road. Turn right and ascend the gravel (watch out for vehicles) to arrive at Cyrus Gates Overlook, the day's high point, 3 hours in. An interpretative panel helps identify Orcas Island, Chuckanut Bay, and "Canada."

Winter hike on the Fragrance Lake Trail.

Find a trailhead at the other end of the overlook and keep right to drop down the steep and fun Double Black Diamond Trail, with its mountain-bike twists and turns. Turn left when you hit Fragrance Lake Road to loop back, with a waterfall for eye candy, to the Interurban Trail (right) and the trailhead. The Interurban Trail is a link in the multi-use Coast Millennium Trail, a cross-border project that aims to connect Blanchard, Washington, and White Rock, B.C.

Rising in the traditional territory of the Lummi (Lhaq'temish) Nation and straddling Whatcom and Skagit counties, the Chuckanut foothills are overseen by a patchwork of agencies. In 1915, Larrabee State Park became Washington's first state park. Other protected areas include the City of Bellingham's Arroyo Park, Whatcom County's Chuckanut Mountain Park, and Washington Department of Fish and Wildlife's Whatcom Wildlife Area. Meanwhile, logging continues in the Washington Department of Natural Resources' Blanchard Forest Block. Conservation Northwest is one of the organizations working to protect this beloved area.

LONGER OPTION

From the Cyrus Gates trailhead, the Rock Trail plunges east to the South Lost Lake Trail. Built by the Washington Trails Association, the 600 m (0.4 mi) route features sandstone cliffs and caves. Turn right to loop back to Fragrance Lake Road in 3 km (2 mi).

GETTING THERE

Vehicle: From Interstate 5 (Exit 250) in Bellingham, drive west on State Route 11 (Old Fairhaven Parkway). Go left on 12th Street and left on Chuckanut Drive. Follow SR 11 south to milepost 15. Park at the Fragrance Lake trailhead on the left, or turn right into Larrabee State Park's main entrance and park by the picnic area. Discover Pass required (purchase in advance).

96
OYSTER DOME

Distance: 14 km (8.7 mi)
Time: 6 hours (circuit)
Elevation gain: 583 m (1,910 ft)
High point: 627 m (2,060 ft)

Quality: ★★★
Difficulty: ■
Maps: USGS Bellingham South, Bow;
Square One Chuckanut Recreation Area
Trailhead: 48°36'31" N, 122°26'00" W

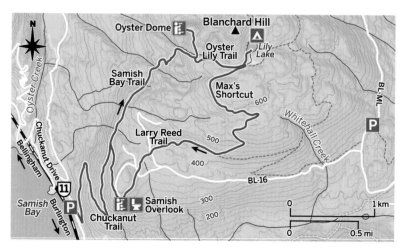

IN HER 2012 memoir *Wild*, author Cheryl Strayed vividly recounts backpacking 40 per cent of the Mexico-to-Canada Pacific Crest Trail. A more recent addition to the U.S. national trails system is the Pacific Northwest Trail in Montana, Idaho, and Washington. To get a quick taste of the PNT—and an excellent south-of-the-border perspective on the Salish Sea—get thee to Blanchard Hill of the Chuckanut Mountains, in Skagit County and the traditional territory of the Lummi (Lhaq'temish) Nation.

The enjoyable loop described here lies in the Blanchard Forest Block, which is managed by the Washington Department of Natural Resources. Begin on the busy Chuckanut Trail, switchbacking up the steep hillside east of Chuckanut Drive and earning a view of Samish Bay. In 2.3 km (1.4 mi), leave the PNT for the time being and turn left on the Samish Bay Trail (1.8 km/ 1.1 mi), which starts out mellow before making a sweat-inducing ascent to the Oyster Dome turnoff. Head left and up to a rocky clifftop (3 hours in) with views of Fidalgo Island and the San Juan Islands.

After lunch, return to the last junction and turn left (east) on the Oyster Lily Trail for 0.6 km (0.4 mi). Go left for a brief side trip to Lily Lake, where

Max's Shortcut, part of the Montana-to-Washington Pacific Northwest Trail.

there's a campground, then return and continue east. With a quick right turn, rejoin the PNT and head south on the quiet Max's Shortcut (2.3 km/1.4 mi) and the Larry Reed Trail (1.4 km/0.9 mi), which crosses a clear-cut. (Conservation Northwest has campaigned to permanently protect Blanchard's core from logging.)

Farmland fills the scene to the south of the vehicle-accessible Samish Overlook (48°36′35″ N, 122°25′34″ W), which has toilets. Back on the Chuckanut Trail, it's just 3 km (1.9 mi) to the trailhead.

Dating back to the 1970s, the PNT runs 1,900 km (1,200 mi) from the Continental Divide to the Pacific Ocean. In 2009, the Pacific Northwest Trail Association celebrated its designation as a national scenic trail. Although a continuous non-motorized route is the goal, roads still make up a quarter of the PNT.

SHORTER OPTION

Foregoing the loop, a there-and-back hike to Oyster Dome via the Samish Bay Trail involves a round trip of 9 km (5.6 mi). This trail can be a highway on weekends and a mudfest after rain; try visiting on a weekday or in shoulder season instead.

GETTING THERE

Vehicle: From Interstate 5 (Exit 250) in Bellingham, drive west on State Route 11 (Old Fairhaven Parkway). Go left on 12th Street and left on Chuckanut Drive. Follow SR 11 south to find the trailhead on the east side just before milepost 10. Park on the west shoulder. Discover Pass required (purchase in advance).

97
PINE AND CEDAR LAKES TRAIL

Distance: 12 km (7.5 mi)
Time: 5 hours (circuit)
Elevation gain: 467 m (1,530 ft)
High point: 559 m (1,830 ft)

Quality: ★★
Difficulty: ■
Maps: USGS Bellingham South, Square One Chuckanut Recreation Area
Trailhead: 48°41'26" N, 122°27'10" W

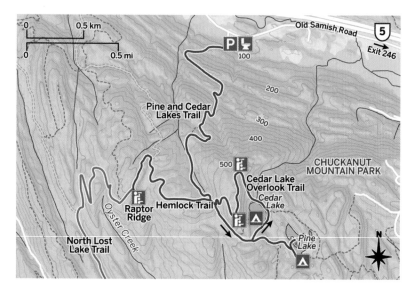

FOR MANY Metro Vancouver residents, Bellingham is synonymous with cross-border shopping and hazy memories of a pizza buffet. However, locals know there's decent hiking immediately south of the 85,000-strong "City of Subdued Excitement," in the sandstone foothills of the Chuckanut Mountains.

One of the pleasant shoulder-season hikes on Chuckanut Mountain itself is the Pine and Cedar Lakes Trail, which begins within earshot of the I-5 but finds peace and quiet in the woods. Located in Whatcom County and the traditional territory of the Lummi (Lhaq'temish) Nation, the trail passes through Larrabee State Park, Chuckanut Mountain Park, and the Whatcom Wildlife Area. (Dogs must be leashed.)

From the parking area, the multi-use trail winds south for 2.6 km (1.6 mi) to a junction with the Hemlock Trail (490 m/1,600 ft). For now, go east (left) to stay on the Pine and Cedar Lakes Trail. Ignore the next few paths going left

Mount Baker (Kweq' Smánit) and Twin Sisters Mountain (Kwetl'kwítl' Smánit) from a viewpoint above Cedar Lake.

and follow boardwalks to one or both of the backcountry campsites (no fires) at Pine Lake, 3.5 km (2.2 mi) in.

Double back to the last Cedar Lake turnoff, and go right to round the northeast side of the lake. Turn right on the Cedar Lake Overlook Trail to visit a few viewpoints. The best vista features majestic Mount Baker (Kweq' Smánit [white mountain] in the Lhéchelesem language of the Nooksack Tribe) and Twin Sisters Mountain (Kwetl'kwítl' Smánit [red mountain]) of the Cascade Range. Past the high point, follow switchbacks down to the Pine and Cedar Lakes Trail and head back to the Hemlock Trail junction.

Before you retrace your steps to the trailhead, a side trip to Raptor Ridge is in order. About 1 km (0.6 mi) west on the Hemlock Trail, turn left on the Raptor Ridge Trail and soon left again for the signed viewpoint. This lovely, rocky spot overlooks the forested valley of Oyster Creek, providing ample reward for your efforts.

LONGER OPTION

From the viewpoint on Raptor Ridge, the trail continues 1.6 km (1 mi) west to the North Lost Lake Trail. Head south (left) to arrive at Lost Lake in another 3.2 km (2 mi) via the East Lost Lake Trail. Turn around at Lost Lake and return via the Hemlock Trail to the Pine and Cedar Lakes trailhead.

GETTING THERE

Vehicle: On Interstate 5, just south of Bellingham, take Exit 246. From either off-ramp, go right onto North Lake Samish Drive. On the south side of the freeway overpass, turn west onto Old Samish Road and drive 4.3 km (2.7 mi) to the Pine and Cedar Lakes trailhead on your left. Discover Pass required (purchase in advance).

98
MOUNT ERIE

Distance: 8 km (5 mi)
Time: 4 hours (reverse lollipop)
Elevation gain: 275 m (900 ft)
High point: 386 m (1,266 ft)

Quality: ★★
Difficulty: ●
Maps: USGS Anacortes South, Deception
Pass; Green Trails 41S Deception Pass
Trailhead: 48°28'03" N, 122°37'46" W

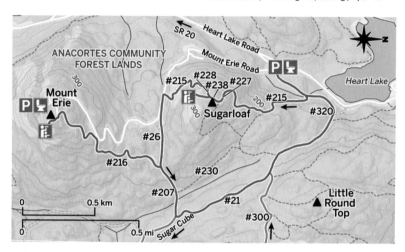

MANY VISITORS drive all the way up to the modest summit of Mount Erie, but its grand views are even more satisfying after a couple hours of hiking. The scenery includes Mount Baker (Teqwúbe7 to the Skagit people), Glacier Peak, Skagit Bay, and the Olympic Mountains—not to mention hawks and rock climbers.

The mountain is in the Anacortes Community Forest Lands, owned by the City of Anacortes on Fidalgo Island in Washington. In the 1980s, a public outcry halted clear-cutting in the forest. Since the creation of a conservation easement program in 1998, donors have protected much of the area from logging and mining. It's easy to get off track in the labyrinth of trails, so pay close attention to markers.

Strike off on Trail 215. Stay right at two junctions, then go left on Trail 227 and right on Trail 238 to reach the delectable viewpoint and grassy ledges atop Sugarloaf (310 m/1,017 ft), the day's appetizer, in 30 minutes. Spot your entrée, Mount Erie, and Skagit Bay to the south, as well as Whitehorse Mountain and Three Fingers to the east.

Briefly backtrack and turn west on Trail 228 and left on Trail 215 to hit Mount Erie Road. Follow the road east momentarily, taking a left on Trail 26.

Rock climbing anchor on Mount Erie.

Go right on Trail 216 and ascend the switchbacking, steepening path for 1.4 km (0.9 mi) to Mount Erie's car-park summit (48°27′13″ N, 122°37′36″ W). Take your pick of viewpoints.

After lunch, double back on Trail 216, but go right (east) on Trail 207 (not left on Trail 26) to vary your return. Keep right at the Trail 230 junction and turn left on Trail 21. Follow the double track for 1.4 km (0.9 mi), then make a left on Trail 320 and a right on Trail 215 to re-emerge at the trailhead.

The Friends of the Anacortes Community Forest Lands and Skagit Land Trust deserve credit for preserving these woods and their all-season, multi-use trails. Camping, hunting, and fires are prohibited. Dogs must be leashed and their poop packed out. Anacortes lies in the traditional territories of the Samish and Swinomish Tribes.

LONGER OPTION

Got room for dessert? Visit the hill known as Sugar Cube on the way back from Mount Erie to add 1.4 km (0.9 mi) to your trip. Head south (right) instead of north on Trail 21. Turn left on Trail 202, Trail 231, and Trail 300 to rejoin Trail 21, where you go right to return to the trailhead.

GETTING THERE

Vehicle: From Interstate 5 (Exit 230) in Burlington, take State Route 20 west to Anacortes. Go left at the SR 20 Spur junction to stay on the mainline. Turn right on Campbell Lake Road, stay right for Heart Lake Road, and go right at the Mount Erie viewpoint sign. Drive about 50 m (160 ft) to the parking lot and trailhead kiosk (don't turn right on Mount Erie Road).

99
HOYPUS HILL

Distance: 10.5 km (6.5 mi)
Time: 3 hours (loop)
Elevation gain: 134 m (440 ft)
High point: 134 m (440 ft)

Quality: ★
Difficulty: ●
Maps: USGS Anacortes South, Green Trails 41S Deception Pass
Trailhead: 48°24'04" N, 122°37'20" W

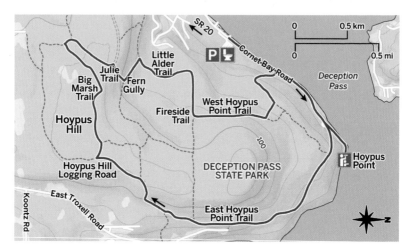

IT'S NO mystery why Deception Pass State Park is one of the busiest state parks in Washington. The historic Deception Pass Bridge—fictionalized as "Desolation Bridge" in the Vancouver-shot TV series *The Killing*—is simply stunning, the beaches have sand dunes, three campgrounds offer 167 tent sites, and a maze of trails explores the woods and shore.

Although the trails are quick affairs, a year-round, kid-friendly loop of sufficient length is possible on the Whidbey Island side of the park. From the gate on Cornet Bay Road, enter the Hoypus Point Natural Forest Area and continue northeast for 1.6 km (1 km), staying left at two junctions. Hoypus Point features the remains of a ferry terminal and views of Mount Erie (Hike 98) in Anacortes and Mount Baker (Teqwúbe7 to the Skagit people) on the mainland.

Double back to the nearest junction, turn left (east), and stick with the East Hoypus Point Trail (part of the Pacific Northwest Trail) for 3.2 km (2 mi) as it ascends Hoypus Hill and visits old-growth Douglas fir trees. Go left on Hoypus Hill Logging Road, right on the Big Marsh Trail, and right to rejoin the logging road.

Forest fork in Deception Pass State Park.

Then it's right on the Julie Trail, left for Fern Gully (ah, memories of the 1992 animated film *FernGully: The Last Rainforest*), and right on the Little Alder Trail, which leads to the Fireside Trail. Finally, turn left on the West Hoypus Point Trail and keep left to return to the Cornet Bay Road gate.

Sadly, the peace of the forest is rudely interrupted by noisy U.S. Navy jets from Naval Air Station Whidbey Island. The Deception Pass Park Foundation raises money to protect the park and support its educational programs. Before leaving the park, make sure to stop on Pass Island for a close-up look at the Deception Pass Bridge.

Interestingly, Deception Pass—which separates Fidalgo Island and Whidbey Island and connects the Salish Sea's Puget Sound and Strait of Juan de Fuca—was named by imperialist voyager Captain George Vancouver in 1792. It lies in the traditional territory of the Swinomish people.

SHORTER OPTION

Alternatively, three brief but superb coastal lollipop routes may be accessed from Bowman Bay on the Fidalgo Island side of Deception Pass State Park. Combine the Rosario Head, Lighthouse Point, and Lottie Point loops for a 7 km (4.3 mi) outing. To reach the trailhead, turn east onto Rosario Road from State Route 20, north of Deception Pass, and then go left on Bowman Bay Road.

GETTING THERE

Vehicle: From Interstate 5 (Exit 230) in Burlington, take State Route 20 west to Anacortes. Go left at the SR 20 Spur junction to stay on the mainline. After crossing Deception Pass, turn east (left) on Cornet Bay Road and drive 2.3 km (1.4 mi) to Deception Pass State Park's Cornet Bay boat launch and parking area. Discover Pass required (purchase in advance).

100
CATTLE POINT

Distance: 8 km (5 mi)
Time: 2.5 hours (reverse lollipop)
Elevation gain: 88 m (290 ft)
High point: 88 m (290 ft)

Quality: ★★★
Difficulty: ●
Maps: USGS Richardson, Great Pacific San Juan Islands
Trailhead: 48°27'49" N, 122°59'56" W

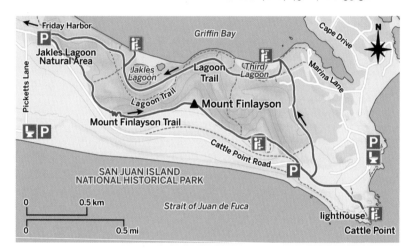

TRUE STORY: Back in 1859, the U.S. and the U.K. came to the brink of war over the shooting of a Hudson's Bay Company hog on San Juan Island. Following the Pig War incident, the two empires carried out a joint military occupation of the island for twelve years, with camps on opposite ends. This state of affairs lasted until their Salish Sea boundary dispute was settled in favour of the U.S., which explains why the San Juan Islands aren't part of Canada today.

Our scenic outing explores American Camp, now preserved by San Juan Island National Historical Park, in the traditional territories of the Lhaq'temish (Lummi), Samish, Swinomish, and W̱SÁNEĆ peoples. From the Jakles Lagoon trailhead, head southeast on the Mount Finlayson Trail. Tackle laughably unnecessary switchbacks (still, don't shortcut!) to the arid ridge, a gentle mound compared to its Canadian namesake (Hike 94) outside Victoria. Paralleling Cattle Point Road, stay right on the double track as it travels across the top of a windblown grassland, dry from the rain shadow of the Olympic Mountains. Rocky Mountain junipers and Townsend's voles inhabit the open environment.

Salish Sea from San Juan Island.

With bent-over Douglas firs on your left and the stunningly beautiful coast and vast expanse of the Strait of Juan de Fuca to your right, pass the summit of Mount Finlayson (48°27′31″ N, 122°58′58″ W). Continue east into the state-managed Cattle Point Natural Resources Conservation Area until you reach Cattle Point Road. Scan the tall grass for Columbian black-tailed deer. Walk down the road's shoulder, soon turning right onto a path to the dunes, bluffs, and lighthouse (48°27′03″ N, 122°57′48″ W) of Cattle Point (TIQENEN to the W̱SÁNEĆ), after 1 hour of relaxed hiking. The promontory is part of San Juan Islands National Monument, proclaimed in 2013.

Head back up Cattle Point Road and go right on a gated service road to continue the counterclockwise loop. Follow signs north to the gorgeous Third Lagoon on Griffin Bay. Backtrack momentarily to go west on the old road known as the Lagoon Trail. Salal and oceanspray shrubs grow in the understory, and downy, hairy, and pileated woodpeckers chisel holes in the trees. Fork right onto a forest trail to view Jakles Lagoon itself before continuing west to the trailhead.

Dogs must be leashed, camping and fires are banned, and Leave No Trace practices are mandated in these protected areas.

GETTING THERE

Vehicle: Washington State Ferries offers daily service to San Juan Island from Anacortes and Sidney, B.C. From the Friday Harbor ferry dock, go right on Front Street South, left on Spring Street, and left on Mullis Street. Continue onto Cattle Point Road for 10 km (6 mi). Turn left into the Jakles Lagoon Natural Area parking lot.

101
TURTLEHEAD

Distance: 8.5 km (5.3 mi)
Time: 2.5 hours (round trip)
Elevation gain: 270 m (885 ft)
High point: 325 m (1,065 ft)

Quality: ★★★★★
Difficulty: ●
Maps: USGS Eastsound, Great Pacific San Juan Islands
Trailhead: 48°40'02" N, 122°56'50" W

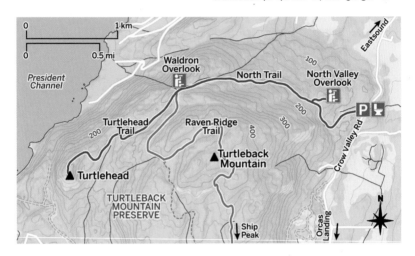

FANS OF shelled reptiles may be drawn to this hike in Turtleback Mountain Preserve on Orcas Island. Hopefully, the tremendous Salish Sea views will suffice in lieu of chelonian sightings. The San Juan County Land Bank, San Juan Preservation Trust, and Trust for Public Land are to be commended for sparing these Garry oak woodlands, meadows, and wetlands from development.

Set off west on the multi-use North Trail. Detour right for the North Valley Overlook in 800 m (0.5 mi) and the Waldron Overlook in another 1.6 km (1.0 mi). The vistas of Mount Constitution (Hike 102) to the east and Waldron Island and B.C.'s Saturna Island to the northwest hint at the splendour waiting at your destination.

Continue west on the Turtlehead Trail, which links Turtleback Mountain Preserve (protected in 2006, after a US$18.5-million fundraising campaign) to Turtleneck Preserve (2012) and Turtlehead Preserve (1990). Over 1.9 km (1.2 mi), the delightful path descends and then climbs to the top of the Turtlehead, officially named Orcas Knob (306 m/1,005 ft; 48°39'41" N, 122°59' 26" W)—no relation to the killer whale.

West Sound from Turtlehead Trail's end.

Burst out of the woods and onto the grassy, south-facing overlook. Behold the grand scene: West Sound and Deer Harbor separating the appendages of horseshoe-shaped Orcas Island, with Shaw Island and San Juan Island beyond. Bees buzz between common camas, meadow death-camas, and other wildflowers. Retrace your steps to the trailhead.

Camping and fires are prohibited, and dogs should be leashed in Turtleback Mountain Preserve. Orcas Island, the largest of the San Juans, lies within the traditional territories of the Lhaq'temish (Lummi), Samish, Swinomish, and W̱SÁNEĆ peoples.

LONGER OPTION

Upon your return to the Waldron Overlook junction, turn right and head south to see more of the "turtle." Keeping left at forks for 5 km (3.1 mi), reach Turtleback Mountain (463 m/1,519 ft) via the Raven Ridge Trail and then follow the Center Loop Trail and Ridge Trail to Ship Peak (284 m/931 ft). Turn around and retrace your steps to the junction at the Waldron Overlook, where you go right (east) on the North Trail to your car.

GETTING THERE

Vehicle: Washington State Ferries offers daily service between Anacortes and Orcas Island. From Orcas Landing, head north on Orcas Road for 5.5 km (3.4 mi). Turn left on Nordstrom Lane and right on Crow Valley Road. In 2.5 km (1.6 mi), find Turtleback Mountain Preserve's north trailhead on the left.

102
MOUNT CONSTITUTION

Distance: 13.5 km (8.4 mi)
Time: 6 hours (loop)
Elevation gain: 460 m (1,510 ft)
High point: 734 m (2,409 ft)

Quality: ★★★
Difficulty: ■
Maps: USGS Mount Constitution, Great Pacific San Juan Islands
Trailhead: 48°39'17" N, 122°49'08" W

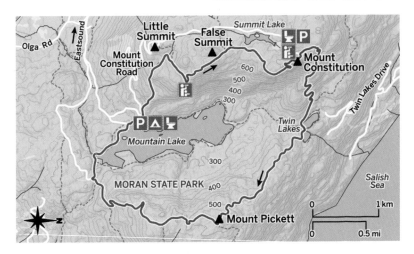

STARING AT each other across Mountain Lake, Mount Constitution and Mount Pickett are decidedly different in character. Sure, both peaks are found in Moran State Park on Orcas Island, in the traditional territories of the Lhaq'temish (Lummi), Samish, Swinomish, and W̱SÁNEĆ peoples. However, bustling Mount Constitution, the San Juan Islands' tallest mountain, has a road to its top, which boasts panoramic views. Meanwhile, quieter Mount Pickett has a treed summit and is largely protected by a natural area preserve. Our grand tour takes in both mountains.

Begin by the Mountain Lake picnic shelter and set off on the trail signed for Little Summit, climbing northwest in forest. In 1.9 km (1.2 mi), go right at a junction to bypass Little Summit and continue north for 3.2 km (2 mi). As the trail gains elevation on the east side of False Summit, bluffs afford a commanding vantage of Mount Pickett across gleaming Mountain Lake. Snow-capped Mount Baker (Kweq' Smánit to the Nooksack Tribe) looms in the background. Stay right at the Cold Springs trail junction, pass Summit Lake, and earn more Salish Sea views en route to the high point of our clockwise loop.

Looking down at Mountain Lake from Mount Constitution (SWEH-luhkh).

Mount Constitution (48°40′39″ N, 122°49′52″ W), known as SWEH-luhkh to the Lhaq'temish, is crowned by a medieval-style stone tower. Designed by Seattle architect Ellsworth Storey, it was built in 1936 by the Great Depression-era Civilian Conservation Corps. Inside, two cabinets showcase the park's history. Up top, five photo plaques identify landmarks in sight, including Lummi Island and Twin Sisters Mountain (Kwetl'kwítl' Smánit to the Nooksack).

Cross the parking lot and, over the next 2.4 km (1.5 mi), drop to Twin Lakes (340 m/1,115 ft), our loop's midpoint. Continue east, passing Big Twin Lake and keeping right at Little Twin Lake, to pick up the Mount Pickett trail. In 2.4 km (1.5 mi), the pleasant forest walk leads southeast to the viewless summit (533 m/1,750 ft; 48°40′00″ N, 122°48′00″ W). Stay right at the next five junctions, and keep your eyes peeled for Pacific chorus frogs. Go left at Mountain Lake, pass below the dam, and follow the lakeshore trail back to the parking area.

Dogs must be leashed, smoking is banned between April and October, and hunting is prohibited. Moran State Park has four vehicle-accessible campgrounds and one walk-in/bike-in camping area.

GETTING THERE

Vehicle: Washington State Ferries offers daily service between Anacortes and Orcas Island. From Orcas Landing, head north on Orcas Road to Eastsound. Turn right on Main Street, which becomes Crescent Beach Drive. Hang a right on Olga Road. After passing Cascade Lake, go left on Mount Constitution Road. Take the right-hand turnoff to arrive at the Mountain Lake parking area. Discover Pass required (purchase in advance).

103
SKYLINE DIVIDE

Distance: 13 km (8.1 mi)
Time: 6 hours (round trip)
Elevation gain: 670 m (2,210 ft)
High point: 2,000 m (6,560 ft)

Quality: ★★★★★
Difficulty: ■
Maps: USGS Bearpaw Mountain, Mount Baker; Green Trails 13 Mount Baker
Trailhead: 48°52'52" N, 121°51'52" W

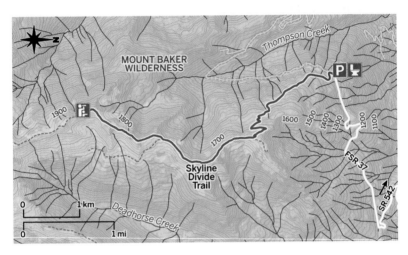

KNOWN AS Kweq' Smánit (white mountain) to the Nooksack Tribe and Teqwúbe7 (snow-capped mountain) to the Skagit people, Mount Baker (3,286 m/10,781 ft) is an iconic landmark to residents of B.C.'s Lower Mainland and Washington's Whatcom County. Composed of andesite lava flows and breccias, the highest stratovolcano in the North Cascades last erupted 6,700 years ago. These days, the U.S. Geological Survey rates its volcanic threat potential as "very high" in terms of risk to people and property. Due to its similarly rated scenic values, Mount Baker's Skyline Divide Trail (open to llamas!) is on many a hiker's tick list.

Good in summer and fall, this popular trail enters the Mount Baker Wilderness and traces the watershed between Glacier Creek (and its tributary, Thompson Creek) and Dead Horse Creek on the northern doorstep of the glaciated giant. Save this one for a blue-sky day to make the most of the dazzling landscape and rainbow of wildflowers, and remember to bring plenty of water. Regulations stipulate a maximum of twelve hikers per group, and no fires. Arrive early in the morning or visit on a weekday to beat the crowds.

Skyline Divide Trail in Mount Baker Wilderness. Photo by Bob Hare

The trail begins by climbing steadily to subalpine meadows and the ridge crest, where you ignore a path on the left. American bistort, fireweed, heart-leaved arnica, leafy aster, and pink mountain-heather star in the floral show. Stroll south, traversing several bumps, with Mount Baker before you and Mount Shuksan (Shéqsan to the Nooksack) to the west.

At a low saddle between knolls where you find an unmarked junction, follow the rugged uphill path to the right. You're aiming for a high point near the end of Skyline Divide, short of Chowder Ridge and about 6.5 km (4 mi) from the trailhead. (The left fork descends to meadows east of the divide.)

Try picking these peaks out of the lineup: Mount McGuire (T'amiyehó:y) across the border, Yellow Aster Butte (Hike 104) to the northeast, Twin Sisters Mountain (Kwetl'kwítl' Smánit) to the south, and the Olympic Mountains to the west. Take a lunch break with an eyeful of the crevassed Roosevelt Glacier and the vertiginous Coleman Headwall below Grant Peak on Mount Baker itself. Retrace your steps.

GETTING THERE

Vehicle: From the Sumas border crossing, head south on State Route 9 (Cherry Street). Turn left on SR 547 (Front Street). Follow the highway for 17.5 km (11 mi) to a roundabout. Take the second exit and go east on SR 542 (Mount Baker Highway). Shortly after passing the Glacier Public Service Center (purchase the required Northwest Forest Pass here), turn right on Glacier Creek Road (Forest Service Road 39) and immediately left on Deadhorse Road (FSR 37). Drive 20 km (13 mi) on gravel to the Skyline Divide trailhead.

104
YELLOW ASTER BUTTE

Distance: 13 km (8.1 mi)
Time: 7 hours (round trip)
Elevation gain: 770 m (2,530 ft)
High point: 1,902 m (6,241 ft)

Quality: ★★★★★
Difficulty: ◆
Maps: USGS Mount Larrabee, Green Trails 14 Mount Shuksan
Trailhead: 48°56′36″ N, 121°39′46″ W

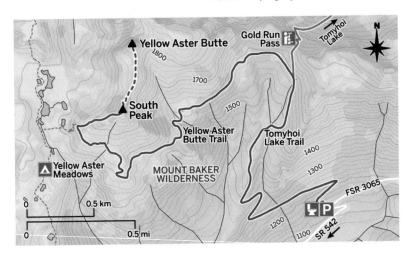

YELLOW ASTER Butte has it all: a rich profusion of wildflowers, berries, and alpine views—and a summit scramble to boot. Starting on the Tomyhoi Lake Trail, switchback up an avalanche path with thimbleberries. Enter the forest and Mount Baker Wilderness (maximum party size: 12), gradually ascending west and then north.

Trading woods for meadows, reach a fork (48°57′07″ N, 121°39′56″ W) after an hour of hiking. Go left on the Yellow Aster Butte Trail to contour around the head of a scenic bowl. Gaze upon American bistort, edible thistle, fireweed, green false hellebore, red paintbrush, subalpine daisy, western pasqueflower, lots of bees and blueberries (save some for the bears), perhaps a sooty grouse, and of course the glory of the North Cascades.

Traverse west and cross a couple of creeks (snow lingers into late summer). Prepare to be amazed by the magical tarns of Yellow Aster Meadows, where camping is allowed on snow, rock, or bare ground. At 5.7 km (3.5 mi) from the trailhead, swing right at an unsigned junction (48°56′57″ N, 121°41′16″ W) and head steeply up the meadowy ridge to the south peak (1,870 m/ 6,140 ft).

Ridge walk on Yellow Aster Butte, with Mount Shuksan (Shéqsan) in the background.

Lunch and savour the splendid panorama: Tomyhoi Peak (Put-lush-go-hap to the Nooksack Tribe), Canadian and American Border Peaks, Mount Larrabee, Goat Mountain (Yi7íman), Mount Shuksan (Shéqsan), and Mount Baker (Kweq' Smánit). The horn rising 500 m (0.3 mi) north is Yellow Aster Butte's true summit (48°57′16″N, 121°40′56″ W).

The easy scramble (best left to experienced hikers) entails a highly enjoyable ridge walk. Watch your step on the steep bits at both ends. From the rocky perch, peer down at Tomyhoi Lake.

By the way, the third principle of Leave No Trace is "Dispose of waste properly"—better known as "Pack it in, pack it out." To help hikers minimize the impact of human waste on this extremely popular trail, the U.S. Forest Service provides blue bags at the Tomyhoi Lake–Yellow Aster Butte trailhead in Mount Baker-Snoqualmie National Forest.

LONGER OPTION

Back at the fork 2.8 km (1.7 mi) from the trailhead, swing north to explore more of the Tomyhoi Lake Trail. Over 3.4 km (2.1 mi), hike up to Gold Run Pass and down to Coyote Flats and Tomyhoi Lake (1,134 m/3,722 ft).

GETTING THERE

Vehicle: From the Sumas border crossing, head south on State Route 9 (Cherry Street). Turn left on SR 547 (Front Street). Follow the highway for 17.5 km (11 mi) to a roundabout. Take the second exit and go east on SR 542 (Mount Baker Highway). At 19 km (12 mi) east of Glacier, turn left on Twin Lakes Road (Forest Service Road 3065). Drive 7 km (4.3 mi) on gravel to the Tomyhoi Lake–Yellow Aster Butte trailhead and roadside parking. Northwest Forest Pass required (purchase at Glacier Public Service Center).

105
CHAIN LAKES TRAIL

Distance: 11.5 km (7.1 mi)
Time: 5.5 hours (loop)
Elevation gain: 375 m (1,230 ft)
High point: 1,640 m (5,380 ft)

Quality: ★★★★★
Difficulty: ■
Maps: USGS Shuksan Arm, Green Trails
14 Mount Shuksan
Trailhead: 48°50'48" N, 121°41'31" W

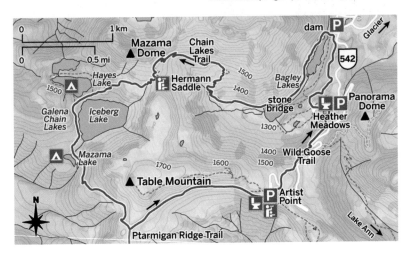

DELIVERING POSTCARD landscapes at every turn, the Chain Lakes Trail enters the Mount Baker Wilderness, within Mount Baker–Snoqualmie National Forest. Wilderness regulations limit the size of hiking parties to twelve. (Consider this a rule for all backcountry areas!) Shortcutting trails is prohibited.

The hike to the Galena Chain Lakes begins at perhaps the most scenic parking lot in these parts. From Artist Point's vault toilets, descend the upper section of the Wild Goose Trail (4 km/2.5 mi)—crossing the highway and passing the trail to Lake Ann—with jaggy Mount Shuksan (Shéqsan to the Nooksack Tribe) before you. At Terminal Lake, admire the reflection of Table Mountain (1,750 m/5,742 ft), the lava plateau you'll be circumnavigating. Head across the parking lot to the Austin Pass picnic area to pick up Wild Goose's lower section, which leads to the Bagley Lakes trailhead and the start of the Chain Lakes Trail in the glaciovolcanic wonderland of Heather Meadows.

Follow the throng of beaming hikers over the old Bagley Dam and head west above the shore of Lower Bagley Lake. (You can thank volunteers with the Washington Trails Association for restoring the tread, improving drainage, and brushing out the path.) At Upper Bagley Lake, a picturesque stone arch bridge spans the outlet. Stay on the north side to ascend a rockslide and

Mount Baker (Kweq' Smánit) and Iceberg Lake from Chain Lakes Trail.

switchbacks to Hermann Saddle (48°51′32″ N, 121°42′36″ W), between Mazama Dome and Table Mountain, 3.8 km (2.4 mi) from the Bagley Lakes trailhead.

Don't resist the urge to stop for lunch here—at the midpoint of our counterclockwise loop and just past the high point. Mount Baker (Kweq' Smánit) and the columnar andesite walls of Table Mountain dominate the eye-popping scene. Then descend south and east, following the trail between Iceberg Lake (1,461 m/4,793 ft) and Hayes Lake, the two largest of the four Galena Chain Lakes. Keep left at two campsite junctions, visiting the west shore of Iceberg Lake (watch out for ice calving) and passing above Mazama Lake.

Turn left at the Ptarmigan Ridge Trail junction. The Chain Lakes Trail's busy homestretch slices across the plunging south slopes of Table Mountain to Artist Point. With rock ledges, waterfalls, a dramatic view of Mount Shuksan, and, if you're lucky, a dozen mountain goats grazing in the meadow below, it's a spectacular and leisurely way to finish.

LONGER OPTION

Before returning to Artist Point, take an out-and-back hike on the Ptarmigan Ridge Trail, which extends 5.5 km (3.4 mi) southwest to the base of Coleman Pinnacle and Camp Kiser.

GETTING THERE

Vehicle: From the Sumas border crossing, head south on State Route 9 (Cherry Street). Turn left on SR 547 (Front Street). Follow the highway for 17.5 km (11 mi) to a roundabout. Take the second exit, and go east on SR 542 (Mount Baker Highway) to the end. At 39 km (24 mi) past Glacier, pull into the huge parking lot at Artist Point. Northwest Forest Pass required (purchase at Glacier Public Service Center).

ACKNOWLEDGEMENTS

THIS BOOK IS a long-time dream that surprised me by becoming reality. Without the help and generosity of many friends and hiking partners, I wouldn't have made it to 105 by deadline.

Special thanks to Svetlana Tkacova, Sarah Palmer, Patrick Hui, Jacqueline Ashby, Colleen Craig, Tara Henley, Bob Hare, Saeed Refaei, Louise Morrin, Matt Horne, Jason Cusator, Trevor Hargreaves, and Stefan, Esther, Verena, and Julius Brysch. I'd like to acknowledge the Wanderung Outdoor Recreation Society, founder Steve van der Woerd, president Andy Gibb, and the club's directors, trip organizers, and participants for greatly enriching and expanding my outdoor adventures.

I am grateful to T'uy't'tanat—Cease Wyss for writing a wonderful foreword for the first edition and to Michael Coyle (Coquitlam Search and Rescue) and Jaime Adams (Forest and the Femme Society) for lending their wisdom to the safety and ethics chapters, respectively. Certainly, I owe Jennifer Croll big time for putting my name forward for this project. Rob Sanders, Nayeli Jimenez, Alice Fleerackers, and the whole team at Greystone Books made my introduction to the publishing process a (relatively) painless one. It was a pleasure to collaborate with masterful editor (and living trail encyclopedia) Lucy Kenward. Steve Chapman (Canadian Map Makers) designed the excellent topographic maps.

Authors Charles Demers (with an assist from Cara Ng), Lydia Kwa, and Travis Lupick shared immensely helpful advice during the writing process. I've appreciated the support of Charlie Smith and Martin Dunphy (*Georgia Straight*), Bob Kronbauer (Vancouver Is Awesome), and Carolyn Ali (Destination British Columbia) over the years. Thank you to Josha MacNab, Karen

Crossing the Lynn Canyon Suspension Bridge.

Tam Wu, and all my amazing clean-energy think-tank colleagues at the Pembina Institute for getting behind this project.

Indigenous place names were gleaned from the work of the Squamish Lil'wat Cultural Centre and Kwi Awt Stelmexw (*squamishatlas.com*), Allan Richardson and Brent Galloway's *Nooksack Place Names* (UBC Press, 2011), First Nations' land-use plans and environmental-assessment submissions, and many other sources. I am also indebted to the numerous outdoor writers whom I interviewed as a journalist and whose work I have devoured as a reader; they provided plenty of inspiration for this book.

I'd like to recognize the Federation of Mountain Clubs of B.C., Wilderness Committee, Powell River Parks and Wilderness Society, Hope Mountain Centre for Outdoor Learning, B.C. Mountaineering Club, and Washington Trails Association for their tireless conservation efforts. Much respect to all the park defenders, trail maintainers, search and rescue volunteers, avalanche practitioners, and outdoor educators.

Lastly, this book could not have made it to trail's end without the support of Nicole Reid and Oliver Hui-Reid—thank you.

INDEX

Hike details are indicated by page numbers in **bold**

ABOUT THE AUTHOR AND PHOTOGRAPHER

Photo by Sarah Palmer

STEPHEN HUI has been hiking, backpacking, and scrambling in British Columbia's Coast Mountains for twenty-five years. His outdoor writing and photography have appeared in the *Georgia Straight*, where he was the web editor and technology editor, as well as in the *Toronto Sun*, *Le Journal de Montréal*, Vancouver Is Awesome, and *Wild Coast* magazine.

Born and based in Vancouver, B.C.—in the territories of the Musqueam, Squamish, and Tsleil-Waututh First Nations—Hui works for an environmental organization and serves as the vice-president of the Wanderung Outdoor Recreation Society. *105 Hikes In and Around Southwestern British Columbia* is his first book.

105HIKES.COM

facebook.com/105Hikes

@stephenhui

@StephenHui

stephen@105hikes.com

#105Hikes